To Ethan

For re[...]

later on.

[signature] Judith Eisen[...]

9/87

RECONSTRUCTING JUDAISM

Isaac and Sadie Eisenstein and their sons
Myron and Ira, 1922

Judith and Ira Eisenstein, 1951

Mordecai M. Kaplan
and Ira Eisenstein, 1958

RECONSTRUCTING JUDAISM:

An Autobiography

IRA EISENSTEIN

THE RECONSTRUCTIONIST PRESS
New York

Library of Congress Catalogue Card Number: 86-60973

International Standard Book Number: 0-935457-37-2 (clothbound)

Dust Jacket by Nina Gaelen

Book design by Alvin Schultzberg

Published by
The Reconstructionist Press
270 West 89th Street, New York 10024

Printed in the United States of America

FOR MIRIAM RACHEL AND ANN NEHAMA

Table of Contents

Foreword

This book is the result of the curiosity of my students. They would ask: what made you decide to become a rabbi? How did you come to work so closely with Rabbi Mordecai Kaplan? How did Reconstructionism begin? I got tired of repeating myself and decided that I had better write it all down. I am glad that I did, for I no longer have that daily contact with students, and those who ask the same questions do not have me around to answer them.

Obviously, the story of my life and its interweaving with the launching of the Reconstructionist movement is by no means complete. Some day a full history will have to be written. But this book recounts at least my part in the early struggle to get things going.

Several people have read the manuscript and have contributed excellent suggestions for changes, omissions and additions. Rabbi David Teutsch did a thorough job on the text, for which I thank him most sincerely. My daughters, Miriam and Ann, have made many constructive comments, and my Judith, with unfailing good judgment, has guided me throughout. I thank her for that, and for more than I can properly articulate. Of course, responsibility for the final version is mine alone. I thank Ruth Sumliner for her typing and retyping the manuscript.

Generous friends have made possible the publication of this

book. I wish to express my gratitude to the following:

Martin Abelove
Frances and Daniel Berley
Bess and Roy Berlin
Adelle and Samuel Blumenthal
Harriet and Sidney L. Feiner
Marilyn and Gene Grayson
Florence and Sheldon Kohn
Irene and Leo Irvings
Jacques Pomeranz
Judith and Arthur Winston
Kay and Jack Wolofsky
Marjorie and Aaron Ziegelman

January 1986   I.E.

1

Harlem and the Bronx

I was born on November 26, 1906, in a walk-up flat at 11 West 117th Street, in Harlem, New York.

When the subway was finished, Jews moved uptown in large numbers, away from the lower East Side where the masses of East European Jews had settled after arriving in this country. The move represented a step up the ladder. Harlem was a fairly large rectangle, extending from the north end of Central Park (110th Street) to 125th Street, from 8th Avenue to Park Avenue. As I grew up, this area seemed to me to be entirely Jewish. North of 125th Street the "Negroes" lived, and we never crossed over into their territory. West of 8th Avenue the Irish were in charge, and east of Madison the Italians were dominant. This Jewish rectangle contained synagogues, kosher butcher shops, Jewish book stores, *talmud torahs* (schools for Hebrew instruction), and many shops catering to the burgeoning Jewish middle class.

My father had to run for the doctor because we had no telephone. Phones were not common in those days, and my father had lost his job shortly before I was born. With a first-born ahead of me, there was no money for such luxuries. My mother frequently mentioned my father's race for the doctor among the hardships she had to endure (sic) in bringing up two children. My brother Myron was two years and three months old when I appeared.

I was what they called a "sickly" child, fed large doses of cod liver oil. From the age of eight, I wore glasses. This meant I could not participate in "rough" games with the other boys on the street. When I was five, we left Harlem and moved to the Bronx.

It was certainly not my mother's preference, for we would have to live next door to my grandmother and grandfather, Aunt Mamie and Uncle Oscar and their three children, and my unmarried aunts and uncles who lived with their parents. My father, being a "good" son, wanted to be near his folks; my mother would have chosen to live elsewhere.

But word had spread that the air in the Bronx was fresher than in Harlem. There was no pollution in either place, really, except for horse manure; but at least there were fewer buildings in the Bronx, and more open space, and that was another good reason for the move. For my mother the fresh air did not compensate for being further away from the department stores where she did most of her window shopping. The people in the Bronx were not stylish, and her in-laws were prosaic, dull, and never went to the opera.

However we moved. Proximity to the Eisenstein clan gave us a chance to get to know our cousins better, but it intensified Mother's ambivalence toward the family she had married into. On the one hand, she had made up her mind, while still in her teens, that she would never marry a foreign-born man (with an accent). The length of time it took my father to decide to marry her led my mother to despairing that she would ever marry at all —for she held out for him, and him alone. But he was either out of a job, or not sure he was earning enough to get married, not quite certain his parents would approve his getting married, either to her or at all. They finally made it.

What did she like about him? First, he talked without an accent. He was actually born in New York; more than that, his mother was born in New York, on Elizabeth Street, in 1854. Practically a Yankee! He was also good looking, sober, a gentleman. His father was a scholar, a Hebrew scholar, whose mother had come to this country before the Civil War and established a shirt business. She was rich by the standards of her time. Judah David Eisenstein inherited none of his mother's business acumen;

2

in fact, when he tried to get involved in the business, he made a mess of things. His son, my father, did not inherit business skills from his grandmother. The genes got lost somewhere. Maybe my brother Myron saved a few.

Grandpa devoted his time to community affairs and to scholarship. His mother had finally made him independent, giving him a piece of property which provided enough for his livelihood. Accordingly, he was free to serve on the committee which brought Rabbi Jacob Joseph to head the New York *Kehillah*, an experiment in communal organization based on European precedents, which failed miserably.

Despite his learning, which he had acquired from his grandfather in Meserich (or perhaps because of it), he neglected totally the education of his children. My father, the eldest, was expected to go to work at an early age to help support the family. Father had attended P.S. 2 and had taken the entrance examinations for City College. When he came home breathless with excitement, eager to report to his father that he had passed the examinations, Grandpa told him he simply could not continue at school. He would have to go to work.

So my mother had ambivalent feelings about her husband's family: pride in the reputation of her father-in-law, pain at her husband's frustrations. Add to this her not always suppressed anger at my father for his meek acceptance of these frustrations, her pride in and anger at his honesty in business. She both admired and was furious at my father's filial devotion—he never failed to visit his parents at least once a week, even when they were 95 and he was 74.

No wonder she suffered from migraines.

———

The Eisenstein part of my family constituted my American heritage. Knowing that my roots reached back to the first half of the 19th century in New York, I sensed a deep kinship between myself and the American scene. I was greatly moved to discover that Grandpa had translated into Hebrew and Yiddish the Declaration of Independence and the Constitution. He did this soon after his arrival at these shores, in order to impress upon his fellow immigrants the privilege which was theirs to have come to a land of freedom and opportunity. My awareness of these deep roots helped to shape my sense of at-homeness in this land. Very few of my friends and contemporaries were spared the pain of cultural estrangement from their parents, and certainly from their grandparents. As I was growing up, my schoolmates simply could not believe that they were hearing right: an old Jewish grandmother speaking English without a foreign accent!

At the same time I developed a strong attachment to the Jewish people. Strangely, it was not influenced by the Eisenstein branch. My Yiddish-speaking grandma was largely responsible for my equally strong attachment to the traditions of the *shtetl*. She was perhaps the major influence in my early life. Without actually meaning to, she instilled in me a love for what is generically called *Yiddishkeit*, for the Yiddish language, for the sentimental associations with certain moments like Erev Shabbos and the twilight hour at the close of Shabbos, for folk wisdom which came from her illiterate but kind and gentle soul.

She was full of gratitude for having a home with us after an unsuccessful marriage to a Mr. Spectorsky, her third husband. Who knew her age? She might have known, but she was not telling. You don't count the years, she said; God counts, and that's enough. We tried to calculate: she had been married in Kalvaria, Lithuania. After ten childless years, she and her husband were divorced, as tradition required. Then a *shadkhan* arranged for her to meet and marry Moshe Yizhak Luxenburg of Kovno, twice widowed, with nine children to take care of. Rochel Miriam agreed, and miracle of miracles, she bore two children, a boy Yaakov and a daughter (my mother, Sonia, later Sadie). Apparently, she was loved by her step-children. When the oldest, Jonas, left for America, and one by one, brought over all his brothers and sisters, he finally sent for Grandma and her two little ones.

There was never a time when she was not part of my world. I loved her with a warmth reserved for very few persons in my life, because she was little and round, with a willingness to laugh at herself, at her inadequate English (*Lach, lach, kinder!*). Even when my brother Myron and I wrote a parody of her favorite Yiddish and non-English phrases, to the tune of *Hatikvah*, and

4

sent the relatives into gales of laughter, she laughed along, enjoying the attention, not minding the fact that the laughter was at her expense. She knew we loved her.

She would lie down on her bed to rest in the afternoon, and frequently I would sit by her as she told tales of the old country. She boasted of her father's household, the guests whom he would always invite to her home for Shabbos dinner, the store he owned ("big, like Macy"), the respect in which he was held by the burghers of Kovno, his ability to hold his own in the *Bes Hamidrosh* with the scholars of the city. They had a country house too, with cows and chickens. And how they would celebrate Pesaḥ and the other festivals! Long before books like *Life Is with People*, I experienced the joys and the sorrows of the *shtetl* on those afternoons while my Grandma reminisced.

She read the daily Yiddish paper, *Der Morgen Zhournal.* When I was five, she taught me the letters on top of the front page. "Daled, ayin, resh . . ." I proudly recited them for company. Later, when I could read the Yiddish and her eyes could no longer cope with the small type, I would read aloud to her. The news of the world made her laugh and cry and say "Oy"; she had a wonderful time, and I practiced my Yiddish.

Most Yiddish-speaking Jewish women read the *Tzennah u'R'ennah*. It was a compilation of stories and legends, homilies and commentaries, based on the biblical text and designed for those who were not encouraged to study seriously, namely women. Grandma read this regularly, and when her eyesight deteriorated, she again asked me to read to her. It may well be that my love of Jewish literature and folklore began with her.

An orgy of tears and sighing accompanied our playing of records on the Victrola. Of course, we bought Caruso, Galli-Curci, Melba, and the rest, but the cantorial renditions of Rosenblatt and Sirota were just as popular with us as they were with Grandma. It was simply that she provided the sound effects. When Yoseleh Rosenblatt cried out for "parnoseh" (in the prayer for the New Month), she would chime in "*Oy parnoseh, oy parnoseh*" ("to make a living, to make a living") as though she had once struggled for *parnoseh*. (Mother often said that Grandma had never "put her fingers into cold water.") But Grandma's heart bled for all those who prayed for a livelihood. Besides, you are supposed to start crying whenever the hazzan begins to sing, no matter what the text.

In tandem, as it were, with Grandma, Mr. Lunevsky introduced me to the mysterious Hebrew letters. He must have had a first name, but we never learned it.

When I was eight, and Myron past ten, my parents decided that we needed a good teacher. They either knew or assumed that the congregational Hebrew schools were inferior; in any case, their boys were going to have the best. When word of Mr. Lunevsky's reputation reached us, he was interviewed. He was a portly man who carried a cane (for effect, we thought), and of course he never took off his fedora hat. He was "modern," that is, he believed that one should learn Hebrew scientifically. Already in Volozhin, where he had studied, he insisted upon learning *dikduk* (grammar), even though to the old-timers this was superfluous, indeed bordering on heresy. My parents were impressed.

They were taken aback by the steep fees: $15 a month, two lessons a week for both boys! But they were determined that their children be properly educated, at least as well as their next-door cousins who had also engaged this expensive teacher.

At the beginning we were encouraged by our rapid progress; but soon what happened to us was no different from what happened to other American boys. He would arrive in the middle of a handball game, and we would either pretend we had not seen him, or we would reluctantly yield. At this point, even Grandpa became interested in our Hebrew lessons. (Was he trying to make up for his indifference to his own children's learning?) Grandpa would send us by mail postcards written in Hebrew, so that we would practice reading *modern* Hebrew. It was something of a thrill to receive these communications, which had traveled all the way from 940 Kelly Street to 944 Kelly Street. But even deciphering Grandpa's handwriting did not provide enough excitement to compensate for a lost hour of playing on the street.

Grandma, however, generated the excitement, for no matter how cool our feelings for Mr. Lunevsky, she saw in him the messenger from God who was destined to prove the accuracy of a prophecy uttered by the Kovner Rov, Rabbi Isaac Elchanan, whom she visited prior to leaving for America. She had brought her two children, my Uncle Jake and my mother (aged ten and eight) for a blessing before their embarkation, and he had said that Grandma would some day raise a child to be a rabbi!

For a time she had hoped that this child would be her Yaakov. But as the boy grew up in New York he showed little intellectual curiosity. He was more interested in the latest fashions, in spending time with pretty young girls and smoking Turkish cigarettes, than in pursuing the talmudic studies which might have led to the rabbinate. He was a sport, a have-a-good-time bachelor who made a nice living as a jewelry salesman. Well dressed and handsome, he could sell anything to anybody. Grandma refused to give up. The Kovner Rov could not have been mistaken.

Then it came to her: what Isaac Elchanan had meant was that a male descendant of hers would become a rabbi. Obviously, he had had in mind a son of her daughter Sadie, either Myron or myself. "A grandson is like a son," she declared; her exegesis of the Rov's prophecy pointed directly to Mr. Lunevsky. He was obviously more than a Hebrew teacher and a provider of an occasional pinch of snuff.*

I did not know whether I was destined to serve as a surrogate for my Uncle Jake until much later, when I was fifteen and had declared my intention of becoming a rabbi. I knew only that, despite the loss of the handball games, despite the fact that I was the only kid on the block taking Hebrew lessons, despite the fact that I could not stand the smell of the snuff, I was enjoying my adventures into the mysteries of Hebrew grammar and the challenge of Rashi's interpretations. Trying to figure out why Rashi offered certain explanations to the verse was like do-

---

*The Rov was actually right after all. Jake's grandson, son of his son Milton, became a rabbi, Jack Luxenberg.

ing puzzles: what was the question to which Rashi was giving an answer?

When I was ten, in 1917, my father experienced one of his brief periods of prosperity. We moved back to Harlem and bought a piano. When I was offered piano lessons, I eagerly accepted. Piano lessons were added to my schedule. Mrs. Forgotson, my teacher, came once a week for an hour's instruction; she was paid $1.25. She thought I had talent, but I knew better. I would always love to play the piano, and music became a very important part of my life. I even studied cello and clarinet at various times, but her dream of my becoming a professional never stood a chance.

Another consequence of the prosperity (caused, incidentally, by World War I) was a month at the seashore. We were installed in one of the kosher hotels in Asbury Park, where eating and playing poker were the major activities. But Myron and I were given to understand that we were not supposed to "waste" the weeks we spent there. We might forget our Hebrew altogether. Mr. Lunevsky suggested that we write letters to him, which he promised to answer. Our first efforts naturally resulted in: "Dear Teacher, we are here at the shore of the sea. It finds grace in our eyes. We are feeling healthy. We go to the ocean each day. (Nothing about poker games.) Please write. Your loving student . . ." Mr. Lunevsky was true to his word. He wrote back, enclosing our all-too-brief notes with his corrections penciled in.

Despite these efforts we did forget much of our Hebrew, and in the fall we had to spend the first few weeks reviewing.

Religious observance in our family was casual. Shabbos consisted of intense cleaning on Friday afternoon, lighting of candles by Grandma and Mother, and Grandma dropping a few coins into the little tin box with the Hebrew letters on them. Kiddush was recited. Challah replaced the usual bread. The house was kosher, but not simply for Grandma's sake. Mother insisted upon observing *kashrut*. She used to tell how, as a young woman, she was the only one of her crowd who stayed away from shellfish and ham-bacon-pork. Keeping kosher was her way of being religious. To be sure, she did not go shopping on Saturday, but that was hardly an act of self-denial because she had all week to do her shopping. She had very little else to do; we always had a maid.

The rest of Shabbos was different, but not as a result of religious observance. For example, we went to the movies, Myron and I, practically every Saturday afternoon. Because we required an adult to accompany us, we would shlepp Grandma along. She neither understood what was going on nor bothered to ask. As far as she was concerned this was a favor to her grandsons who, like the other Americans, somehow found pleasure in sitting in that dark auditorium watching shadows on the screen. She granted that we were at least less addicted than some: "Some," she observed, without any evidence to back it up, "sit in the moompitches day and night." But she invariably complained of a *shvindel* (dizziness) in her head when we got back home.

The major event on Shabbos morning was my going to shul with Grandma. She would put on her Shabbos hat and take my arm, and we would walk the two blocks to the synagogue slowly. I cannot remember her ever walking fast; she was an old lady (to us) as long as I can recall. Why was I the only one in the family to go to shul? The congregation (Shaare Zedek) had no regular rabbis. The stories I heard later were to the effect that no rabbi with any self-respect would stay here. Its last permanent rabbi had actually left the rabbinate altogether and gone into the silk business. (He was no happier there and subsequently returned to the rabbinate, and to that particular congregation.) Every week, then, a different preacher delivered the sermon. These were the first sermons I had ever heard, and it may well be that listening to them made me think I could do as well. I proved that by delivering, at home around the lunch table, a half-serious half-mocking summary of the talk. The family thought I was witty.

But the sermon was not the main attraction. It was Mr. Lunevsky. He *davened* at that shul, and he invited me to sit down next to him and, during the reading of the Torah, solve grammatical puzzles. He would point to a word, and ask: root?

9

gender? tense? number? I was good at it; I got many a pinch on the cheek, and the people around us were full of praise. On the other side of Mr. Lunevsky would sit a girl whom he pronounced a marvel. Why? She also took lessons from him; she was also good in grammar, and her parents were very rich. Mr. Lunevsky told my parents that with her went $25,000; the match seemed made in heaven. But her interest in Hebrew grammar dwindled after a while. We lost track of each other. In fact, we never actually said a word to one another.

It was fun. Mr. Lunevsky, as I recall, did not recite the prayers any more than I did; we were both more interested in the language of the *Siddur* and the Bible. We were even a bit unruly. During the reading of the Torah, the *shammes* would frequently bang on a book to plead with the congregation to be quiet. We were not the only offenders. There was a difference however. They talked business, and we talked *dikduk* (grammar). But we contributed our share to the hubbub. My teacher would conceal his embarrassment by taking a pinch of snuff and giving a tremendous sneeze. His neighbors, front and back, were frequent "borrowers" of a pinch, as was Grandma.

There were moments when we really behaved. During *Yizkor* (memorial services) on the final days of the festivals, when all the kids were asked to leave, Mr. Lunevsky thought I ought to stay. He was modern enough to know that this was all superstition, having the youngsters absent themselves if they were not mourning the loss of parents. The folk belief was that if you stayed while *Yizkor* was being said, the Angel of Death would arrange for you to *have* to stay. I was not too eager to remain, but there were no other kids I knew with whom I could play ball on the street in the interval.

It was pretty harrowing. The hazzan would recite individual prayers, especially for the important members of the congregation and for the families who had only recently been bereaved. His wailing and crying induced similar wailing and crying in the survivors.

Why did I go through the torture of listening, both to the hazzan and to the families? Was I already, in a vague sort of way, acting like a rabbi, empathizing with the mourners? And why did I (without verbalizing my feelings) object to the fact that the hazzan made a fuss over a few people and combined all the rest in summary repetition of the prayer? Was I already unconsciously planning to change all that when . . .? My mother called this my sympathetic nature. It was why, when she suffered an occasional migraine headache (the prospect of one always cast a pall over us), I was the one to wring out the hot towels and apply them. It was why, when my Aunt Theresa fell on the ice and broke her wrist, I was the one to take her to the hospital. My reputation as the "good one" got me into taking my Aunt Marcus (Grandma's sister who lived alone near us) downtown to buy a pair of shoes at the one place where they had the kind of shoes that fit her, or bringing her to the doctor periodically to remove a skin cancer from her cheek with an electric needle.

How did I get myself into these situations? How much was it out of my genuine desire to be helpful, and how much out of my desire to be praised? Did I not enjoy rollerskating as much as I thought I did, that I responded to these calls? Was it perhaps because I had few friends (actually none for whom I felt a real affection)? Was my enlistment in good deeds as great a deprivation as my parents and others (active public relations at work), considered it to be? Taking Grandma to shul was listed as one of my self-sacrificing acts, yet I was fully conscious that I would have gone without her (and sometimes did when the weather was bad or she did not feel up to it) to show off my Hebrew grammar.

We did not belong to Shaare Zedek; in fact, we did not belong to any congregation. On the High Holidays we most often went to Ohab Zedek on 116th Street, just opposite my school, P.S. 184. We chose this "Hungarian" shul, as it was popularly called, because the hazzan there was the greatly loved Yosele Rosenblatt (whose recordings made Grandma cry). He had a sweet, powerful voice, and his *davening* was equivalent to a concert. Being very pious, he turned down offers from the Metropolitan because he would have had to perform on Friday nights.

The rabbi was a Dr. Phillip Klein who, they said, was a fine scholar; but he preached in German, and when he rose to address the congregation, there was a rush for the door. "Like

11

from a fire," my father used to say. My heart once sank at this remark because I thought he had said there *was* a fire. The men would gather on the street chatting, and the boys would play handball until the signal emanated from inside that the sermon was over.

The women sat upstairs. Getting Grandma up those stairs was quite a performance. My mother held her arm, and I would be appointed to ascend slightly behind them, to catch one or the other if she toppled. The problem was complicated when Grandma had to go to the bathroom. This meant coming down to the main floor and descending still another flight of steps, into the basement—and back. I was not around for those maneuvers.

Since the World Series usually coincided with the High Holidays, immediately after the *kedushah* prayer we took off our *taleisim* and sneaked out, my father, Myron, and I. We would walk up to 125th Street to watch the progress of the game. In those days, before radio and TV, World Series fever could only be treated by standing in front of one of the stores on 125th Street which kept a telephone line open, and with white soap filled the spaces for each inning as they were concluded. We saw no action between the time one side was retired and another was put out. But the conversation, even with strangers (which was unusual for my father) was all baseball talk. When the game was over, the three of us would hurry back to 116th Street, take our places, and put on our *taleisim*—and the women upstairs did not know the difference.

This passion for baseball I acquired early. Father would tell us that when he was a boy he would cut Hebrew school and go up to the old Polo Grounds on 110th Street to watch Christy Mathewson pitch. This iron man, this legend of baseball history, retired before I had a chance to see him, but Father's enthusiasm for a good game was transmitted early. I must have been about ten (it was before we moved back to Harlem) when Father took us on the 163rd Street crosstown trolley over to Coogan's Bluff to see a game. He told us later that he knew the game had been postponed on account of the weather, but he thought we might enjoy taking a look at the grounds anyway. I was very pleased that Father, this timid man, had once broken the rules and cut Hebrew school for Mathewson.

2

De Witt Clinton High School

The fall of 1919 began a new chapter of my life; I
entered high school. The choice of a school appeared to be pre-
ordained. It was De Witt Clinton because Myron went there, as
did most of his friends. We were amazingly ignorant of the op-
tions available, but that was not as odd as the unchallenged
assumption that I was to study Spanish. Why Spanish? In 1919
there were no Puerto Ricans living in New York, and hence no
need for the spoken language. My father urged me to take
Spanish because he was doing business in Cuba and Puerto Rico,
and he required a knowledge of Spanish for his correspondence.
He blithely assumed that one of us would go into business with
him.

I could not imagine myself a businessman at any time,
though one summer while at high school I did try it out; that is,
I went down to the place of business and thought I might make
myself useful. The machines fascinated me, the typewriter and
the adding machine especially. But I was bored, bored to death.
I sometimes went to the bank to make a deposit. Having a lot of
checks in my pocket was exciting, but when I returned to the office and spent the next hours checking off the labels to see
whether all the size thirty-eights and all the forty-fours were
together, I got sleepy and was soon ready to call it quits.

I was certainly mistaken in thinking that this was the essence of the business life. Not until much later did I appreciate the talent of those who had to plan and calculate and demonstrate shrewdness and courage. But what I saw of business then was enough to convince me that I had neither the talent for business nor the interest in the commercial life.

I did very well that first semester of high school. But it did not last. In the second semester at the main building on 59th Street and Tenth Avenue, I was a total loss. The annex at 52nd Street had been small and intimate, but the main building was enormous. I was totally bewildered, and being too shy to ask my way around, I experienced moments of intolerable panic. Everything I had learned of Spanish in the first term I completely forgot; I passed by the skin of my teeth. I kept confusing Hebrew with Spanish and found myself writing Hebrew words in Latin script.

My head was full of Hebrew because I had just completed my bar mitzvah ceremony. Whatever blows I suffered in the second term of high school could have been regarded as punishment for the swelled head I developed as a result of my virtuoso performance in the synagogue. First, I had no trouble at all learning the chant for the Torah and the *Haftarah*. Having sat in on Myron's bar mitzvah lessons two years before, I had mastered the trope, the singing notes, and I was ready to chant my portion before I needed to be.

But then came the climax—the speech in Hebrew which Mr. Lunevsky had written for me. I was all set to show off, but I insisted on one condition: I would deliver the talk only if I understood what I was saying. Mr. Lunevsky agreed, and we proceeded to spend the following weeks studying the speech as part of my Hebrew lessons. The speech was written in a clear simple style, but the text reeked of sentimentality. This was just after the first World War, and the Jews of Europe were as usual being killed in pogroms. The adults were aware of the tragic fate overtaking the Jews of Poland; I was not. What I knew about it was what I learned from my bar mitzvah speech.

The synagogue was crowded with our families and with the many regular attendees who knew me from my weekly visits with Mr. Lunevsky. Surely he did a bit of advance advertising. ("Wait until you hear this boy; he is giving a speech in Hebrew.")

But practically no one understood a word. My grandfather, my Uncle Oscar, who had been raised in Jerusalem, the rabbi, and my teacher—that was it. I was so obsessed with articulating each word clearly and not making a single mistake that I was hardly conscious of the emotional impact of the words on those who understood and those who did not.

When I finished, I shook hands with those on the *bimah*, the president of the congregation, who whispered in my ear: "You should be a rabbi," and the rabbi himself. The rest was an anti-climax. We walked three blocks north on Lenox Avenue to a catering establishment, where a heavy dinner was served. I sat on the dais between one grandma and the other. Myron, his friends, and mine, sat together at their own table, and as I glumly ate I could hear them laughing and having a good time.

My mood was not improved when the family urged the hazzan to sing a number or two. He chose *Eli Eli*, the popular Yiddish song of that day, in which reference is made again and again to the pogroms and the suffering of the Jews, concluding with a melodramatic and defiant *Shema Yisrael*. More crying. Then we went home to take a look at the presents which had been brought to the shul.

It is not difficult to understand why, after the triumph of that Hebrew speech, I should have been plunged into an energetic drive to advance more rapidly in my Hebrew studies. There surely was a connection between my post-bar mitzvah spurt of interest in Hebrew and my almost total collapse in high school. I have a strong suspicion that I found it cozier to concentrate on matters closer to home than to compete comfortably in the large world of De Witt Clinton. I could count on Mr. Lunevsky's approval. I did not need to prove myself to him. And the Hebrew lessons gained fulsome praise from the family.

By the end of the school year, I managed to come through with respectable grades, but I still felt like a stranger there. The other fellows stayed after school to join clubs—the Math Club, the History Club, and others. They got on committees of the student government, working on the Late Squad and other student activities. At the end of each day, I dashed off, either to Hebrew lessons or to piano lessons, or to practice.

I knew a few students casually, but I either did not have

15

time to spend with them or, if they lived in the neighborhood, my mother discouraged me from getting too chummy with them. They came from poor homes. They were not dressed properly. One way or another they were regarded by my mother as unworthy companions. I thought she was being unfair. But I did not put up a strenuous fight. I blush to think that I acquiesced in this snobbery.

One of the boys lived in our apartment building, and we did become fast friends, even though the family disapproval persisted. His name was Emanuel Eisenberg, a talented poet highly unconventional in his views, a natural-born critic of everything that represented the status quo. He was appalled by my middle-class respectability and said so in strong language, yet he seemed to like me enough to defy my mother's disapproval, which she did not bother to conceal. Grandma liked him because he knew a few Yiddish words and repeated them again and again, relevant or not. He also banged on the piano, which she thought was amusing. The only other boy whom I spent some time with was Al Newman, in the same building, who was not much fun. He had no sense of humor, but was available for a walk or a game of catch in front of the house if he happened to need a respite from his studies.

Soon after my bar mitzvah ceremony, I was attracted to a Conservative temple, Ansche Chesed, then located on 114th Street and Seventh Avenue. Myron had joined a group of fellows with whom he would play ball on the street. They formed a club which met at the temple and would meet for services on Friday evening. Since he seemed to enjoy this new attachment, I began to go along. It was quite different from the shul on 118th Street. There was an organ and a choir, quite Reform I thought, but after a while I found it more to my liking, and soon the family developed the habit of attending quite regularly.

The sermons were delivered by Dr. Jacob Kohn. He was the first rabbi I ever heard who made reference to Einstein and Freud and Marx, who in addition to his knowledge of Talmud and Midrash had a Phi Beta Kappa key on his watch chain. He seemed to be attracting a large number of young people, and although I did not always understand what he was saying, I revised my notion of what a rabbi is like.

In the meantime I became involved with a group at school called the Hatikvah Club. I cannot recall exactly how I came to work with this group, but I do remember that it was brought together by a League of Jewish Youth, organized by the Bureau of Jewish Education under the leadership of Dr. Samson Benderly. The man who came to the high school was William Kolodny. He wore pince-nez glasses; he was slight of build and quiet of voice, and generated much excitement among a small group of students. He was organizing Hatikvah clubs in many of the schools around the city, and somehow at our school he found a few who wanted to be active. I was elated, for until then I had not discovered any peers who were at all interested in anything Jewish.

Perhaps I knew Hebrew better than most of the others, or maybe in the company of fellows who did not make fun of Jews or Judaism, I found my tongue and was more articulate. In any event, I was elected president. At once I began to formulate plans for a series of cultural meetings. We would discuss major events of the day; we would invite important people to come and speak to us. We might even start a Hebrew class, which I thought it would be fun to teach.

But I soon discovered that the others were not as serious about the Club as I was. They wanted something more social. I didn't see anything wrong with being social, but I had the feeling that sociability ought to be a by-product of something else. When you had interesting things to do or talk about, sociability naturally followed. What was the stuff of sociability? What did you do? The others (not all—otherwise I would have given up quickly) had the answers: plan a dance, go on a picnic, organize a baseball team. That was fine, I argued, but that was recreation which you engage in *after* the business of Hatikvah was behind you.

Hatikvah means "The Hope." It was the name of the Zionist hymn, which later became the national anthem of Israel. I guess the people at the Bureau for Jewish Education proposed the name because we young people were expected to be the hope of the Jewish people. I took the name seriously, so they elected me president, but they were not happy about *my* hope of making the Club into something worthwhile. We never did grow into more than a coterie of ten or twelve, but when the Inter-High School Hatikvah Council was organized, I was naturally asked to "represent" De Witt Clinton High School.

We met on Sunday afternoons at the YWHA on 110th Street, and Mr. Kolodny was our leader. There were about five schools represented, but I believe the delegates "represented" their student bodies about as legitimately as I did mine. We all pretended (and I among them) that we were meeting to discuss our common problems. But the meetings of the Council were, for those of us who went to all-boys schools, the only informal, casual way to meet girls. And while we did talk about our respective clubs, the agenda was less important than the fact that we could get together.

Indeed, the Council provided me with my first encounter with girls, and I immediately fell in love with the representative of Hunter High School. She was blonde, and she was soft-spoken, and she laughed at my jokes. To impress her I bought a ridiculous bow tie, which I wore only to meetings of the Council; to impress her further, I would sit down at the piano before the meetings began and play a bit of Chopin with lots of shmaltz. Mr. Kolodny had it all arranged in his mind; the two of us would surely marry when the time came (this he told me later when his plan didn't work out).

The same conditions which catapulted me into the presidency of the Clinton Club got me elected president of the Inter-High School Hatikvah Council. I was articulate about the purposes of the Clubs, I urged that we have serious discussions, I insisted that sociability was a by-product—and I impressed all the girls and boys. Most of all I impressed my blonde beloved. But the upshot was that the debate remained the only item on the agenda of the meetings—and the Council decided to run a dance, and on Decoration Day to run a picnic, to Staten Island.

I had never invited a girl to go anywhere with me because I was too shy. I believed that I was unattractive: my nose too long, my ears still sticking out. But that was only one side of the coin. The other was my snobbishness, which Manny certainly encouraged. I was not going to spend time being bored with some dumb girl who probably did not read Heywood Broun, and maybe never even heard of him. Besides, my mother did not think that boys my age should waste their time with girls. They, the boys—maybe not all boys but certainly her son— should be studying or playing ball for exercise. My fear of her disapproval was paralyzing, and no matter how disdainful I thought I was of female company, I wished that I could get myself to ask a girl—at least for a walk in the park.

When the picnic to Staten Island was planned, I ostentatiously remarked that I did not think I was going, mostly because I did not "have someone to go with." I made sure that Miriam, my blonde, would hear me. She did, and her response threw me into a panic. She too, she said, was not sure she wanted to go to the picnic, for the same reason. With palpitating heart I said, "Well, maybe we could go together." Having committed myself I decided that come what may I would go through with it because I desperately wanted to, and in spite of the fact that I knew my mother would object. There was only one thing to do: I would not tell her. She would learn (casually) from me that the Hatikvah group was going on a picnic, and that I was going along. "Be sure to come back early," said Mother, "and be careful not to get too sunburned."

The picnic was glorious, but throughout the day I was trying to calculate just when I could get home. Staten Island was at least thirty minutes from the tip of Manhattan, and then I supposed, I would have to take her home. She lived in the Kingsbridge section of the West Bronx. On Memorial Day, the subway schedule was surely curtailed. Of course, it all turned out to be as I had feared. The train took forever, and I was beginning to sweat. I could see I was not going to get home before midnight, and that was not "early."

When we arrived at her home, I was greeted by her family— father, mother, grandfather, and grandmother. Even her younger sister joined the party. They were sure we were starved, so they had prepared a really nice dinner. I was frantic. I could not eat. I wanted to say, "good night" and run. But they would have none of that. Miriam had told them how well I played the piano. Would I play for them? Whatever could I do? It was getting later and later.

The train ride back was slow, and I was sunk in fear of Mother's disapproval and Father's upset stomach. When I reached home at last, my parents, relieved but greatly worried that I had perhaps gotten too sunburned, asked how it had gone. I said "fine," and fled to my room.

At Mr. Kolodny's insistence, the delegates from the Hatikvah Club came to the YWHA on Sunday mornings to join other high school students from around the city (who attended Hebrew High Schools or Sunday Schools), to listen to talks by Dr. Benderly himself.

Thus every other Sunday morning we would hear Dr. Benderly, a man whose career and extraordinary mind I learned about later on. I found myself fascinated by his talks, which centered for the most part on the drama of Zionism, the vision and courage of the pioneers, the dream of a Jewish people revived. His lectures generated great excitement in me; they brought my Hebrew lessons into a world of reality. Those lessons were unrelated to the normal course of our daily lives. It was past history in an esoteric language, irrelevant, as we came to say subsequently. You were a bit peculiar if you were interested in all that stuff. Dr. Benderly, on the other hand, was telling us about real people who were living real lives—as Jews in Palestine drying up swamps, building roads and houses, establishing schools, and defending themselves against marauders. These were brave people whose ideals were not buried beneath tons of ancient books, who did not just meet once in a while to discuss whether to have a dance or a picnic.

I became a Zionist on the basis of Dr. Benderly's talks long before I knew very much about a Zionist movement. He fired my imagination, and I knew then that some day I was going to visit Palestine to see with my own eyes the *halutzim* and their work. I knew that my Hebrew lessons were going to come to life there. Hebrew was spoken by these people; the places they were

20

rebuilding were places I had come across at one time or another in my work with Mr. Lunevsky. Between the Volozhin of his boyhood in Eastern Europe and the settlements in Eretz Yisrael, Dr. Benderly constructed a bridge which I could traverse.

He was built, Dr. Benderly, like a barrel. His sparse hair was parted in the middle; his eyes peered from behind very thick lenses. He spoke with a pleasant accent, leaning forward as he spoke as though to get closer. I did not have the nerve ever to speak to him. When the talk was over, he left, and the boys and girls began to dance the horah, which they had apparently learned at their various schools. It was easy enough to pick up, but for reasons which I did not analyze at the time, and which I am not sure I understand even today, I did not join in. Why? I think it was because I sensed that they had no right to dance so joyfully and with such abandon when they had not done anything yet—if they were to do anything at all—about building up the Land. I guess it was in the same category as objecting to the picnic and sociability. Those should be the reward, not an end in themselves. Dancing the horah, said Dr. Benderly, was what the *halutzim* did after a day of hard labor, expressing their exultation at the achievements of their sweat and blood. But what had these kids done?

I suppose I was a pain in the neck to the others, too damn serious, but I simply did not join the circle. I stood around feeling superior. I was also stalling until the group disbanded, so that I could walk Miriam to the subway. Yearn as I might to ride back to the Bronx with her so that we might have some time together, I stayed as long as I possibly could and dashed home for lunch. If I came home late, I was scolded—either because the food was getting cold, or because they were worried. Where was I? What was I doing that was so important? I reported about the lecture but not about the blonde girl the mention of whose name would make me blush painfully. In fact for many years I avoided using the name "Miriam" around the house. If anyone else spoke of a Miriam so-and-so, I blushed. The family must surely have known that I had a crush on a girl named Miriam whom they had never met, but I persisted in pretending that nothing was going on while I blushed and blushed.

The problem of getting home on time and reporting where I

had been, what I had been doing, and with whom became one of the tortures of my adolescence. I would develop nausea and stomachaches, to the point where I was afraid I would throw up at the most embarrassing moments. My father was given to these attacks of nausea whenever he was worried, especially when one or another of us was late. He would imagine the worst, being run over by an automobile or becoming ill. In those days we did not think in terms of muggings. When Myron and I were invited together to a party and did not make it home by the deadline (a deadline incidentally which was much earlier than most of the kids we knew), we could be sure that my parents were not asleep, that my father was bending over the basin vomiting, and my mother was getting a migraine. As a result I would develop the same symptoms. My parents never knew, and I never told them, that their worrying virtually ruined every party we went to.

My Sundays at the meetings of the Council or at the lectures by Dr. Benderly could have been pure pleasure, but I was always conscious of the time. Could I or could I not squeeze in a little stroll with that girl, or even with a couple of the boys? I was expected home, and home I went. I was discouraged from eating out because I had a "delicate" stomach. I believed that I really did have a delicate stomach.

About this time my theological troubles began. I had never questioned what I read in the Bible about the creation of the world, the revelation of the Torah at Mt. Sinai, the chosen people and the rest of the fundamentals of traditional Judaism. I had assumed that there was no reason to doubt any of them. But Myron had already moved on. While he and I had been brought up in the same household and been exposed to the same influences, he matured sooner and made it clear that he had outgrown the old beliefs.

Was I headed for the same fate? I recall that my father was on a business trip and I sent him a poem which I had written. It was one of the very few I ever wrote. In a burst of candor, I confessed that I was disturbed by what had happened to Myron. His tower of faith had been undermined. Would mine suffer a similar collapse? The poem turned into a sort of prayer, asking that if indeed my faith were to crumble, God help me build a new one as strong as the old.

I was by no means ready to let go. In fact, I fought off the onslaught as well as I could. I recall two incidents. One was hearing a sermon by Rabbi Stephen S. Wise at one of his Sunday morning services in Carnegie Hall. My parents were virtually addicted to Sunday morning lectures, preferring Wise most of the time, but once in a while going to hear Rabbi Nathan Krass at Temple Emanuel. They used to encourage me to come along, and from time to time I did. The experience left me a bit confused. There was a rabbi conducting services without a hat, mostly in English; how goyish could one get? On the other hand he fascinated me by his voice, his eloquence and his courageous denunciation of political chicanery and civic dishonor. He roared like a lion, and one could not help but be impressed and deeply moved.

On this particular occasion he spoke on a biblical theme, and that was for me the most outrageous talk I had ever heard. He referred to the fact that the books of the Bible were written by various authors at various times, and he attacked the "fundamentalists" who did not seem to understand that they were dealing with human documents!! When we returned home I declared that that was the last time I would ever expose myself to this sort of heresy. His talk shook me up. I got very emotional about it, as would a young believer teetering on the edge of heresy himself.

The other time I was outraged was when my father took me to hear a Rabbi Mordecai Kaplan on a Saturday afternoon. Father always enjoyed hearing a variety of preachers and lecturers, and when I thought I was sufficiently mature to enjoy them too I would go along. This stern and forbidding man with a black goatee was giving a learned talk on the mythical and pagan origins of some of the laws in the Bible. I think the subject was the red heifer, but it does not matter. Here was another arrogant disbeliever. How in the world could he say those things about one of the most important institutions in biblical days? All the way home I excoriated that Kaplan.

The inevitable, of course, happened. It seemed sudden

23

though it had surely been brewing for some time. I too stopped believing. Obviously, the whole religious thing was the product of ancient minds who were burdened with ignorance and superstition. The world had not been created in six days; God did not speak to Abraham; and whatever happened at Mt. Sinai, it certainly was not what the Torah described. The Shabbat had nothing to do with God's resting on the seventh day.

The tower of faith was crumbling all about me. There was nothing left. Yet could it all have been for nothing? The long history of the Jews could not have been built upon an illusion. I felt in my bones that there must be an answer somewhere, an answer which could justify all the hours and weeks and months I had spent studying Hebrew, all the efforts I had expended on the Hatikvah Club and the hours spent listening to Dr. Benderly.

Then I saw it. Zionism! That was the answer. Zionism was what Jews had to substitute for all the things they could no longer believe in. I was not sure I knew just how Zionism was to serve as that substitute, but that there was a connection I was sure.

Among Myron's friends from Ansche Chesed was a fellow named Milton Steinberg. He was three years older than I, but he was tolerant enough to include me in the world of the young people who came to services to hear Dr. Kohn. Milton was already a legend in my high school years. He had been to De Witt Clinton, arriving with his family from Rochester, N.Y. early enough to have attended high school with his new-found friends. He was brilliant, by all reports. He never got less than an *A* in any subject. He had taken Latin and Greek and was already regarded as the genius of City College. His father had been a student at the Voloszin yeshivah, like Mr. Lunevsky; his mother was a native American. When Milton met the fellows on the block (they lived across the street from us), he was taken along with them to Ansche Chesed.

There he came under the influence of Dr. Kohn. This rabbi was an eye-opener for Milton who had, during his Rochester days, been exposed more to socialism than to Judaism. In fact, he had been given only enough Jewish training to become a bar mitzvah. Immigrant garment workers often discarded their religious observance and neglected their children's Jewish education. However, Dr. Kohn knew about socialism and about evolution, philosophy, and the classics. Milton was impressed. Apparently it was possible to be an educated person and a good Jew at the same time. He had by no means resolved his own philosophical problems, but Milton was willing to explore them with Dr. Kohn. He would read with the rabbi and return to City College armed with what he had learned, prepared to take on the great and challenging Prof. Morris Raphael Cohen, the ex-yeshivah student who had totally rejected Judaism. In fact, Cohen considered it his duty to enlighten innocent Jewish boys who came to his classes with naive notions about religion.

I was told that the classroom debates about Milton and Cohen were virtuoso performances. Milton's friends reported that Milton came through dazed but unfazed. He would go back to Dr. Kohn to pick up more ammunition. These reports came to me third hand, but I was so stirred by them that I dreamed about the time when I might be able to get close enough to Milton Steinberg to be able to discuss these matters with him. I did not seriously expect that this would ever happen because Milton was the star of the Ansche Chesed community. They had a debating team which challenged other synagogue youth groups, and crowds would turn out to watch the blood flow. Milton demolished all comers, taking either side of any issue. Debates centered on problems like: Resolved that the Balfour Declaration Is a Tragedy; Resolved that Capital Punishment Be Abolished; Resolved that the Jews Are a Race. . . . Of course, dancing and refreshments followed the serious part of the program.

In the midst of my spiritual dilemma, I decided that I wanted to become a rabbi. I blurted out this startling decision one Shabbat after services at home during lunch. I had not given much thought to the rabbinate as a life profession. I had pondered the questions of God and faith and the Jews; but all this had not come together, it had not coalesced into a clear purpose. But there it was, full grown, articulated with calm assurance!

My family was amazed. Myron said, "If you want to spend the rest of your life talking to a lot of empty seats and a few old ladies, go ahead." My mother was delighted. Grandma declared that this was exactly what the Kovner Rov had predicted. Later I told Mr. Kolodny; he sniffed. "A rabbi?" he said. "Why should a nice intelligent fellow like you want to be a rabbi? Social work yes; there you could be of use. But a rabbi? That is only for the unenlightened." Manny Eisenberg said he simply would not believe it. I must be demented. My Aunt Ray said, "A rabbi? What a waste. Ira could make a fine lawyer, and he would at least make a good living." Grandpa said, "Well, in America a rabbi doesn't need to know so much. But you can get a good job if you go to the Jewish Theological Seminary. I don't agree with the ideas they teach, but you can get the training to earn a good living."

Having made the announcement, I trembled. What was I doing? What had I committed myself to? Would I now have to change my whole way of life? And how would I reconcile my doubts with my new commitment?

Overcome by confusion and utterly bewildered, I thought perhaps I might talk over this momentous question with someone in the ministry. I would try to find out just how a doubter could fit into this kind of career. I sensed that there might be a function one could perform without having to subscribe to beliefs which demanded surrendering one's rationality.

On 110th Street there was a community church whose pulpit was occupied by a preacher whom my father and I had gone to hear on one of our church-synagogue-hopping expeditions. (I am ashamed to confess that I do not recall his name.) When I called him on the phone, he was cordial and invited me to come over. He listened gravely, giving respectful attention to this serious-minded teenager wrestling with his theological problems. Then he said that I had a long way to go and that I might resolve some of my religious doubts; that I ought to study philosophy at college; that there was room in the pulpit for men with a vision of a better world whose voices could influence the course of society; that there were many people who needed ministers and rabbis and would appreciate having one who had gone through some of the spiritual agonies I was experiencing. . . .

I left him feeling much better about my decision. It seemed strange to me at the time (though I understood better later) that I had had to go to a stranger to pour out my heart. I did not discuss the problem with Dr. Kohn, whom I respected greatly; I guess I was too embarrassed to unburden myself to someone to whom I felt so close. Whether it made sense or not is now beside the point. The Unitarian minister did not think it was horrible to be a rabbi.

Nor did Milton Steinberg. I learned that he too was considering the idea of going to the Jewish Theological Seminary. He was in his third year of college. While he was still trying to decide whether to enter the academic world as a professor of Latin and Greek, the rabbinate was a live option for him. It occurred to me that I had been foolish not to consult with him. Surely he must have been through a similar difficult period.

One evening at the temple, I asked Milton whether he would be willing to talk over with me a problem I had—about Judaism. He was most gracious. He suggested we meet at his house, where we could talk undisturbed, and the following Friday night we did. I was shocked to see the general condition of the apartment in which he lived. The furniture was shabby; the rooms seemed to be small and dingy. I suddenly felt very rich by comparison. But then we came into the dining room which doubled as a library, and I was bowled over. I had never seen so many books in all my life.

He took down a few to show me what he had been reading recently. The text was underlined, the margins were crowded with his own notes. At the back of the books on the inside cover were hundreds and hundreds of notes in his handwriting. Never had I read a book with that degree of care. No wonder he got all A's while my average at high school was not good enough to qualify me for the Honor Roll. I was a rank amateur, a mediocre kid with pretensions to scholarship. If I had had to meet Professor Morris Cohen in combat, I would have turned and fled.

But Milton turned out to be a sweet guy. Was he doing it for Myron's sake? Diffidently I told him that I was thinking of becoming a rabbi. But how could I if I had stopped believing in what Tradition had taught? Milton then smiled and said that he too had gone through exactly the same crisis and had come out of it. The process was slow. One had to study and study. One had to read and read. Perhaps he would suggest some books for me to start on. He told me that he had not yet made up his mind definitely, but he was leaning toward the rabbinate. He was studying with Dr. Kohn. Perhaps Dr. Kohn would allow me to sit in.

I left that evening walking on air. If Milton Steinberg thought it possible for me to be a rabbi, that was enough. But of course it was not all that easy. For days, months, even years, I had my ups and downs. I fluctuated between faith and skepticism, between becoming a rabbi and something else vague and undefined.

3

Columbia College

That summer I was admitted to Columbia College. My mother had made it quite clear that in spite of my father's money troubles (he had had to liquidate a business in 1921 and in 1923 was working for someone else), I was going to a "pay college" and not City College. Myron had entered NYU two years before. I was to receive no less, even if it meant pawning her diamond ring. Fortunately, she did not have to resort to such heroic measures; I managed to get a state scholarship which paid $100 a year for four years, and the tuition was only about $250 per year. Not only were the fees absurdly low by current standards. I also earned some money teaching at the Ansche Chesed Hebrew School.

Milton had spoken of me to Mr. Marcel Katz, the principal of the school who was also the cantor, and I was assigned the job of helping the slow kids with their reading. I had never taught anybody anything before, but this assignment did not require any greater skill than I had mastered at the age of not-quite-seventeen.

Staying on at the campus during the afternoon might have helped me to get to know some of my classmates. I might have become involved in some campus activities. But I found myself in the same pattern as at De Witt Clinton. After classes I had to rush off, this time to teach in addition to having to practice the piano. I no longer studied with Mr. Lunevsky because I had entered the evening sessions of the Seminary, but that took preparation and occupied two evenings a week. Fortunately, I was taking only twelve points by special permission of the student advisor. He agreed that I might be able to make up for the other points by assuming a heavier burden later on. Even so, I had little time to read my assignments, especially in Contemporary Civilization, a somewhat new course at that time at Columbia. As a result, I did poorly, despite the excellent instructor, Harry Carman, who later was known as one of the outstanding professors on campus.

In Freshman English I had Mark Van Doren. I was determined to excel in his class, but I tried too hard to be clever. We did brief essays in class each day on any subject we chose, and I chose the kind of themes that Manny and I would have picked for our entertainment. My attempts at humor were not too successful. Mr. Van Doren was not amused; he thought I might try something more serious. I was embarrassed and disappointed, as anyone might who is told that his humor is not so funny. I persisted, however, longer than I should have because I was intent upon not letting my status as a future rabbi influence me. Myron had warned that I might start taking myself too seriously and become a stuffed shirt.

The truth is that I already was something of a stuffed shirt, and a snob despite my feeble attempts at humor, for I was attending evening classes at the Seminary, and that impressed me greatly. The fact was, however, that these sessions turned out to be depressing. Classes were held at a modest building on 123rd Street that was later replaced by the large campus of the greatly expanded institution across the road. The street was quiet and poorly lit. I walked there from home twice a week from the other side of Morningside Park. The building was empty, except for the half-dozen students who were taking the courses. They and I were tired after a day's work at college and teaching, and the instructors must have felt the same way about having to be there.

Two courses were offered, one in Bible, one in Talmud. The Bible instructor was Professor Jacob Hoschander, a very thin man with a large head, a droopy moustache, and a Hungarian accent which was all but unintelligible. He had been brought in a short time before, from Dropsie College in Philadelphia, an institution which concentrated on graduate work in Hebrew and Cognate Languages, and he therefore assumed that his students were prepared for a discussion of the fine points of biblical criticism. His method of teaching was to read, slowly from a manuscript—clearly a work in progress—on the books of Ezra and Nehemiah.

In the first place, I could not understand what he was saying. In addition, I had never read either Ezra or Nehemiah, either in the original Hebrew or in translation. I had expected that I might get an introduction to some of the biblical literature I had not yet covered; certainly I was totally unprepared for the sometimes heated, even bitter and sarcastic remarks Professor Hoschander would make about the other Bible scholars who were, without doubt, altogether wrong in their theories about Ezra, not to mention Nehemiah.

The second class was in Talmud, and the instructor was Louis Finkelstein (later Professor, still later Chancellor of the Seminary and a world renowned scholar and administrator). At that stage he was a young instructor whose main occupation was serving as the rabbi of a congregation in the Bronx. He too must have been tired because he kept his feet on the desk, with his yarmulke pushed to one side constantly in danger of falling off.

He was a likable man, apparently native born (one could note traces of a Brooklyn accent), educated in this country, himself a graduate of the Seminary and thoroughly trained in Talmud. His father was an Orthodox rabbi from whom he must have acquired a great deal of knowledge. Dr. Finkelstein had a Ph.D. from Columbia University. In contrast with Dr. Hoschander, he recognized with whom he was dealing and led the students through the intricacies of the text with patience and understanding. But even he forgot from time to time how elementary was our knowledge of Talmud, and he would launch into complicated cross-references to other treatises, quoting easily and rapidly. His diction was not entirely clear, so for minutes at a time we just sat back and let him go on, until he realized he had lost us. He would then push his yarmulke back toward a more secure spot on his head, and we would proceed.

Was I unprepared for these classes? I thought not, judging by what the catalogue had said and by the intensive summer I had spent with Mr. Lunevsky getting ready for admission to the sessions. I was examined by Professor Louis Ginzberg, the renowned Talmudist. Mr. Lunevsky had taught me to translate many phrases into Yiddish. Professor Ginzberg must have understood my predicament; after all, many students came directly from the yeshivahs to the Seminary, and had been trained the same way. Nevertheless, he could not resist a remark: "Don't you speak English?" With some effort I managed to switch to my native tongue. But that was hardly enough to qualify me for a Talmud class.

Despite the unrewarding hours at the depressing empty building on 123rd Street, I did have the distinct impression that I was on my way to becoming a rabbi. My commitment had been reenforced, though my intellectual problems were more insistent than ever. I tried to read some of the books Milton had recommended, but I was not helped by them. Either I did not understand what they were about, or they spoke to issues about which I was ignorant. For example, Milton had loaned me a copy of Ahad Haam's essays translated into English titled *Lo Zu Haderekh*. It seems that he was refuting some of his Zionist contemporaries with respect to the future development of the movement. Unacquainted with the issues, I was lost.

Milton was immersed at that time in Maimonides' *Guide to the Perplexed*. In all fairness I must report that Milton did not suggest I read that book. But it sounded like the kind of work one should read if one were perplexed. I met a girl who said she was perplexed about Judaism. "Oh," I said casually, "I have just the book for you. It's by Maimonides and it's called . . ." Later on, when I learned what that medieval treatise was all about, I shuddered at the pretentiousness of a seventeen year-old future rabbi.

My lifestyle during this period was limited by my decision to become observant, especially with respect to Shabbat and *kashrut*. In addition to rushing off to teach as soon as my classes were over and spending two evenings a week at the Seminary, I was virtually a prisoner from Friday evening to Saturday night.

As I look back, I try to analyze what was going on in my mind at the time. Was it a sort of adolescent religiosity which overtakes kids, whether or not they have chosen to become religious leaders? Or was it the notion that I would appreciate better the Jewish way of living by actually adhering to it and in some mysterious manner recapture the innocent faith which I had lost? Or that, having committed myself to becoming a rabbi, I should begin at once to exemplify the life of the rabbi?

This meant, for practical purposes, no more movies on Saturday afternoon, no more vaudeville shows to which I had graduated; no riding; no spending money; and now that I was at college, no football games on Saturday afternoons. Not going to the games was particularly alienating, since virtually every other freshman went and on Monday morning became the proverbial Monday morning quarterback. I listened to the football talk and was filled with a mixture of envy and superiority. I was definitely out of the mainstream, but (I laid this unction to my soul) I had better things to do than to waste an afternoon shouting for a team.

What was better? I determined to read through these portions of the Bible with which I was still unfamiliar. With Mr. Lunevsky I had concentrated mainly on the Ḥumash, the five books of Moses. Of Joshua, Judges, Samuel, Kings, the later Prophets, and the Hagiographa I was shamefully ignorant. I set a schedule for myself and tried to cover as much ground as I could on my own. Sometimes Manny would come over, and we would walk in the park. Sometimes I would take a nap (like a regular rabbi, said my mother). Sometimes I would join Dr. Kohn and Milton at the Kohn household and sit in on one of their discussions. What I genuinely enjoyed about those sessions was the *idea* of spending time in the company of those two brilliant people, but I was out of my depth and had enough sense to sit and listen and keep quiet.

They seemed to be discussing proofs of the existence of God. In a vague way I knew that this pointed to my perplexity, but I did not understand the vocabulary they were using. When they got onto the subject of theological rationales for ethics, I thought I knew what the subject was supposed to be about, but again I floundered. It was apparent that I needed some courses in philosophy. The next year I would begin to major in that field.

My teaching career began with part-time work at the Ansche Chesed Hebrew School. Marcel Katz, the principal, needed someone to work with the children who had fallen behind in their reading of Hebrew, but I was also pressed into service as a substitute for Milton, who was a full-time teacher. It was a dreadful experience, for I knew nothing about teaching. I had many a difficult moment because the little monsters sensed my inexperience and made the most of it.

One day stands out; it was awful. I took over Milton's class, which consisted of some twelve year-olds, six girls and a solitary boy. They were reading the story of Joseph in the Bible. Instinctively those brats knew what to do with a seventeen year-old substitute.

We had not progressed very far when the questions began to pour in. Mr. Eisenstein, what did Potiphar's wife really want from Joseph? Why did he run away? Why did she hold on to his cloak until it tore? (Milton subsequently married the ringleader of this pre-delinquent gang.)

There were no final examinations at the Seminary, but I did not need them to know that I was pretty deficient in Talmud. With Mr. Lunevsky I had covered only a small treatise, and during that year much less. Grandpa now came forward and offered to teach me. Several times during the following summer I traveled to the Bronx with my tennis racquet, planning to join my brother at the public courts after the lesson. Grandpa was certainly a scholar in all branches of Jewish literature, but he had not the slightest idea how to teach Talmud. We would pore over the text, and he would read and translate while I sat by and listened. The idea, I guess, was that I would gradually acquire the skill of making out the text from watching him. From time to time, however, he got stuck on a difficult passage (much to my amazement) and for five minutes I would sit by while he plucked his short gray beard, and mumbled. Of course, he eventually figured out the line of argument, but by then I was bored and discouraged. I left wondering what in the world I was

34

doing, sweating it out on a hot summer day when I could have been playing tennis for longer than the remains of an afternoon.

John Herman Randall, Jr. and Irwin Edman were my first teachers in philosophy. Randall's course was an introduction, virtually a primer in logic; Edman's course was a lecture survey of great thinkers from Plato and Aristotle to Santayana and Dewey.

Professor Randall was a stocky, bright-eyed young man who brought an enthusiasm to the articulation of ideas which matched the sophomoric eagerness of his students. In his History of Philosophy course, which I took next, he impressed us with the great breadth of his knowledge and his way of establishing similarities and contrasts among the philosophers, sometimes to our delight and sometimes to our puzzlement, while always smiling and seeming to enjoy the intellectual exercises he was putting us through.

Irwin Edman, on the other hand, was very thin, walking with a slight tilt to one side, his head seeming to be too heavy for his body. His voice was thin, and he spoke with a lisp— altogether an unprepossessing young man. But he was one of the wittiest men I have ever known, and his students reveled in his quiet but sometimes devastating comments.

As the semester progressed I became a Platonist, then an Aristotelian, then a neo-Platonist, completely won over to each in succession by the lucid and fascinating presentations Edman gave. I began to read in earnest. The world of philosophy was irresistible. Those writers were dealing with the really important issues of life, the meaning and purpose of existence. I shall never forget how I almost wept reading Socrates' *Apology* and farewell before drinking the hemlock. I was deeply moved by the *Meditations* of Marcus Aurelius. I was intrigued by Lucretius, though I hesitated to arrive at his conclusions. My Jewish-Puritanical nature was challenged, and I struggled to regain my equilibrium. By the end of the semester, I knew that I had to learn more, dig more deeply. I discussed my readings with Milton and resumed occasional sessions with Dr. Kohn, finding myself much more capable of participating in the conversations.

I continued to go to temple, mainly to hear the rabbi and to listen for references to some of the writers I had been studying.

My preoccupation with being Jewish and preparing for the rabbinate added to my self-consciousness about being a Jew in the midst of a gentile environment. In the twenties, Columbia had a tacit quota. Jews comprised about ten percent of the student body, and except for a rare exception like Irwin Edman, there were no Jews on the faculty. These facts alone would have been sufficient to convince me that I was in a hostile world. But I could not understand how other Jews on campus managed so well to conceal or at least to ignore their Jewishness.

Not living at school, I came to know very few students; those I sought out were themselves Jews. But they irritated me by their ignorance of Judaism and their calculated indifference to the whole subject of their identity.

Fraternities played a large part in student life, and one day during my freshman year, much to my surprise I was invited to attend a smoker at Kappa Nu, one of the Jewish fraternities. I knew it was futile for me to accept because even if I were to be rushed I had neither the time nor the money to join. But I went anyway.

The evening was a disaster. Most of the upper-class men were older and far more sophisticated. Cigarettes were passed around, and to avoid embarrassment I took one. I really believed the ad which advised people to "light up a Murad" in such circumstances. Actually it made things worse. I did not know how to hold the thing. I coughed and choked, just like in the movies and stories.

This was Prohibition time, and liquor was supposed to be out of bounds. But Kappa Nu, like (I assume) other fraternities, had access to liquor. I was horrified, first, that college students should violate the law; second, that Jews should drink at all. My education had convinced me that Jews confined their drinking—as we did at home—to Kiddush on Shabbos and to Purim, when tradition called for indulging immoderately. We even broke with tradition on Purim.

The smoking and liquor were only a prelude. Soon the students gathered around the piano, and one of the brothers played and sang a series of outrageously obscene songs. Some of the allusions escaped me altogether; I laughed when the others did. The lyrics which I did understand made me blush.

I left early, explaining that I had to do some work at home. The experience made me more miserable than ever. That I did not feel at home with the non-Jewish students was painful enough. Here were (for all I knew) typical Jewish men. There was nothing Jewish about them. They smoked, drank, and sang dirty songs—and that was their idea of sophistication, and of having a good time. This is what fraternity meant to them. I had nothing in common with them.

There was no Jewish student organization on campus. I had heard of the existence of a "Menorah" movement. City College had a chapter. The thought occurred to me that I might try to organize a chapter at Columbia. Surely there must be some students whom I had not met who shared my interests. I spoke to Chaplain Knox, the official religious leader of the university. As I look back I realize that my shyness disappeared altogether when I was in the presence of anyone (in this case the Chaplain) who was religious or who took religion seriously. Strange that those who encouraged me to become a rabbi were the Unitarian preacher at the Community Church, the Chaplain (with whom I became friendly) and my non-Jewish professor Mark Van Doren (of whom I will relate an incident later). My Jewish friends— Manny, Mr. Kolodny, Elie Siegmeister, a classmate in philosophy courses—all either ridiculed the idea or thought it was just a waste of good human material.

The Chaplain assured me that I could count on using space at Earl Hall. He would assist me in any way I might need. Emboldened by this friendly response, I traveled down to 13th Street and Fifth Avenue, the headquarters of the International Menorah Association. There I met Frances Grossel, the executive secretary. (We remained close friends for many years. In fact, I recruited her to serve in a similar capacity in the synagogue.) After a few moments I was completely won over by her charm and her eagerness to help. She agreed that it was a shame there was no chapter at Columbia. She suggested I put a notice in the *Columbia Spectator* inviting interested students to meet at a given hour at Earl Hall.

About five students showed up. They will forgive me after these many years if I say that my first impression of them was that they were misfits like me. They did not belong to fraternities; they did not live on campus. They were lonely guys who felt out of things and welcomed an opportunity to huddle together "under Jewish auspices." I had no particular agenda in mind (shades of De Witt Clinton!), but we agreed that we might come together and discuss. . . . In the meantime we would join the Menorah movement by subscribing to the *Menorah Journal.*

The *Menorah Journal,* now defunct, was an elegantly published monthly magazine of superlative quality. My excitement at discovering it is indescribable. The writing was as polished and sophisticated as the appearance of the book. Distinguished names appeared among the contributors: Louis Golding, Philip Guedalla, Horace M. Kallen, Professor Harry Wolfson of Harvard, and, to my amazement, Irwin Edman! Professor Edman had written a series of essays entitled "Richard Kane Looks At Life," for one of the literary journals. They depicted the typical American college man of the 20s, including the hip flasks, the raccoon coats and the flaming part of flaming youth. This was clearly a parallel series, entitled "Reuben Cohen Looks At Life." The style was the same, slightly ironic, patronizing. I did not mind Kane getting that kind of treatment, but I objected violently to seeing Cohen depicted that way.

I asked Dr. Edman after class one day whether I might discuss his series in the *Menorah Journal* with him. I was not sure from the expression in his eyes whether he was humoring me or took me seriously. (He was albino, virtually without pigmentation, and his sensitive eyes moved rapidly back and forth all the time.) When I came to his office, I plunged right in. I was in his class, of course. Yes, he had seen me. My family knew his family. Really? He seemed annoyed, I thought. I was planning to become a rabbi. Oh, one of those professional Jews with a chip on his shoulder, super-sensitive, taking offense where there was no reason to! Well, he was Jewish by descent. He did not believe in organized religion. He was a philosopher or more modestly, a teacher of philosophy, and he saw virtue in many approaches to life. He was not an activist, only an observer of the passing scene.

In this generation we would say he had no commitment. We did not use those terms in the twenties, but the equivalent was a reality to me. I had made a commitment, and I was impatient with Jews, or anyone else, who stood on the sidelines observing. Was he really that indifferent to his identity (another new word)? Or was he deliberately playing down his Jewishness, knowing that Columbia had been willing to appoint him despite the fact that he was a Jew?

I was puzzled. If he was indeed indifferent to the whole enterprise of being Jewish, if he could take it or leave it, why then did he bother to write a series of articles in the *Journal*? When I suggested that he might come and speak to us at the Menorah Society, he begged off. Nothing personal, mind you. He just did not have time for extra-curricular assignments. He tired easily, and he had a heavy schedule, and so on. He might have been telling the truth, but my intuition told me that he was avoiding any association of a formal nature with Jews or Jewish organizations.

And what did he mean by saying he objected to, or was not interested in, organized religion? I had heard this from some of the other students. In general, it was assumed that religion had been left behind in the forward march to civilization. I knew of my own struggles with ideas of God and of the specific theological dogmas of the Jewish tradition to which I could not reconcile myself. But I also knew that those questions were real questions. They had troubled thinking people throughout the ages (at least, I was beginning to get a sense of the chronic character of these issues). How could it be that suddenly the central questions of human life were no longer to be pondered?

Irwin Edman was one of the most popular instructors on the campus. His courses were fully subscribed. His Philosophy of Art course always had auditors lining the walls. I was among them. What an influence he could be, I thought, if he were to assert his Jewishness openly, honestly, wholesomely. Students took their cues from the teachers they admired. Was it not his responsibility to show the way? I thought of Morris Cohen at City College. He at least engaged the Jewish students there (and they were almost all Jewish) in heated debate. He wanted them to begin thinking for themselves, and not merely parroting what they had heard from their parents and rabbis. In that respect he was engaged: he believed passionately in coming to terms with whatever the past had handed down. But Edman was altogether different. He took the aesthete's position, dispassionately, coolly and amusedly observing the human comedy. It made me furious, yet I was devoted to Dr. Edman and moved by his meticulous prose (which I proceeded to imitate), by his wit, and by his erudition.

After some consideration I realized that I should not have been surprised to find Irwin Edman in the pages of the *Menorah Journal*. The entire publication reflected his attitude. The articles on art, richly illustrated, unconsciously were demonstrating how far Jews had made it in the artistic world. The travel notes, brilliantly done by Marvin Lowenthal, covered Jewish communities which were exotic, far away, quaint—rich morsels for the connoisseurs. Cecil Roth's pieces on Jewish history called attention to "golden ages" at other times and places. And Elliot Cohen's notes for a future history of the Jews in America were funny but bitter commentaries on the Jewish "booboisie" as H.L. Mencken would have called them. Indeed, Cohen appropriated the tone and method of the *American Mercury* and applied them to the foibles of Jewish life. Cohen was brilliant and cutting, and what he reported was true. But I can recall, despite my amusement, wishing that instead of saying "ha ha," he had said "oy veh."

The Menorah movement, established by Henry Hurwitz at Harvard during the teens of this century (it was about ten years old when I came upon the *Journal*), was the intellectual Jew's delight, for it reveled in the fact that Jewish culture could take its place side by side with other cultures. But what troubled me was that it was a form of snobbery rather than a way of grappling with the problems of Jewishness. I discovered later that only a few years before my introduction to the *Journal*, Mordecai Kaplan had written a series of articles for it, outlining the basic problems of Judaism in the modern world. These laid the foundations for his later work.

The big problem at Menorah was arranging programs. We had no money, and we had to rely on the good nature of busy individuals to come and speak to a handful of undergraduates. I approached Milton Steinberg and asked whether he would give us a short series on the Prophets. Though he was very busy with his Seminary work, he agreed. When he came, I regretted having troubled him, for only a few students showed up. My friend Miriam (who had by now entered Barnard) thought we might get some of the girls to join us. They did not have a formal organization (like us?) but she did manage to corral some of her friends. Milton's talks were fascinating, as I expected they would be.

Miriam introduced me to Mirra Komarovsky, a very knowledgeable person who later became head of the department of sociology at Barnard. Another participant was Shalmith Schwartz, whose mastery of Hebrew and Hebrew literature produced a sense of painful inferiority in me. Her grandfather had been the famous Rov Masliansky, the fiery Zionist preacher and mentor of those who later assumed the leadership of the Zionist movement.

Mirra had an idea. She thought she could persuade Vladimir Jabotinsky to come to Columbia–Barnard. I did not know who Jabotinsky was, but I naturally did not let on. We chipped in and paid for printed posters, which we put up on all the bulletin boards, and we inserted a notice in the *Spectator*. On the appointed day, Mirra and I went to pick him up at a brownstone house on 88th or 89th Street. He welcomed us into his furnished room with old-world courtesy. I let Mirra do all the talking. I ran to get a taxi, and we brought him to the campus. Apparently, there were many hundreds of students who *did* know who Jabotinsky was. The students stormed the auditorium. I remember only that he spoke rapidly in a staccato, peering defiantly through his pince-nez glasses. He was not tall, but he gave the impression of overwhelming energy. No wonder he became a world figure. He could transport his audiences in a dozen languages, and his militancy (the implications of which I did not grasp for several years) aroused great excitement in those who listened.

A somewhat lesser triumph was achieved by bringing Morris

Raphel Cohen to speak to our combined group. We were helped in convincing him to come by name-dropping: I said I was a good friend of Milton Steinberg. (Prof. Cohen was another Jew who thought Milton was wasting his time by becoming a rabbi.) Cohen's talk had virtually nothing in common with Jabotinsky's. He spoke slowly, quietly, in a semi-Yiddish intonation. He was not a spellbinder.

Instead of giving a prepared talk, he asked for questions. Applying his razor-sharp mind to whatever subject came up, he gave us an intellectual treat. Naturally, I did not care for much of what he said. There was too much cynicism, or at least skepticism, woven into this intricate reasoning. But this was my deficiency. I was still at a point where I waited for the speaker to say what I would have liked him to say.

The 1926 convention of the Intercollegiate Menorah Association was held in New York, and Columbia Menorah, along with a few others, was to be the host. I had a sense of déjà vu representing Columbia. I was a general without a real army—as I had been in the Inter-High School Hatikvah Council. As the host school, we were given the honor of presiding at the climactic event of the convention, a debate held at the Great Hall of City College. Two visiting delegations were to take opposite positions on some theme. I have forgotten the subject; I have forgotten who the other speakers were. All I do recall, with horror, is the miserable failure I was as presiding officer.

I had rented a tuxedo for the occasion. It was too large for me because I was so skinny that they could not find one narrow enough for my size. I was petrified with fright. Though the audience, including my family, was only some hundred people lost in that great hall I could not be heard. My casual way of speaking did not magnify my voice, so it died at about the third row. Of course, my feeble attempts at witticisms were a total failure.

When we came home that evening, I was told that if I had any hopes of becoming a rabbi, I had better forget them, or learn to open my mouth. I was depressed for several days.

My attachment to Mark Van Doren grew from semester to semester. He was the kindest and most intelligent man I had ever studied with. I took every course he gave from English authors to American literature. When I was admitted to the General Honors program, I was in his section. My enthusiasm for literature and my particular admiration for him, rendered perfectly clear by my enrollment in all his courses, created a bond between us which I deeply cherished. He was the first non-Jew with whom I felt entirely at ease. I knew that if I had a problem I could confide in him. His warmth and kindliness gave me the courage to approach him at the end of one semester when a problem did arise. The final examination was scheduled for Shavuot. I explained that it was a Jewish holiday and that I would appreciate taking it at another time.

He smiled and said, "If the Dean approves, it's all right with me. But tell me," he added, "how is it that in this very large class where there must be quite a number of Jewish students, you are the only one who has mentioned this conflict?" I suppose he meant it as a compliment; but I was ashamed for the other Jewish students, and I tried to soften the implied criticism by remarking that I was planning to become a rabbi, and maybe that was why I was especially sensitive to the sanctity of the Jewish festival. Then he said something which moved me greatly: "I know that Henry Rosenthal is also studying for the rabbinate, at the Jewish Theological Seminary. If two men of your calibre choose to attend that school, it must be indeed a superlative institution."

One professor to whom I owe much is Herbert W. Schneider. He was in the philosophy department but taught, along with Horace Friess, the first courses in religion. There was not yet a department of religion; the course was included among the philosophy course offerings. Schneider was warm and modest, like Van Doren, and he was greatly interested in my absorption with the phenomena of religion and its institutions. With Schneider I was not exposed to the cheap and superficial jokes of the free thinkers. Religion was a serious matter, a scholarly discipline to be studied and analyzed like any manifestation of human effort. The notion that religion is being left behind seemed absurd when one studied comparative religions, the psychology of religion or the sociology of religion. Religion was an integral part of every known civilization; and it was foolish to dismiss it as a vestige of an earlier time. Schneider introduced me to the tremendous power which religions could and did exert.

When it came to Judaism he was unnecessarily modest, deferring to me as the expert. I welcomed the compliment but insisted that I had yet to learn what Judaism was all about. That would come after my graduation from Columbia.

When the end of the 1925–1926 academic year rolled around, I felt a strong need to get away, to do something else besides studying. I sensed that this would be the last chance I might have to spend the summer away from the customary round. Next year I would be on the threshold of entering the Seminary, and I would have to do some last-minute catching up on my Jewish reading, which had been neglected. I also wanted to get out from under the scrutiny of my parents. This was my twentieth year, and it was about time for me to withdraw from my usual surroundings and develop some perspective.

The idea of a summer of good hard physical work occurred to me. Remaining in the city would not achieve the purpose; it would have to be out of town. Something like a farm? I had heard there was an agency called the Jewish Agricultural Society which encouraged Jews to get back to the soil. Perhaps they knew of a farmer who could use a summer hand. At that time I had a friend named Jack Rifkin. He was one of those high school fellows whom my parents looked down on. He was poor and could not afford to go to college; he was talented with electrical gadgets and had begun to work for a radio manufacturer. In fact he had put together a radio for us, the first we ever owned. I liked Jack, but I must admit I was prompted to think well of him because of his opinion of me. He was not intellectual; therefore he was less interesting to me than someone else might be. But as a companion working on a farm, he seemed the most likely candidate.

I put the idea to Jack. He agreed to try the experiment instead of looking for some other summer employment. So off we went to the Agricultural Society. Sure enough there was a Jewish farmer near Fishkill, N.Y. who needed help. He was willing to give food and lodging to a young man prepared to work hard. Neither of us would go without the other, and we decided to take a chance riding upstate to the farm on the chance that the farmer would take us both. He did, and we lasted three days.

The two city boys had not known that work on a farm starts at sunrise, and in the summer that is quite early indeed. In addition, we had no skills whatsoever. The farmer was patient the first day or two; he sent us out to the field to watch the cows. There were nine; we were supposed to see to it that they did not wander beyond the pasture. The cows seemed to us to be sufficiently docile, so we lay down in the grass and soon got to talking about religion, my work, his work, gazing up from time to time to check. We counted—gevalt! There were only eight. What happened to the ninth? We finally persuaded the ninth to return, having found her at last.

This exhausted us, at least me. But the real test came when we were charged with cleaning the barn. Neither Jack nor I had ever had to shovel manure. I can still smell the unbearable stink. I got nauseous. Jack did most of the shoveling. By the end of the second day, we knew we were not cut out for this kind of work, but we were determined not to return to the city. I had another idea: we should hitch-hike to the mountains. Perhaps in a place like Tannersville, where my family had spent some weeks at a kosher hotel, we might get jobs as waiters. It was early in the season, and we might succeed in being placed before the usual summer applicants arrived.

Between us we had about ten dollars. We bought a couple of cheap blankets, which we rolled up and placed across our shoulders, as we had seen others do, and we set out. By Friday evening we found ourselves on the outskirts of a town on the west side of the Hudson River and decided to spend the night on the side of the road, rolled in our thin blankets. We both almost froze. In the morning we faced a new problem. I would not ride on Shabbos; there was to be no hitch-hiking until the end of the day. Jack, who was not himself observant, respected my wishes, and we began to walk. Strictly speaking we walked further on the Sabbath than is permitted by Jewish law. But we could not simply stand around and make no progress toward our goal.

As the afternoon progressed, it got hotter and hotter. We got grimy and tired, and I finally capitulated. A car picked us up, and we arrived in Kingston, N.Y. as the sun was beginning to set. We could not face another night sleeping on the hard ground, and then my Jewish education came to the rescue. I had read that in the Jewish communities in Europe, the *kehillah* (Jewish community) provided help through a fund called *hakhnasat orehim* for the purpose of giving temporary lodging to strangers. It was meant for people like us: honest Jewish boys passing through on their way to somewhere else looking for a job.

I suggested we try to find the local synagogue. We soon found it. About twenty men were there *davening maariv*, the evening prayers. We took our places, picked up prayerbooks and joined the services. Several men looked around at us, somewhat suspiciously, but we repeated the Hebrew loud enough to impress them with the fact that we were Jews and not bums. After *havdalah*, I asked one of the men for the *shammes*. He pointed out a man who turned out to be the president of the shul and the one in charge of taking care of strangers. Indeed they did have a *hakhnasat orehim.* He motioned us to the butcher shop (his), which he opened for business. Then he went to a drawer and drew out a small notebook, on which he wrote our names. He tore out the page and told us to present the page at a house down the street. A woman there was in charge of the flat where strangers were housed for the night.

The little old lady, who reminded me of my grandma, showed us our room, and we flopped into bed, exhausted and soon asleep. In the morning, on an impulse, I reached for my *tefillin* (phylacteries worn by males after they become bar mitzvah. Small boxes attached to a long, thin, leather strap are placed on the head and the left arm.), which I had taken along to the farm. I began to put them on. At that moment, the old lady knocked on our door, and, invited in, she opened it to find, to her surprise and delight, that we were indeed good Jewish boys. As soon as we were ready, she said, she had a special breakfast for us—special, she added, because of the *tefillin*. We had been saving our pennies and not eating much, so the meal was devoured with gusto.

Then to *our* surprise and delight, she handed us each a dollar bill. This was routine and had nothing to do with the *tefillin*. Our gratitude was so great, however, that we actually refused to take the money. We thanked her and hurried off. By evening we had made it to Tannersville. We got jobs as busboys in a small hotel named La Vela run by a widow and her two sons. She had been an opera singer in Russia, and her husband had been a famous cantor named Russotto. One son was a doctor and the other a musician who worked at Roxy's in New York.

We got the job, she said later, because she liked my face; she knew she could trust me. Poor Jack she did not like so well. In fact she did not need more than one busboy, but she took us both. Jack soon left for home. I was promoted to waiter and spent the entire summer working. It was one of the best summers of my life up to that time because I did not look at a book, though every once in a while I suffered a moment of guilt. Milton, I thought, would have read a dozen books by now. I learned to play bridge (not very well), and I had a chance to hear good music, played by Dan Russotto (from Roxy) and a variety of his talented friends. One sour note: my mother decided to come up and see where her boy was. She stayed a week, complaining to the other guests that the future rabbi had, against her better judgment, gone ahead with this crazy plan to work during the summer, and for what? For the twenty-five dollars or so he might earn?

What she did not know was that I had been initiated into a criminal career that summer. It happened in the following way. The waiters—all of them young musicians except one older chap, who had written music criticism for a New York Russian-language paper—heard that there was a crap game in the village of Tannersville where one could, and some did, make a lot of money. A couple of them investigated and came back thirty dollars richer. With tips coming in at the rate of one dollar per person per week, one might slave all summer and not make much more. So off the group went to the crap game; all except me. I was, after all, a future rabbi.

But when I learned as we set the table for breakfast the next day that several of them had struck it rich, I decided I would go along that night to watch. I did not know how one played the game, and since the least amount one could bet was one dollar, I was planning to get better acquainted with the fine points before I risked my hard-earned money.

The game was run in a garage behind one of the smaller hotels. We stood around the long green table as the players took turns tossing the dice. The betting was done with large silver dollars which you acquired from the dealer. I watched, fascinated. Suddenly we all heard a gruff voice saying, "OK, everybody. Don't move. This is the police. You are gambling without a license. Line up. Give your name and plead either guilty or not guilty."

We were, of course, stunned. We lined up against the wall as the man in uniform (with an impressive revolver at his side) took out a notebook and started down the line, recording each name.

The man who ran the game paid the fine of ten dollars for each player; that was part of his overhead. He knew that if he did not pay the fines himself, the customers would never return. One of my waiter-friends, in the meantime, had turned to me and whispered, "Don't give your right name!" Under the stress of the moment I could not make a quick decision. Naturally as a future rabbi I was deeply inhibited about telling a lie.

Before I could arrive at a wise decision, he reached me, and I blurted out "Eisenstein. Guilty." As he dropped a ten dollar bill onto the notebook, the man who ran the game gave me a dirty look, and I knew why. He recognized me as the fellow who had merely stood by and had not played a single time. Instead of making a profit on me, he had lost ten dollars. I could not explain to him that I had come not as a kibitzer but as a potential gambler, that I was merely trying to learn the game.

"I guess that's the end of the game," I said as we made our way back to the hotel. "Don't be silly," they said. "You must have noticed that the boss was not surprised. This happens every couple of weeks. It is part of his overhead. He'll open up again in a few days." But I knew I had better not show my face there again. I also knew that my name would be forever inscribed in the annals of the County Courthouse in Catskill, N.Y.

———————————

That fall I began my final year at Columbia. I was more confused than ever. My religious views had not been clarified. Philosophy and history, literature and science had done their work; the tower of faith had crumbled, as I had fearfully predicted. I was no longer an innocent and naive believer. But I still found joy and comfort in my Jewish studies, in my unswerving Zionist convictions (though I had done nothing about them) and in belonging to the Jewish people. I wanted to learn more about Judaism, even as a religion in which I no longer believed. But on the other hand I was beginning to chafe at the restrictions which I had imposed upon myself.

There was little comfort in missing football games or in not going out to restaurants and experimenting with other than kosher foods. If, I thought, I had really outgrown the disciplines of religious observance, why continue them, especially when they deprived me of perfectly legitimate pleasures while offering me none of the satisfaction of knowing that I was conforming to a sacred obligation. I decided I would go to the next game, Columbia against NYU up at Baker Field. Myron had since graduated from NYU, but his enthusiasm for the team had dimmed but little; I would go and root for Columbia.

Since I had not been attending these games, I had not developed a circle of friends who were in the habit of going together. I had to go alone. That in itself dampened my enthusiasm, but not my determination to break out of the confines of the restrictions which make up so large a part of Shabbos observance.

The next hurdle I had to overcome was putting money back into my pocket. On Friday afternoons, like all good pious Jews, I emptied my suit of all work-a-day items, especially money. There was no need of them. Actually they were a temptation to violate the Sabbath. Most of all they interfered with the sensation of being "*shabbosdick*." On this momentous Shabbos, after attending services at the Temple and eating lunch at home, I quietly announced that I was going to the football game! By now my piety had been considered taken for granted, and it came as a shock to my parents. Myron had begun working at an advertising firm, and he was no longer at home on Saturdays. "I thought you were going to become a rabbi?"

Well, I am not so sure, I said as calmly as I could. I added that I was still seriously considering the Seminary, but I would go there to continue my studies, not to become a rabbi. In those days Jewish studies at colleges and universities had not yet been introduced, and the only way one could pursue a program of advanced Jewish studies was to attend a seminary. Columbia did have a Semitics department, headed by Professor Richard Gottheil, but the courses were oriented toward language study in Hebrew, Arabic, and Syriac, and that was not what I had in mind. I don't think I was sure what I had in mind; I did not discover the wide variety of subject matter available until I actually began my work at the Jewish Theological Seminary. But Columbia was not suited to my needs as I vaguely conceived them.

My parents seemed disappointed. They had already begun to visualize themselves as the parents of a rabbi, perhaps sitting in the pews and listening to him deliver sermons while the congregation praised him for his learning and his eloquence. Their fantasies were not really so different from my own. But as long as I had not ruled out the Seminary altogether, they were still hopeful. They suggested that I carry out this plan, and if, after four years, I still did not wish to be a rabbi, I could go on to other things, like law school perhaps.

Off I went to the subway station. I recall to this day the sound of the coin, a nickel to be exact, dropping into the turnstile. I almost did not walk through. I never expected to experience such a combination of emotions: regret, shame, alienation from the years prior to that moment, as though I had suddenly become someone else, someone I did not altogether recognize. I felt as though a spirit had departed, the spirit of the Shabbos. It suddenly became just Saturday, another day, a weekday. I was going into the subway to travel to do something connected with school. The joy went out of my freedom; no more was there exhilaration at breaking away from the restrictions.

I almost turned back. All the way uptown I was in turmoil. I arrived at the station not knowing which way to go; it was actually my first trip to a football game, and I felt like an intruder. The people moving toward the stadium seemed to be going where I was headed, so I followed them. But I felt alien from them. They were carrying banners. Some of them had begun drinking from flasks. They were in groups, laughing. I walked alone, wondering what I was doing there. I had lost both worlds, one which I had possessed, the other which I had never entered fully.

The game itself was strange. I knew baseball well; football I understood only in the most primitive terms. The team had to make a touchdown in order to gain six points; you had a chance at a seventh. There were eleven on a team. That was about all I knew. I watched the people around me more than the game itself. Who were they? Were there Jews among them? Did they know it was Shabbos? Did they not care?

Columbia lost. I was astonished to discover that I was indifferent. Is this what young people like myself really get excited about? I assumed that they were generally intelligent and that they were concerned about the world, or at least knew what was going on. If so, how could they expend all that energy on football?

I look back now and realize that I was not so aware of world events myself. Yes, I spent much time discussing eternal values, concepts of God and religion, the spiritual dilemmas of modern man and the like. But if someone had asked me directly what was going on at the time in Europe or Asia or Latin America or even in Washington, I would have been at a loss. In addition, whenever the World Series rolled around, I got as excited as they did about football. Was it not that football was a game I had not ever really learned? Was not its conflict with the Shabbos at the heart of my indifference to it?

In short, I had built up a case about my own generation and its putative faults around my own tensions resulting from an act of rebellion, which I was regretting before the day of the rebellion had passed.

My work had improved greatly since the first disastrous year, and I began to hope that I might make Phi Beta Kappa. I had begun German the previous year and was getting A's. As usual, in the special honors seminar in philosophy, with Edman and Schneider, I was doing very well, or so I was assured.

Why Phi Beta Kappa loomed so important is not difficult to understand. I was intent upon impressing upon the Seminary faculty that I was coming with a rich secular education and that what I lacked in my Jewish studies—especially Talmud—I could make up with hard work. I had the potential of being a candidate for the rabbinate. Had not Milton also come with less background than many of the other students? They had certainly made no mistake in taking him. I felt especially insecure about my Jewish studies because, apart from desultory sessions with my grandfather, I had done virtually nothing to improve my preparation during the past three years—even four, since that first year at evening session counted for little.

I did not make Phi Bete on the first round. Out of the class of 300, they elected 15 purely on the basis of grades; the other 15 were to be chosen from a pool of those who had achieved the equivalent of a B plus average for the four years. I later learned that a number of professors had spoken up for me as had some students (one non-Jew, by the way, who was preparing for the ministry). They acknowledged that I was not the best student in the world, but I was serious, even earnest, and I might make a contribution to the profession of my choice. Thus I was elected in the second fifteen.

My parents were jubilant, and Grandma most of all, though she didn't know what Phi Bete meant. We ordered ice cream, and Milton joined us in an impromptu party. Just to show that we were not just intellectuals, we played poker and included Grandma, who won all the money.

I sometimes think that winning the Phi Beta Kappa key did me harm. It reenforced an already growing snobbery which, in the summer of 1927, caused me much heartache, as I shall recount. As soon as I received it, I got myself a chain and attached the key and spread it across my narrow chest. It made a good impression on Professor Israel Davidson, the Registrar of the Seminary, when Milton introduced me as a candidate for admission, but it gave the wrong impression. The fact is that I was not a good student. I had not been selected in the first round; a number of people liked me and said nice things about me, but that was beside the point. Of course, I had done well and brought my average up. But the truth is that I really did not understand as much as I thought I did, especially in philosophy. I gave the right answers on the exams. But my limited life experience had shielded me from truly knowing what the basic issues were.

I had learned to make a little go a long way. Through a kind of cleverness, I was able to infer much from the little I actually knew. Perhaps this was a strength which would serve me well in later years, but as of 1927, I fancied myself an intellectual, and that produced (along with all the other influences which I have tried to describe) an unjustified sense of superiority, which should have made me unbearable—and did, as the summer proved.

In June I attended the graduation exercises of the Seminary at the old Aeolian Hall on 42nd Street. It no longer exists. Since I was to be a student, I was curious to watch and be among the people who were to be my environment, as it were, for the next four years.

After the exercises, standing on the sidewalk with several people, I met a young man whom I had known from Ansche Chesed. He asked me whether I was planning to enter the essay contest conducted by the Young People's League of the United Synagogue. I had not heard of it. He urged me to write something, on either of the two themes announced: the Sabbath or *Kashrut*. But I must hurry because the deadline was the next morning.

When I reached home I sat down and wrote an essay on *Kashrut*. I recall that I was then very much under the influence of Irwin Edman's prose style, and I composed a prose-poem, describing the observance of *Kashrut* in semi-mystical terms. One would have thought that the experience of avoiding the flesh of the swine had the same ability to elevate the soul that Santayana ascribed to a painting or a symphony. I ran down to the mailbox and mailed it. I won second prize; the first prize had gone to the chap who had called my attention to the contest.

The prize was a fifteen dollar credit at the Bloch Publishing

Co. I chose three volumes of Schechter's *Studies in Judaism*, and several others. In those days one could get five or six books for fifteen dollars. These were to be my summer reading; surely I should know more of Schechter if I was going to "Schechter's Seminary," as it was still called; and considering how I had squandered the previous summer (waiting on tables), I resolved not to indulge any further whims but to get down to the serious business of reading.

When I was called, therefore, by Rabbi David Goldstein (who, I believe, had just graduated) and asked whether I would like to serve as the camp rabbi at the kosher Boy Scout Camp in New York State, I hesitated. I was nervous about serving as a rabbi when I had had no experience whatsoever, and I was concerned about whether I would be able to do the reading I had promised myself. Milton had apparently recommended me when it became apparent that no one else among the Seminary students was available. I was assured that the only thing I had to do was to conduct services on Friday nights and check the kitchen to see that nothing too obviously non-kosher found its way onto the menu. And I was to be paid something, not much to be sure, but I would have a summer in the country with lots of leisure time.

I agreed. I had never been a boy scout. Without knowing anything about the movement, I had nothing but contempt for it. It was a childish game, getting into uniform, playing soldier, learning to tie knots, saluting, marching, rubbing two sticks against one another—altogether a sort of goyishe nonsense. But who cared? I had a tent all to myself. I could bring my books. And I didn't have to fraternize with the counsellors, who surely must be equally moronic.

The first service did not go so well. The boys did not have books, so I tried to get them to sing the familiar songs, like *Shema* and *En Kelohenu*. I gave a five-minute talk in compliance with the instructions I had received. The subject was "The Moral Equivalent of War," straight out of William James. The boys looked blank. When we gathered at the staff tent later, I asked how they thought it went. They said I would have to come down to the level of the scouts. For this I got a Phi Beta Kappa key?

The second week went worse, and at the staff meeting I

complained that I was not getting the cooperation of the counsellors. They did not help round up the kids; they sat together and talked throughout the service. I demanded better cooperation. Then the lightning struck. I shall never forget the shock and humiliation. The head counsellor spoke for the staff: who did I think I was? Why did I consider myself superior to everyone and to the boy scout idea? What right did I have to sit in my tent by the hour and not participate in the activities of the camp? If I were the last man on earth, they would refuse to cooperate with me when I flatly refused to cooperate with them. And who needed a Phi Bete attached to one's shorts?

No one had ever attacked me like that before. I could not sleep. I paced up and down the campus for an hour or more, crushed, depressed, deflated. Was it true? Was I such a snob? Was I blind to the wholesome effects of the camp? Had I isolated myself from the company of my peers? Was I actually superior to them? Around and around the tongue-lashing echoed in my ears.

I was ready to quit, go home, and try to forget the whole nightmare experience. A fortunate circumstance saved me. Across the lake there was another kosher camp; the rabbi was a little chap with a funny moustache and a well-developed, muscular body. Actually he was a gymnast from McGill University, a first-year student at the Seminary who had entered only the previous January. His name is Lavy Becker, and to him I owe whatever transformation I was able to effect that summer. I did not in so many words tell him my troubles, but I watched him at work. I observed his manner of relating to the counsellors of his camp, his warmth, his friendliness, his patience with the kids, his participation in their games, his willingness to serve as an examiner (to test whether the scouts had mastered a set of skills before being elevated ·to the next category). He told folksy stories. He laughed a good deal, his good humor was infectious.

I am happy to relate that, at the seventieth birthday celebration of Lavy in Montreal, given by the congregation he organized (more of that later), I had the opportunity publicly, for the first time, to acknowledge the debt I owed him, and to thank him for making me a "mentsh"—if I have indeed achieved that status.

The rest of the summer was sheer delight. I plunged into the work. I did *not* read Schechter (until much later). I learned the knots. I tested the scouts. I played baseball. I went on hikes. And when the summer ended and we made our way back to the city, I glowed with deep satisfaction at the compliment I received from the head counsellor.

I was lucky to have learned my lesson before the new semester began because at the Seminary I would have been catapulted from my illusory heights if I had not already climbed down. The students were all much better prepared than I. I was put in Talmud C (the third of four grades). Humility was very much in order, and I owe it to Lavy that I came prepared to place myself into the proper niche—among these yeshiva-trained, richly educated fellow-students.

4

Jewish Theological Seminary

During the spring of 1927 I was trying to make up my mind whether to go to the Jewish Theological Seminary or to another rabbinical school which had been established only a few years before by Rabbi Stephen S. Wise of the Free Synagogue, the man whom I used to go to hear frequently on Sunday mornings and who, only a short time before, had shocked me by his heterodox views. His institution, called the Jewish Institute of Religion, was intended to bring into existence a new kind of rabbinical education, one which was not affiliated with any of the established denominations but whose graduates would be trained to serve any or all of them.

Dr. Wise was not himself a scholar. He had been ordained by his father, and he had received a Ph.D. from Columbia's Semitics Department for a thesis whose true authorship was the subject of some smirking remarks by scholars. But he was a magnificent person, an impressive figure physically with a booming voice that sounded like an organ; he had great charm, and he was endowed with a remarkable capacity to enlist supporters among liberal wealthy Jews. Among his communal achievements were the establishment (with others) of the American Jewish Congress, the World Jewish Congress and his own Free Synagogue. Among Reform rabbis of that time, he was a rare combination of ardent Zionist and religious reformer. That combination is no longer so rare.

He brought together a brilliant array of scholars to serve on his faculty, including people like Chaim Chernowitz and Salo W. Baron. To serve as chairman of that faculty, he invited Mordecai M. Kaplan. Kaplan had been running into frequent storms at the Seminary, where he was Professor of Homiletics and Dean of the Teachers Institute. He had been brought into the Seminary faculty by the first president of the newly reorganized Seminary, Dr. Solomon Schechter, who had been impressed by the young Kaplan's views on Torah and Zionism. But after Schechter's death, when the Seminary was under the leadership of Dr. Cyrus Adler, the essentially Orthodox faculty had made Kaplan's life difficult. They regarded his views as representing a basic discontinuity with normative Judaism and sought, at every possible occasion, to denigrate and refute his interpretation of Judaism. It reached a point where Kaplan decided to resign from the Seminary, and it was then that Wise offered him the position.

From the peripheral position which I occupied as a senior student at Columbia College, receiving my information from infrequent, second-hand reports by Milton Steinberg, I was unable to follow the course of these developments step by step. But of one thing I was certain: If Kaplan goes to the JIR, I shall go there too. If he stays at the Seminary, I shall go to the Seminary as planned.

What did I know of Kaplan that made me so certain that I wanted to study with him? Not very much more than I was able to glean from a few talks I had heard him give at various Zionist gatherings, and from a very occasional visit to the synagogue which he had organized in 1922, the Society for the Advancement of Judaism. Living in Harlem, I found it too far to walk; the SAJ was on 86th Street. But from time to time I would attend services to hear Rabbi Kaplan preach.

These exposures, few and far between, were enough to impress me with the fact that he was attempting to formulate a conception of Judaism which would come to grips with my theological doubts. Unlike Dr. Kohn, who tried to bridge the gap between historical Judaism and modern thought, Rabbi

Kaplan would speak about the need to *change* some aspects of Judaism in the light of contemporary knowledge and insights.

Admittedly, that was not much to go on, but I had never heard anyone except Reform rabbis speak of change, and I knew that the kind of change they talked about was not for me. It had resulted in a Protestantized kind of Judaism, deprived of the spirit which I had grown to love from my Grandma and Mr. Lunevsky and the Shaarei Zedek congregation, and even, in a somewhat cosmeticized version, at Ansche Chesed. I had noticed a few actual changes in Kaplan's services: the last stanza of *En Kelohenu* had been replaced by a verse the words of which I could not catch. In the *Alenu* there was a verbal change too. The revolutionary changes of which Kaplan had spoken, on the few occasions I had heard him, were still in the realm of theory.

But I had made up my mind: if Kaplan moved over, I would too. He did not move, and I entered the Seminary in the fall. For many years the debate has been carried on by rabbis and others on the subject: what would have happened if Kaplan had accepted Wise's invitation to head the JIR? Would a Reconstructionist movement have developed? If so, would it have been launched sooner? Would it have resembled the movement which actually did come into existence? Why did Kaplan turn down the offer? Was it because of the pressure exerted upon him by students and alumni and the laity of the United Synagogue? Or was it because he did not have faith in Wise's ability to finance the JIR sufficiently? The debate goes on.

I believe that no one will ever know the precise truth of Kaplan's decision, but I have a theory which has two parts to it. First, I believe that Kaplan (and his wife, Lena) had by that time had enough of changes. He had left the Orthodox synagogue which had been his first pulpit after graduating from the Seminary; he had organized and then left the Jewish Center; had organized the Society for the Advancement of Judaism in 1922; and it was only a few years later that he was invited to make another change. These changes had left him little time to work on his major opus, long overdue, the book which finally came out in 1934. He needed more stability in his life.

The second part of the theory deals with his powerful attachment to the Seminary. He enrolled there while still a young boy; he spent years studying there; and it was there that Solomon Schechter gave him the golden opportunity to teach, and to administer an institution for the training of teachers called the Teachers' Institute. His roots were there. And while he had serious disagreements with the philosophy of Conservative Judaism, he felt thoroughly at home there. He respected the level of scholarship represented by the faculty—and I believe he had some doubts about the level of learning at the JIR. Certainly, the prestige which the JTS had earned over the years was not to be matched by a newly established school, which, at that time had no record of achievement. The years that followed were increasingly difficult for him at the JTS, but despite the heartaches and the insults he never again showed any sign of stepping down. A psycho-historian might have much to explore in this phenomenal demonstration of loyalty to an institution which made his life so full of anguish, an institution to which he clung with a mysterious passion.

From the first moment in the Seminary I was happier than I had ever been. Milton Steinberg personally escorted me to the office of the Registrar (there was no dean), Professor Israel Davidson, and introduced me as his friend applying for admission. Dr. Davidson soon identified me with my grandfather, whom he had known for many years—and I was home at last, among Jews. I reveled in the intimate and friendly environment. The school comprised some 60 students altogether, quite a change from the vast university from which I had just graduated.

The faculty in 1927 was substantially the same group which Dr. Schechter had assembled when he led the reorganization from 1901 until his death in 1915. Professor Louis Ginzberg, the great talmudist, taught Talmud A and gave lectures to the entire student body on special occasions. He was short and round, with deep-set eyes beneath bushy brows and a constantly quizzical expression. His learning was unbelievable. He had mastered not only all of Jewish literature, but also economics and many languages. When we once asked him whether he knew Chinese, he replied in that squeaky voice, "I read it a little." Who knows what he considered a little?

When he lectured, he held in his hands an envelope on which he had scribbled some notes. That was all. From these he developed erudite lectures, with copious references to all phases of Hebrew literature. He would sit half turned on his seat, glancing out the window, seemingly not aware of his audience. When students thought they could take advantage of this apparent unawareness of his surroundings and cut class, they were astounded to receive a notice from the Registrar that they must improve their attendance. How in the world did Ginzy know they were absent? Apparently he would, from time to time, glance over the whole group and make a mental note of who was there and who wasn't.

Professor Davidson was the expert on medieval Hebrew literature. He also taught the Talmud B class and lectured on Liturgy. Liturgy was one of the subjects I had not known existed. It never occurred to me until then to think of the Siddur and the Maḥzor as having developed over a period of centuries. Despite the dull manner of Dr. Davidson's presentations, I found Liturgy fascinating. I found Jewish history fascinating too, although Dr. Alexander Marx lectured on the subject by reading from his voluminous notes, keeping his head close to the page, and pronouncing the language in a German accent which was virtually unintelligible.

Though both were pretty inadequate teachers, I preferred Marx's sweetness to Davidson's cynicism and sarcasm. I felt that Marx was a true believer, while Davidson, with a twinkle in his eyes, would never quite answer a question directly if it concerned such matters as faith or belief. Outwardly he, like all the faculty and students, adhered conscientiously to the letter of the ritual law, but I could never figure out what was going on beneath the surface. The same was true of Ginzberg. I could not believe that a scholar who knew so well the evolution of Judaism could continue to teach and act as though it had all emerged out of one divine revelation.

Rabbi Moshe Halevi Levine taught Talmud and Midrash to the students who needed more help with the text. He was referred to as Rabbi rather than Professor or Doctor because he had committed the unforgivable sin of not having earned a Ph.D. He was patronized as a scholar because he had never edited a text, recording all the variants in manuscripts found in Oxford and Rome. But Rabbi Levine was the best pedagogue I had in that first year, and under his tutelage I progressed rapidly. He was rarely known to smile, and when a student failed to prepare, or claimed to be prepared and was faking, his wrath was as the wrath of ten prophets.

One did not discuss ideological matters with Rabbi Levine. He was strictly observant, but that proved nothing about his philosophy. It only indicated that he, like all of the faculty and students, was following the rules which the institution had imposed. I always suspected that he was something of an *epikoros* (agnostic), a product of late nineteenth century *Haskalah* (Enlightenment), which had invaded the small towns and villages of Eastern Europe and corrupted the innocence of the yeshivah students.

Professor Moses Hyamson, who taught Codes, had come from England and spoke with a combined Yiddish and cockney accent. He was enormously nearsighted, and when he read a text at his desk, stroking his white beard, his nose reached within two inches of the page. Obviously, he did not see beyond the first row, and the students behaved accordingly.

Dr. Louis Finkelstein was the opposite of Hyamson in virtually every respect. While he too served a congregation for his major source of income, he was alert to every nuance of student behavior and attitude. He was the youngest of the faculty, raised in New York and educated to the ways of Americans. Hyamson had no ambition other than to instruct the students and to earn their love and loyalty. Finkelstein, it seemed to us then, had ambitions of another sort.

His academic achievements were already impressive. But he had the capacity to do many things at once and do them all well. He was a practicing rabbi, a research scholar, and a busy instructor, and he was already carrying out administrative duties for Dr. Cyrus Adler, the president, who resided in Philadelphia and came to the Seminary only once or twice a month.

There were two schools of thought among the students: those who believed that Dr. Adler was priming Finkelstein to succeed him, and those who believed that Finkelstein was preparing himself, whether or not Dr. Adler knew it. In any case, everyone agreed that he would not remain forever just an instructor of Talmud and a rabbi in the Bronx.

To complete the roster: Dr. Hoschander. He has already been introduced to the reader. His classes were well attended, but few paid attention to what he said. His lectures were full of fascinating data, but they were presented in so lackluster a manner that most students used the time either to prepare for their next Talmud class or to read *The Nation* or the *New York Times.* One could always count on one or two students to take notes; when necessary those notes would be mimeographed and circulated among the rest. Dr. Hoschander was much impressed with anyone who wrote English in an elegant manner. I won the Bible Essay Prize that year with an essay which did not deserve the prize, but I was still under the spell of Irwin Edman's prose, and Dr. Hoschander, who always asked the students to read their essays to him to save his eyesight, could be—and was—seduced by long words and cadenced sentences.

Finally, Kaplan: with him you didn't fool around! When he marched into the building on Wednesdays to teach first his class in Midrash and then the plenum class in Homiletics, the students began to shake and shiver in advance. His reputation was terrifying. He would bellow and roar if he thought you were talking without first thinking the matter through. He would call off the class altogether if the students became lax about promptness. He would tear a sermon apart mercilessly if it did not meet his standards of organization and clarity. Most of all, he demanded intellectual honesty of us as he demanded it from himself. He would settle for nothing less.

I was not sufficiently prepared when I entered, so I had to wait until the second year to qualify for his Midrash class. But everyone took Homiletics. It was a two-hour session. The first was devoted to his exposition of his philosophy of Judaism, the second to the student sermon. When he was invited to teach homiletics (the art of preaching) he told Dr. Schechter that he would teach it in a different way: the students would not come to learn *how* to preach, but *what* to preach; he would stress content rather than style.

For those who had come from Orthodox backgrounds and had not gone through the philosophical and spiritual *sturm und drang* which I knew so well, Kaplan's class was like plunging into the icy waters of the Hudson River in the middle of February. It was what later came to be called culture shock. Belief in the infallibility of the Torah he assaulted with particular relish, for Kaplan believed that no rabbi was worth his salt who had not been an atheist for at least some period of time. He was not deliberately trying to produce atheists, but he believed that you had to unlearn before you could learn properly. You had to remove the rubbish before you could reconstruct the building on a new foundation. Thus was I introduced to Reconstructionism, without knowing yet that it had—or would some day have —a name. But I sensed from the first that *this* was what I had come to the Seminary for. I was going to have a great time, and I was going, at whatever cost, to make an impression on that man.

That, in brief, was the faculty. The student body consisted for the most part of men who had attended yeshivahs. In this respect I was in the minority. Milton and Henry Rosenthal were two others who had never experienced the traditional yeshivah. By and large the students came from underprivileged homes. Their parents were immigrants who had arrived in this country either during the last decade of the nineteenth century or at the latest before World War I. Once again I was different. Yet I had never before felt as comfortable in a group. The differences existed within a framework: we were Jews, we were preparing for the rabbinate, we shared an intellectual curiosity concerning the heritage of Judaism, and we had chosen to go to the Seminary rather than to Hebrew Union College or a yeshivah.

My interest in music drew me to Ario Hyams, also a first-year student. He loved to sing, and he composed a bit, especially songs based on texts from the *Song of Songs*. We soon discovered that before and after classes we could have fun at the piano in the Student Room. It was always noisy there, and few paid any attention to us. I believe we were the only two students at the school then who had any active interest in music. My playing was not expert, but for lack of better, I was asked to play at the Freshman Reception before the faculty, the students and their dates.

My date was Miriam, whom I had been seeing off and on through the College years. (Shortly thereafter she fell in love with a glamorous cantor named Leib Glantz. They married and later both settled in Israel with their children.)

I will not comment on the quality of the performance, but it had nothing to do with the tumultuous applause which followed it. As Dr. Samuel Johnson put it in another connection, "it (was) not well done, but you are surprised to find it done at all." Faculty and students alike were amazed that a rabbinical student could tackle with even modest results anything from the classical repertoire. (It was the first movement of the Beethoven violin and piano sonata, known as the "Spring." A friend of mine named Belmont Fisher played the violin.)

We moved out of Harlem that year (1927) to the Upper West Side, 103rd Street to be exact. Except for five years in the Bronx Harlem had been my home from birth to my graduation from Columbia. But the neighborhood had definitely changed. 125th Street had once been the border for colored people as we called them then; now they had moved down as far as the north end of Central Park. I can honestly say that while we were no paragons of tolerance, we did not move because the Negroes were coming in. We found, simply, that our friends and the temple were no longer in our area. While I was in college during the twenties, the change gradually occurred. But we could not afford to move until Myron and I began to earn enough to make a difference.

Once we were on the West Side, I began to attend services at the Society for the Advancement of Judaism (SAJ), where Rabbi Kaplan preached every Shabbat. The walk was not excessive, and of course I was now more eager than ever to hear his sermons.

In my first year at JTS Rabbi Kaplan devoted the first hour of his double session in Homiletics to an analysis of the contemporary Jewish problem, how it arose, and what were its manifestations in the lives of modern Jews. These lectures were to form the opening chapters of his major work. In a sense he was utilizing his class to test some of the ideas and observations which he had written in those pages of his manuscript. Growing out of these sessions came an assignment: to portray three contemporary Jews who were victims of the circumstances he was outlining, namely, the Enlightenment and the Emancipation. He asked us to describe the "problem of Judaism" in terms of actual case histories, of men and women who had rebelled against traditional ways of thinking and acting.

The more I listened to Kaplan, the more eager I became to write a character study of three people who had played an important part in my life: Manny Eisenberg, Elie Siegmeister, and William Kolodny. These were the people with whom I had argued interminably, who had challenged my Jewish interests, and who (especially Kolodny, who had once attended the Teachers Institute of the Seminary) questioned the validity of the entire Jewish enterprise. I sat down to do a job on them—and to impress Kaplan with the fact that I knew exactly what he was talking about. What a thrill to get the paper back with an "A + —Excellent!" I had accomplished my mission sooner than I had expected. Kaplan now knew who I was.

The next time I attended the SAJ, he motioned me to remain after the others had left. He invited me to return home with him for Shabbos lunch. We walked together up to 89th Street, where he lived with his family. When we arrived, we went directly into his study and talked about the sermon of the day. As we conversed (I recall being so overwhelmed that I must have sounded like an idiot) I heard noises in the other rooms, high pitched voices, many of them.

I had no idea what his family consisted of. So when Mrs. Kaplan came in, greeted me, and invited us both to come to the table, I followed into the dining room. Rabbi Kaplan stood at the head of the table, which had been set for a large number of diners. One by one they entered, and I was introduced. One, two, three, four, five young women (five daughters?) followed

66

by an old lady (obviously a grandmother) and finally Mrs. Kaplan herself. I was twenty-one, shy, bewildered. I kept my eyes on my plate and after *Kiddush* I, sitting next to Rabbi Kaplan, looked only his way. There was much conversation, much laughter, some screams. I concentrated upon the food and my private conversation. As soon as possible after the *bentching* (grace after meals) I fled. That was how I met my wife, my three sisters-in-law, my mother-in-law, Rabbi Kaplan's mother, Anna Kaplan, and Sylva Gelber, a friend of the girls.

Toward the end of the semester, Rabbi Kaplan had to go out of town to lecture; he informed the class that he wished them not to absent themselves but to come anyway and listen to me read to them the "Three Portraits" which he believed illustrated the points he was making. Shortly thereafter, I wrote a review as part of an assignment. Its topic was a new book by Maurice Farbridge, a work which purported to deal with the intellectual challenge to Judaism in the modern world. I took great pains with that review, exposing the fallacies in Farbridge's thinking. The book is surely forgotten, even by those who read it. Once again Kaplan thought well of my efforts. I was in the student room one day when I was told I was wanted on the telephone—by Professor Kaplan. My heart sank. In his deep voice, which always sounded deeper on the phone, he asked my permission (!) to publish the review in the *SAJ Review.*

The *Review* started out as a supplement to the usual synagogue bulletin issued by virtually every congregation. It soon developed, however, into a weekly miniature magazine containing segments of chapters Kaplan was working on. For a dollar a year, virtually every student subscribed. Others who received the *Review* were members of the congregations which had affiliated themselves with the SAJ. This requires a word of explanation.

When Mordecai Kaplan agreed to establish a new institution, he had in mind a society of men and women who would be interested in "advancing" Judaism, that is, spreading the ideas which he would be propounding. It was to be a kind of society for the propagation of the faith, and not merely a congregation to serve the immediate needs of its local members. It was an exciting idea, but the families which comprised the breakaway group insisted that they wanted a place where they could pray every Shabbos and *yom tov*, where their children could become bar mitzvah, where they could gather for their leisure time activities as many of them had gathered at the Jewish Center. What resulted was a compromise. The Society would have two kinds of membership, one in the *Congregation* of the Society, and one in the Society (the extended institution) itself. The expansion of the *SAJ Review* into a periodical was the outgrowth of this arrangement. It gave Kaplan a place where he could publish regularly, and it provided a service to those synagogues which chose to join the SAJ association.

My first published essays appeared in the *Review*; I was naturally proud. But I recognized at once that I had come to the point of testing what I had learned the summer before from Lavy. The danger of being set apart, of turning back into a snob, worried me. Kaplan had already singled me out for that public reading of my three-part story; now I was chosen to have my class assignment published. The danger was real because, as I mentioned, I was conscious of my inferiority in Talmud and of the need to compensate in some other endeavor. Writing on the problem of Judaism, a problem which was extremely close to home, gave me the opportunity to shine but also provided the temptation to think I was better than the others.

I went out of my way to cultivate humility. I would deliberately and openly declare my ignorance, asking other students to help me in those subjects in which I was weak. Ario Hyams and I became close friends, for example, as a result of my suggestion that we prepare Talmud text together. His father had been a *rosh yeshivah* (headmaster, as it were), and Ario had been inducted into the intricacies of Talmud at an early age. I was pleased that when we studied together he could treat me like a slow learner. He in turn respected my ability to handle philosophical and sociological texts, and I coached him in return.

The campaign seemed to work. I felt the gap between me and the yeshivah-people closing. The highest compliment I received came from Ben Zion Bokser, a classmate whose command of Talmud was truly extraordinary. We were not in the same group, by any means. He went into Talmud A immediately, but we enjoyed one another's company. And he invited me to spend a Shabbos in his home in Brooklyn.

My visit to Ben Zion's family was my first experience with Hasidism. His family were not Hasidim, but they lived near Hasidim, and Ben Zion thought I ought to be introduced to the world I had never known. It should be noted that in the twenties, Hasidism had not yet undergone the resurgence which characterized the period after World War II. There were few Hasidim, and they were regarded as the last vestiges of an age which was rapidly receding into the oblivion of the past. The little we knew of Hasidism we had gleaned from the westernized historians like Graetz, who shuddered at the very thought of this sect of Jews, of whom historians were ashamed. From the point of view of enlightened western scholars, who (it transpired later) knew virtually nothing of the historical sources of Hasidism, Hasidim were ignorant, superstitious, given to excessive use of liquor, sunk in the virtual worship of their rebbes; in brief, primitive Jews who had abandoned the traditional Jewish reverence for learning and had lapsed into a latter-day paganism.

The scholarship of the last fifty years, pioneered particularly by Gershom Scholem, has radically revised this image of Hasidism. But for Americanized Jews like me, a visit to them constituted a sort of intellectual slumming expedition. I had read Schechter's essay on Hasidism and was prepared to give them the benefit of any doubts, but I looked forward to going to the *shtibel* with a combination of curiosity and condescension. Ben Zion led me to the *kabolas shabbos* (Friday evening) services.

They took place in a small room which seemed to have no front and no back. Men stood around swaying and mumbling, chanting or merely humming, facing in all directions—until they came to the *Borkhu*, when they suddenly all faced one way—to the east. They were not led; each one went at his own pace, yet somehow at important junctures they seemed to come together. In one corner stood an elderly man with a gray beard whom Ben Zion identified for me as the Rebbe. The men showed their respect for him by not proceeding beyond the *amidah* until they saw that he had concluded the silent prayer.

As we walked back to the Bokser apartment, I remarked that I had never seen so patently pious a group of people in my life. They gave the impression of meaning what they were doing —quite a commentary on my previous experience with Ansche Chesed and even Shaare Zedek and the SAJ. This was due, I thought, to the fact that they were uninhibited in their body language (as it is now called). They did not hesitate to bend and bow and shake and sway and chant and mumble and otherwise transform the words they pronounced into an actual physical experience.

The next morning, we attended services at the Brooklyn Jewish Center. It reminded me of the shul of my boyhood, set on a higher economic level. The main feature was the sermon by Rabbi Israel Levinthal, whose reputation for homiletical skill had already reached my ears. In the Center one found oneself midway between Hasidism (sharing a little of its fervor but not much) and the challenging intellectual atmosphere of the SAJ. I confess that I left Brooklyn to return to my home that night filled with greater respect for the "real thing," for the unadulterated traditionalism of the Hasidim, than for the half-baked modernism of the Center, which, I soon realized, was typical of the Conservative movement.

In my review-article on Farbridge, to which I have referred, I described his Judaism as walking into the future with his eyes looking backward into the past. This was certainly no way to progress, I believed. It resulted only in stumbling along, without a sense of direction or purpose. Keeping one's eyes glued to the past could never achieve what Kaplan was urging upon us, namely, to face the future boldly. If this meant radical adaptation, so be it; the law of survival, we had learned, is adapt or die. Clinging to the past is not to be confused with living in the past. The Hasidim are content to live in the past. They eschew the present. If that is their choice, so be it. I would respect them for that commitment.

But the "moderns" were neither here nor there. And that was why they could not pray with the same fervor. That was why they were inhibited about throwing themselves completely into their worship, abandoning themselves to the genuine emotions which the words they were pronouncing should have been generating. Authenticity was lacking; in Kaplan I found it, and I was more than ever determined to explore the road he was traveling.

I had obviously not resolved my spiritual problem, the central problem of how to live as a Jew in the modern world. While Kaplan was preparing our minds for the method we should have to adopt, the process was slow, and I was naturally impatient. At that point, a course in Modern Hebrew Literature taught by Mr. Hillel Bavli (a well known poet and faculty member) opened up for me another new world. Modern Hebrew Literature was then almost completely preoccupied with the Jewish people and its fate, and almost not at all with theology. Modernism had eroded traditional beliefs and had put national aspirations at the core of Hebrew literature's concern.

One of the first assignments Bavli gave us was a novella by Zeev Feierberg, entitled *L'An* ("Whither?"). Feierberg, I learned, had died at the age of twenty-six of the consumption which usually afflicted Jewish intellectuals who could not afford adequate nourishment. He had been the fair-haired boy of writers like Bialik until he went the way of other geniuses like Keats and Schubert.

When I finished reading *L'An*, I was in a fever of excitement. Here was a story of a young radical who had lost his mind in the conflict between the faith he had abandoned and the vision of a new and better way for the Jews. Nahman the Madman became an obsession with me, and I could not rest until I had undertaken to translate the book into English. I was transported particularly by the climax of the story, an impassioned speech by Nahman in which he envisions the revival of the Jewish nation on its own soil, resurrecting the national spirit and serving as a bridge between the East and the West, a beacon of freedom and justice in the world.

I do not know how I managed to do the translation, given the overloaded schedule I was following; at least twenty-five hours of classes a week, teaching the bar mitzvah boys in the afternoon, doing my assignments, and—taking cello lessons

71

once a week. (This last *meshugas* I added to the program simply because I had for years yearned to play a string instrument. A fine time to realize that ambition!)

Feierberg was completed in about six weeks. I sent it on to the *Menorah Journal*, but it was turned down. The letter I received from Lionel Trilling, then working for the *Journal*, said, "it is an excellent translation, . . but I think the theme has lost point because of time." Lost point?! So much for the Jewish perspective of the young Trilling, who later became so famous as a literary critic and teacher.

I could think of nowhere else to send it, so I put it away. (It was finally published by Abelard–Shuman in 1956 after having lain in my brother Myron's house on a bookshelf, all but forgotten for almost thirty years.)

L'An transported me back to the days when I used to listen to Dr. Benderly. The Zionist fever gripped me. Yes, this was the way. Rebuilding the nation was the way to bypass all the theological problems; in a home of our own we Jews could resume where we had left off. The long dispersion was only an interlude, an interruption in the ongoing collective life of the Jewish people! Surely it was unnatural for us to persist in maintaining our separate existence among the goyim. Every sociological law denied the possibility of success.

If we had indeed managed to survive as a people, it was because we had believed, really believed, that we were God's chosen, that we were in exile for our sins, that in God's own time we would be redeemed from that exile, and in the meantime we would live our own lives, apart from the non-Jewish nations. Eventually, the Messiah would come, the dead would be revived, the Temple would be rebuilt and a totally new chapter of history—not natural history, but supernatural history— would begin.

But that was all gone now. We did not believe any of it any more. We had to erase the two thousand years and return. Feierberg was right: somehow these centuries had endowed us with the potentialities to serve mankind. The struggle of the future would take place between the advanced, industrial West and the long somnolent East; our land lay between the two. We had served more than once as the link between cultures. We had translated the Greek and the Arabic civilizations and made them available to the Christian world. Now we had a new mission to perform, one which grew naturally out of our unique history. . . .

I needed to talk about these ideas with someone who might perceive them from a perspective different from mine. Who else but Manny? It was a mistake, for Manny had become a communist. That is to say, he had been converted to Marxism. When I discussed Feierberg with him, I met an unexpected hostility. This time my enthusiasm was not dubbed stupid or irrelevant; it was dangerous. Did I not know that Zionism was merely a device of the British imperialists to maintain control over the Suez Canal, and to suppress the social revolutions which were bound to put an end to Great Britain's imperial ambitions?

The Balfour Declaration, followed by the issuance of the Mandate in 1922, had combined both to pay off the Jews for their support of the Allies during the war, and to use the Jews as a strategy of divide and conquer, keeping the Arabs from further revolt in the desert.

But I could not believe that the matter was reducible to such simple terms. Was no part played by Jewish dreams, by Jewish energy and self-sacrifice? Was it all a cynical scheme, bereft of any moral values? Were the *halutzim* Dr. Benderly had talked about merely pawns in the hands of politicians and capitalists?

Now I had not only theological but geopolitical troubles.

Before that first year ended, Rabbi Kaplan approached me with a proposal that I write book reviews for the *SAJ Review* during the following year. I could not believe my ears. What an opportunity to read, write, get paid $10 per review, and to associate myself with the professor whom I most admired! That was not all: would I lead the Junior League (the rather pretentious name for the youth group at the SAJ)? This would yield $20 every two weeks. Climaxing the whole, I learned that Henry Rosenthal was to serve as Literary Editor of the *Review*, and that meant that I would be working very closely with him.

The financial picture brightened even more when I was awarded a Brush Scholarship for the following academic year.

Mr. Brush, a friend of the Seminary, made these funds available to a limited number of students. I was to be given $900 a year. This meant that I could now give up my teaching at Shaare Zedek and even begin saving. And to cap it all, I was asked by Rabbi Samuel M. Cohen, the executive director of the United Synagogue and part owner of a camp in the Poconos, whether I would be interested in a camp job that summer. The year ended in a blaze of glory.

It had been the best of all the years at school or anywhere else. I had found a niche in the Jewish student world. I had won at least one prize (the Bible essay referred to before); I had been given two jobs and a scholarship; and most of all, I had broken into print. I went off to camp proud of my record but fortunately conscious of the dangers. I wanted desperately to avoid the painful experiences of the previous summer at Boy Scout Camp. With what I had learned from Lavy Becker, the summer of 1928 proved to be as satisfying as the year at school had been.

While I had not yet completely made up my mind about my career, the summer at camp plunged me into the role of rabbi. I conducted services daily and on Shabbos, and I was regarded as the expert on all things Jewish. This was a ridiculous burden to place on anyone who had completed only one year at the Seminary. (The summer before had been even more ridiculous.) In addition, Rabbi Cohen spent considerable time at camp. He was a veteran rabbi and consultant to many Conservative congregations, and I hesitated to give answers to questions in his presence. But he treated me with great pedagogic skill. At no time did he publicly minimize my authority; at times he took me aside to correct a misstatement, but always with tact and kindness.

If I came through without disgracing myself, it was because (and this was shocking) I discovered that one could function as a rabbi without knowing too much about the subjects to which I had been devoting much time during the year. You did not need to know Jewish history except in the broadest outlines. Liturgy was regarded by everyone (e.g., the counsellors and the parents, not the kids—who were totally indifferent) as fixed and immutable, transmitted by tradition in the form in which it was found on the printed page. They did not know how the prayerbook had evolved, nor did they care to know. Medieval Hebrew literature was a closed book; modern Hebrew literature did not exist at all. The Talmud was something students were compelled to learn, but all they seemed to know about it was that it involved hair-splitting arguments over inconsequential issues. The holidays like Tisha B'Av (which is observed during the summer—and mostly at summer camps) were related to simple events, with no implications for either Jewish or general history. On the 9th of Av, the Temple was destroyed. On Hanukkah a cruet of oil lasted eight days. On Pesaḥ the Jews (sic) left Egypt for the Promised Land. Could one blame the kids for asking, "Why do you have to go to the Seminary for four years? What is there that takes all that time to learn about?"

Obviously, one year was enough to qualify me to make like a rabbi. What impressed them most, I think, was not how much I knew, but the fact that I was a regular guy. I played tennis, I swam, and I learned to dive; I knew how to umpire a baseball game. What broke down the barriers was what I had learned the summer before and had put into practice during the year—how to behave like a human being. We were pals. They had never before known a rabbi who was so human. I wasn't yet a rabbi, and I had become human only a short time before. But they didn't have to know that.

What I did not enjoy at all was rounding up the boys who were supposed to attend the morning minyan. Their reluctance, and the demeaning position in which my pestering them placed me, had a lasting effect upon my future distaste for morning services in general. They were hurried. The people who came were either mourners who would have felt guilty absenting themselves, or others who were dragooned into attending since their presence was required to fill the necessary quota of ten. There was no time for instruction or discussion, or even for a slow meditative rendition of a musical theme. In a word, it was sheer drudgery. In all my career as a rabbi, I practically never attended morning minyan. If I was criticized, the complaints never reached my ears. After a while my congregants knew that this was one rabbinical duty they could not count on me to perform.

At camp I was expected to round up the ten kids. They and I were both deprived of the morning dip in the lake, adding injury to the nuisance of putting on *tefillin*. Not one of us enjoyed it.

I was therefore both disappointed and enlightened by the summer's experience; disappointed (again) to realize how remote young Jews were from the culture and civilization of the Jewish people, and how undeprived they felt; enlightened because I understood for the first time what people seemed to need and want—the warmth and friendship of one who was a symbol to them of ethical and spiritual ideals. They certainly wanted the rabbi to be educated; the esoteric knowledge the rabbi possessed must, they sensed, be important; otherwise he would not take it so seriously. But the rabbi was a repository, a library, the place you went if you wanted to look up something. As long as the source was intact, they felt reassured. But for themselves, for their own consumption, they wanted guidance in those rituals which they deemed essential for high moments in their lives or in the Jewish calendar. And they looked to the rabbi to boost morale in those moments when they were confused or discouraged. They wanted to know that a rabbi was available to represent them to the gentile world. Every Jew knows, or has heard, that Jews are maligned or disparaged, either for not accepting Jesus as the savior, or for allegedly acting in an anti-social manner. They seemed to plead, "Tell them, Rabbi. You know the answers. Speak for us. Refute their accusations."

Contact with the parents and counsellors revealed something else about their conception of the rabbi which puzzled me then and still does: the conflicting signals they send the rabbi. On the one hand, they want the rabbi to be apart from them; they want to respect a rabbi, and hence they prefer to keep a distance between the rabbi and them. On the other hand, they want rabbis to be regular guys who are not stand-offish. The narrow ridge which a rabbi must traverse makes it very difficult to maintain equilibrium.

People are clearly ambivalent about the rabbi, who represents authority which they crave but also resent. The rabbi represents scholarship which they respect but which also underscores their own ignorance. They want rabbis to be fallible because they are fallible, but they also want rabbis to serve as models. They want the rabbi to be courageous and independent without forgetting who pays his rabbinic salary.

Returning to the Seminary after camp did not produce the usual after-vacation letdown. Usually one is reluctant to get back to work in the crowded city after the freedom and relaxation of the summer. This time I was even more eager to resume my studies since the problem of adjusting to a new school was behind me and new challenges were ahead. Writing for the *Review* and leading the youth group added zest to the program.

But even before I was to undertake these new duties, a major experience was before me. I was to conduct High Holy Day services for the first time, at a synagogue in Brooklyn known as the 9th Street Temple. The congregation had no permanent rabbi, but they were amply equipped with a cantor, choir, and organist. Apparently these people attended shul largely to hear the hazzan; they did not sorely miss the presence of a rabbi except on the High Holy Days. Then they sent for a student from the Seminary. Since I was asked by the student placement committee to take this assignment, I assumed that the compensation was more modest than most and that the synagogue was not considered important in the hierarchy of the United Synagogue. Otherwise they would not have placed a second-year student without any experience whatsoever in that post.

My experience with the liturgy of Rosh Hashanah and Yom Kippur had been limited until then. Remember that due to the World Series I had missed completely some sections of the service with which I did not become familiar until much later. I planned the services in what I considered an original way. I would take the opportunity when so many congregants were present (having been absent all year) to teach them some of what I had learned at the Seminary. It is characteristic, I learned later, for rabbinical students to spill their newly acquired knowledge directly from the classroom to the sanctuary. If this makes for an academic atmosphere, they think, so much the better. After all, the synagogue was first and foremost a place of study, only secondarily a place of worship and a place of gathering.

I therefore spent considerable time after the end of the camp preparing comments and explanations which I carefully typed out and inserted between the relevant pages of the holiday prayerbook. Since I found it difficult to articulate the prayers themselves with genuine conviction, I chose to use the occasion of their recitation as an appropriate opportunity to teach. How much the congregation absorbed of my researches I do not know; I do know that I learned much more from these preparations than from many hours spent in the classrooms.

Since I was not yet twenty-two years old, I had to resort to some artificial means of impressing the congregation with my maturity. In those days, rabbis wore striped pants and cutaway jackets, sometimes even adding a wing-collar to complete the costume. I omitted the wing-collar but conformed to the rest. If the people who saw this skinny guy in that get-out did not make snide remarks, I attribute their good behavior to the speechlessness with which the sight left them.

But I soon succeeded in catching their attention. Between one section of the service and another, I explained the origins and history of the various prayers, *piyutim* (medieval poems) and readings, transmitting all this erudition, hot off the griddle, to an astonished congregation. To be sure, there were some who grumbled and wanted to get on with the service. They had come to *daven*, not to attend a seminar on the history of the liturgy. But others, after the evening service of the first day, complimented me, saying that no one had ever taken the trouble to explain to them what these texts were all about and why they were included in the *Maḥzor* (holiday prayerbook).

The next morning, I spent considerable time interpreting the Torah reading, drawing upon my meager knowledge of the midrash and commentaries. After the Torah scrolls were replaced, I launched into my sermon. This was the straw that broke the camel's back, the camel in this case being the hazzan. Prior to coming out to Brooklyn, I had asked Rabbi Kaplan how he would suggest I treat the subject of God in my Rosh Hashanah sermon. He was kind enough to spend more than an hour coaching me on the most effective way of presenting the problem of theology in the light of current challenges and approaches. I took notes furiously. As a result I developed a clearer notion of what my own theological position might be, and I was most eager to share it with the Brooklyn congregation.

How was I to know that in my enthusiasm for the theme, I would get wound up and forget what time it was? Virtually in the middle of a sentence, at a crucial moment in my exposition, I heard what I thought was an explosion behind me. It was the hazzan, loudly demanding that I finish up *at once.* He had prepared an elaborate *Musaf* service for himself, choir and organ; he had rehearsed for weeks. It would take at least three quarters of an hour to render the composition, and what right did I have to monopolize the whole time and more. Thus was I introduced to the war between rabbis and cantors, one which I later discovered has raged, and continues to rage, in virtually every synagogue. It is perhaps inevitable when two performers compete for one spotlight.

Whether out of an innate sense of diplomacy, or just ordinary shock, I stopped without even finishing that sentence. I returned to my seat, and the hazzan took over. Before the end of the service, however, I rose to make a few announcements; among them I declared my intention of concluding my talk on God at the *minḥah* service, later that afternoon. As a rule only a few of the faithful return later in the day for the afternoon service, but this time, to my amazement, more than a hundred men and women came back to find out how it all came out in the end. The large attendance impressed the officers and, surprisingly, the hazzan, who apologized for his rude interruption of the morning.

I had learned that people who come to the synagogue are really more interested in learning about Judaism than in merely reciting uncomprehended words. I had also learned that intellectual stimulation, however desirable, is not enough; when worshipers come to hear a good hazzan they are conveying the message that the ear and the heart must be nourished, not the brain alone. I had learned that one key to success in the rabbinate is the establishment of a mutually respectful attitude between the rabbi and the cantor and that for rabbis to be able to enter into such a relationship, they must not be musically illiterate. Unfortunately, too many rabbis know virtually nothing about music in general or Jewish music in particular.

Later that year Kaplan asked me to lecture to the young people (most of whom were older than I) on Moore's *Judaism,*

79

the three-volume work by the Harvard non-Jewish professor which had just appeared. I welcomed the opportunity to study that important work carefully, but I had my doubts about the appropriateness of the choice. It was scholarly and lengthy, and I had never lectured before. But he knew these people, I thought. I did not, and besides, I was not about to question the wisdom of the Professor's orders. So I prepared thoroughly and sallied forth, hoping for the best. I don't mind saying I was pretty scared.

My fears were based not only on my inadequacy as an un-tried lecturer. Memories of my experience at Ansche Chesed only five years before still haunted me. I was also intimidated by the thought I would have to make my way in a social world un-familiar to me, inhabited, according to my parents' estimate, by people richer than practically anyone we knew. The SAJ, accord-ing to the gossip, consisted of families prominent in the Jewish community who went to Europe in the summer, attended the opera, and lived in expensive apartments on Central Park West and Riverside Drive. Some even lived on Fifth Avenue! As far as my parents were concerned, mingling with this "high class" circle of Jews was a privilege and an opportunity. My mother did not say so in so many words, but she intimated that it wouldn't do me any harm to break into those circles profes-sionally and socially.

The prospect did not attract me. I had long since adopted the reverse-snobbish attitude which looks down on people with money. Money was vulgar. Money was associated with igno-rance. I had been brought up to ridicule the rich who could not speak English correctly; I had grown accustomed to believing that wealth and ignorance were inevitably wed. In fact I men-tioned this at home. The answer was that the SAJ people were different. They were intellectuals; after all, Rabbi Kaplan was their rabbi.

This myth persisted for many years. It may still actually be held to be a self-evident truth that the level of the laity may be judged by the quality of the rabbi. Thus, the logic ran, any con-gregation that listened to Rabbi Kaplan week after week must be highly educated. In later years, I met individuals whose claim to scholarship was based on the fact that their rabbis were Milton Steinberg and Solomon Goldman. There is no evidence to indicate that the people either listened and learned, or that their intellectual growth was any different from that of most other Jews. Soon after my first encounter with the SAJ Junior League I was convinced that they were like most other privileged young people, interested more in their cars, their night clubs, their parties and their clothes than anything George Foot Moore might have to say about the origins of Pharisaic Judaism.

It was worse than that: they acted as though I had been hired to come, give my talk, and go home. After my first lecture, I wandered about hoping that someone would engage me in conversation or ask a question. I recall only that one of the young women came over and asked whether I would have a cup of tea. I accepted, drank my tea, and despairing of establishing any social contact, I went home angry and depressed. They seemed totally indifferent to what I had to offer. I had gone to the barber for a fresh haircut and a shine on my shoes, and I had prepared conscientiously. But I was outside their circle, and they were not going out of their way to bring me into it. My contempt for the rich was intensified.

It did not occur to me that I was being snubbed for other reasons. One, they had no voice in the selection of the Junior League program. Moore had been foisted upon them. Two, I had reverted to my Boy Scout mood—a prior rejection of them which they may have sensed as soon as I made my appearance. Let the record show that many of the young people in that group, now no longer young, are among the men and women who supported Rabbi Kaplan and me in our pioneering efforts to launch the Reconstructionist movement.

It is true that their association with Kaplan did not prevent them from self-indulgence during the decade of the 20s, and that their sense of values was not entirely to my liking. It is equally true that through their generosity they demonstrated an unusual degree of Jewish commitment and loyalty, both to a new approach to Judaism and to the leaders who urged their support of it. I am not as contemptuous of money as I once was.

My assignment to review books for the *SAJ Review* did not involve getting haircuts and pressing my suits. Reading was a genuine joy. Writing about what I had read intensified the pleasure of every book. Seeing what I had written in print was best of all. Part of the satisfaction came from the approval of Henry Rosenthal, who made very few changes in my manuscripts and gave my reviews the kind of provocative headlines I could never have thought up. The only fly in the ointment was the silence of Professor Kaplan. Each fortnight when my reviews appeared, I went to classes and to the SAJ services, hoping to hear a word from the stern man who had commissioned them.

After several weeks I could wait no longer. Casually, I remarked to him one evening at his home where I had gone to have my sermon outline approved, "By the way, Professor, how are the reviews? Are they what you had in mind?" His answer was, "If they were less than satisfactory, you would have heard from me by now." I left pleased but puzzled. This was not exactly a pat on the back, but I was at least getting a passing grade. On the other hand, why was he so stingy with compliments? Of the Seminary faculty, he was perhaps the only one who prided himself on his knowledge of psychology and pedagogy. He understood—or should have—how important it is to encourage other students. I was disappointed, but the experience stood me in good stead. I learned not to expect compliments from Kaplan. If you did the right thing, you were only doing what was expected of you. Heaven help you if you did the wrong thing.

It was in the second year, too, that I delivered my first sermon at the Seminary. I gave it, as all the students did, on Wednesday to the student body and on the following Shabbos to the congregation at the Seminary consisting of the faculty, some students, and a group of Jews who lived in the neighborhood. Kaplan liked the talk; it was based on the story of the golden calf, and the main proposition was that idolatry is, in effect, the fallacy of mistaking the symbol for the reality. It won the Homiletics Prize that year, but what most impressed the congregants at the Seminary synagogue was that Professor Marx did not fall asleep during my delivery of it. There was a standing joke in the school: Marx always slept during the sermon, and only those who kept him awake were considered effective preachers.

I mention this because Dr. Marx symbolized the attitude of the faculty to the rabbis they were themselves responsible for training. Sermons were a waste of time. They represented no scholarship, and scholarship was the only accomplishment the professors respected. As for the other functions the rabbi was called upon to perform, no real knowledge was needed. If you were a hail-fellow-well-met, you could be a successful rabbi. Hence the members of the faculty treated their role in the institution as just a job. They were not able to produce genuine scholars, so they patiently endured the hours spent in class as a means to making a living. Their real interest was in their own specialized researches; teaching was an interruption in their pursuit of the only goal that mattered. *Wissenschaft* was king.

As a result, the graduates of the Seminary always labored under a burden of inferiority: they knew their former teachers looked down on the Conservative rabbis they had trained, and the rabbis therefore deferred to their professors in all matters involving scholarship. When I graduated and became active in the Rabbinical Assembly, I saw the devastating effect of this denigration on Conservative rabbis. Their expertise was in question, their authority to deal with important issues of Jewish law was undermined. One of the first cracks in the solid wall of my high esteem for the Seminary came with the realization that the faculty had no respect for the students and their future profession. I had thought that the scholars were merely occupying an ivory tower. I learned that the situation was worse: they seemed deliberately to inculcate a sense of inadequacy in their students—at least, in all but those who demonstrated a potential for scholarly research.

What Professor Marx had betrayed by his short nap during services was merely an overt demonstration of what the rest believed but were too polite to reveal. In all fairness, however, it should be said that the problem of combining professional training with scholarship is not an easy one, nor has it been solved either in rabbinical schools or in any other professional institutions. The practitioners and the researchers require different training, and very few schools are geared to a two-track course of study. Rabbis (as I had learned the previous summer at camp) do not need to know very much in order to function, but they also resist lapsing into the role of mere functionaries. They have gravitated toward the rabbinate, as a rule, because they have a love for the intellectual life. At the Seminary they get a taste of what scholarship is like, but they are soon frustrated. Their teachers offer them only what there is time for, a superficial glimpse into the world of genuine learning. Then they must give their attention to the practical aspects of the work. When they graduate and go out into the field, the days of systematic study are over for the rest of their lives unless, with extraordinary effort, they set aside several hours each day for the cultivation of their own intellectual growth, come what may. I know of a few rabbis who have succeeded in doing this, but they can be counted on the fingers of a pair of hands.

As a result of this frustrating set of circumstances, many young rabbis are moving directly from the seminaries into further graduate work and finding their fulfillment in the academic world. Many of them unofficially and tangentially perform rabbinical functions, like guiding young people through their difficult years of groping. But the ordinary people, the masses who need the services of rabbis, are deprived of them. More and more communities are struggling along without rabbis: the demand far exceeds the supply.

One of the pleasant byproducts of a student appearance at the Seminary congregation to deliver the sermon was to be invited to the home of Professor Louis Ginzberg for lunch. As we walked down Broadway that Shabbos, Mrs. Ginzberg took me by the arm and hurried me along ahead of the others who were on their way to the same home. Mrs. Ginzberg was what everyone has called a character, for want of a more descriptive term. In her younger years she was an extremely beautiful woman whom the brilliant young Louis had imported from Germany. She never lost her accent, nor did she ever forget that, being beautiful, animated, charming, and the adored wife of the world-famous scholar, she could take privileges not vouchsafed to others. In other words, she was one of the bossiest women one could meet. And if she said to me, "I have to talk to you privately" and grabbed my arm, there was no escape from her.

The subject was her son, Eli, then in his teens. Like his

father he was a remarkable student, but his interests were not in Jewish scholarship. He was majoring in economics, and later became one of Columbia University's most famous authorities on manpower. Mama was troubled: how to get Eli to become interested in Judaism? I am not at all certain that every student preacher was not treated to the same importunate appeal; nevertheless I was flattered to think that she ascribed to me any possible power to influence Eli. What in fact, did she want me to do? "Talk to him," she said.

I promised, but I did nothing about it. On further thought I realized that one of his father's students was probably the last person to attempt any religious rehabilitation on Eli Ginzberg. I mention the incident, however, because it throws light on a condition which, in the 20s, was only beginning to become widespread. Coming from an intensely Jewish home in which Jewish learning and Jewish rituals abounded did little to bind children to the ways of their parents. It is true that Eli Ginzberg's home was not at all typical (his book on his father is both fascinating and revealing), but to the extent that many Jews still believe that one can retain the loyalty and commitment of young people by creating a Jewish home, it is necessary to issue a caveat: the pressures of the outside world are far too powerful. Judaism is attempting to survive in a vacuum; the home cannot fill it. Unless an environment is created in which families can live their Jewish lives, they strive in vain to supply the environment alone. Some aspects of this sociological truth were conveyed to me in Kaplan's approach in class to the problem of Judaism; isolated incidents of the kind just described helped me to appreciate what he was talking about. He was criticized—and often still is —for being more of a sociologist than a theologian. What his critics fail to understand is that theology often follows sociology; ideas of God grow out of the context of culture, which, in turn, is the natural product of a society.

Lunch at the Ginzberg's was memorable only for one experience. When he had chanted the *Kiddush* and recited the blessing over the ḥallah, Ginzberg broke off pieces of the bread and threw them across the table to his guests. I was unable to believe my eyes. This was what Grandma had always considered a sacrilege!

That spring I was asked to return to Pocono; I was offered an increase of $25. This increase in my salary may have changed the course of my life. All if's, of course, are pure speculation, but it is intriguing to ask what would have happened *if* I had not had those $25 to influence me as they did. Kaplan had recommended to Dr. Dushkin and Mr. Schoolman, two of the educators who ran Camp Modin in Maine, that they interview me for a job as a counsellor at their camp. The third owner was Dr. Isaac Berkson. I was naturally pleased to meet with them and hear them say they thought I might well spend the summer at Modin to take the place of Milton Steinberg, who had graduated in 1928 and was now occupying a pulpit in Indianapolis. He would not be able to return.

Perhaps it was not just the $25 they did not offer me ($100 instead of $125); perhaps I was really frightened of trying to fill Milton's shoes. Word had reached me of his great popularity in camp—the way he held the kids spell-bound with his stories, the plays he wrote for Tisha B'Av. He was a hard act to follow, and I was reluctant to surrender a sure thing for a probable failure. I knew that at Pocono I had already achieved a reputation; I needed only to repeat the triumph of the previous summer. So when they mentioned the fee, I protested. How could I take less than I was being offered elsewhere?

Dr. Dushkin explained to me what a privilege it was to work at Modin. The camp was a gathering place for the sons and daughters of well known Zionists, rabbis, and other Jewish leaders. Modin was the camp where Rabbi Kaplan's own daughters went, or had gone. Tremblingly I suggested they add on another $25; if they had said yes, I would have had to accept and take my chances. They were adamant. I went back to Pocono.

5

The Year of Decision

Little did I know during the academic year of 1929–1930 how radically everything would change during the latter part of 1929. The nation seemed to be riding on the crest of prosperity. Then came the Crash, suddenly, devastatingly. Those of us who had been spending our lives in the cloistered halls of the Seminary, who were shamefully ignorant of world affairs, awoke to find that all aspects of life were to be different for years to come. The depression was merely the first act in a tragic dilemma which, one may say, has persisted until our day. After the Crash came the crises in the economic and political life of Europe, the rise of Hitlerism, the Second World War, followed by a cold war and innumerable small wars in new areas of the world—Africa, the Middle East, the Far East. With the end of the 20's, the age of innocence came to an end for people like me.

The High Holidays arrived as usual. The Crash did not come until the Days of Penitence. I was invited to go to Norwich, Conn., to organize a congregation out of a small group of dissidents who had seceded from the Orthodox shul demanding a more modern type of service. By modern they meant the introduction of some English prayers and readings, and the presentation of sermons in English by an American-born rabbi who would better understand the needs of the younger people. I traveled to Norwich some days before the Holidays and was put up in a private home, the Gordons'.

The experience turned out to be one of the most exciting and satisfying I had ever had. Dozens of details had to be attended to: we needed to negotiate with a local church to use their facilities; they were prepared to cover over all Christian symbols. We had to find a carpenter who would design and build an *aron hakodesh* (Ark for the Torah scrolls); we had to borrow the Torahs from the next town, New London; we needed to buy prayerbooks, *taleisim* and *yarmulkes*. We had to print posters announcing the services, placing them in store windows.

And we had to establish policy: would the men and women sit together or apart? Heated discussions revealed that habit was strong in many of those who thought they wanted a modern service, but who could not quite adjust to the thought of sitting in family pews. I came up with an idea I had brought with me from my one visit to the Brooklyn Jewish Center: the room would be divided into three sections, one for the men alone, one for the women alone, and one, in the middle, for those who wanted mixed seating. (We found that after the first service, the middle section became the most popular.) We needed a ḥazzan, and I brought Morris Margolis, a student colleague of mine at the Seminary who had a lovely voice.

We needed to persuade the wavering group that we were not causing a rift in the community but rather recognizing that such a rift already existed, providing a home for those who would otherwise have felt uncomfortable in the Orthodox shul or would have been compelled to stay home altogether. This was my first exposure to the *realpolitic* of synagogue life. In Norwich I learned the realities of congregational competition and of individuals' selective and arbitrary preferences in Jewish observance (some would ride but would not smoke, some would smoke but would not ride, some would do both but would not eat any but kosher food, some would eat anything but would not ride, etc.). I saw families divided, in some instances for long periods of alienation, over minutae of ritual observance, disputes which broke a community into fragments, leading to the creation of multiple institutions whose only differences were the wearing or doffing of the hat. It was all sobering but exhilarating at the same time.

I also learned that an Orthodox Jew with a little learning could be won over to radical innovations through his confidence that the rabbi really was knowledgeable and loved the Jewish people, though his proposals appeared at first designed to lead to total assimilation. I shall never forget a sweet old tailor who could not believe that this callow youth from New York with the goyish-college education could harbor a warm Jewish heart—until he heard me quote a few words from the Rabbis, comparing the Jewish people to a *seh pezurah*, a group of scattered lambs. His heart melted at the thought that I knew the reference and identified myself with those lambs.

When I returned home I realized the full impact of what had happened, starting with the Crash. People we knew were losing their jobs. Some were actually throwing themselves out of windows. Still others, like my father, were wiped out, their stocks having become worthless overnight.

As for the SAJ, the money ran out, and the *SAJ Review* had to be discontinued. Fortunately for me I was still getting my $900 per year in scholarship, and I was assigned to lead the Junior Society, the teenage group (at the rates I had received for the Junior League—now disbanded).

In spite of the crisis, our studies had to go on. Professor Kaplan invited a selected group of students to meet in his home for a seminar on Ernest Hocking's newly published book, *The Meaning of God in Human Experience*. The group met on Saturday evenings. Rabbi Kaplan did not hold that evening "sacred," as it was to virtually every young person. Who ever thought of studying philosophy on Saturday night? He did, and we did too, however much we might have wished we had been out on a date.

But it was far from a total loss. Studying Hocking with Kaplan was one of the turning points in my spiritual odyssey. I was helped to formulate an approach to the problem of belief in God which could satisfy me and which I believed I could offer to those who might come to me for help.

Human experience was the key to my understanding of the theological issue. I had never been able to grasp how it was possible to prove the existence of God. In my philosophy courses at college, and in the classes in medieval Jewish philosophy taught by Dr. Finkelstein, I had always had the impression that the cards were stacked, as it were. No one had ever undertaken to prove God's existence who did not already have a strong belief in the existence of God. The philosophers always ended up with their prior commitment. Obviously, the proof was no proof in any serious sense of the term.

Especially with respect to the medieval thinkers, I could not accept that they were philosophers at all. It seemed to me that philosophy must begin with the fewest possible axioms—only those which were absolutely self-evident, as in mathematics. But everyone, from Saadia to Maimonides, had apparently begun with a firm belief in the historicity of the Torah, its revelation on Sinai, and, inevitably following, its absolute infallibility. These were not by any means self-evident truths. If they had been, they would have been immediately acceptable to non-Jews. But such was not the case. Christians, to be sure, were prepared to accept the Bible's version of its own origin; but they went further to assert the equal truth of the New Testament, which they considered the basis of their faith and which Jews rejected. Surely the Gospels were not self-evident truths. Otherwise the Jews would have had to concede their validity.

With Kaplan's guidance, I began to discern the distinction between philosophy and theology. The latter consisted in the effort to reconcile philosophy with a prior belief in the authenticity of Scripture. This was true of both Jewish and Christian theologians. Accept the basic premises, and the rest follows, though not always easily and not always without some twisting and squirming.

In any event, Hocking, as Kaplan guided us through the book, opened up an entirely new perspective. He began not with arguments for or against the idea of God, but with those human experiences which people interpreted as manifestations of the presence of a God in the universe. In different cultures, and often in the same culture at different times, people identified various events as God-at-work; they are of varied kinds, but underlying all these events and their interpretations is a striving after what people regarded as the ingredients of salvation. What a study of religions reveals is that human nature is uniform, that, with variations, all people experience the same needs and seek evidence in their experiences for the presence of forces or powers which assure them that those needs can be satisfied and indeed are satisfied. To know human nature, to understand human needs, is to achieve an insight into what God means to people. It explains why, despite diversity, there prevails a fundamental unity.

The universality of these strivings seems to point to a reality which all peoples sense. They do not prove that God exists; but they *know* that God exists just as they *know* that water exists because they are thirsty, or they *know* that food exists because they are hungry. The Hebrew prophets made a startling discovery: they proclaimed that justice and mercy exist because they were hungry and thirsty for those experiences. Furthermore, they were convinced that eventually all nations would awaken to their potential for justice and love, and would ultimately acknowledge that God is the assurance of the eventual manifestation of these human qualities. It is no accident that some ten years later, Mordecai Kaplan wrote a book entitled *The Meaning of God in Modern Jewish Religion*.

By the end of my third year at the Seminary, Kaplan had evidently concluded that I might be interested in working with him, for he asked me one day to walk him home. The route was a familiar one to any student who had occasion to discuss a matter with the Professor; in fact he was a familiar figure on Central Park West, where twice a day he could be seen striding along the park side of the avenue. Kaplan walked at least five miles each day, partly for his health, partly because he got some of his best ideas when walking. It would never have occurred to him to walk just for pleasure. That would have been a "waste of time."

As we made our way toward his home on 89th Street and Central Park West, he said he had a proposition to make: I should become executive director of the SAJ during the following year (my senior year). After graduation I was to become assistant rabbi for two years, followed by promotion to associate rabbi. Actually, the title was "Leader." (In 1930 the term Leader had not yet acquired the horrible association with Hitler. Kaplan had borrowed the word from the Ethical Culture group, which referred to Felix Adler and his associates as Leaders.)

The SAJ had come into being in 1922 as a result of a split between Rabbi Kaplan, who had founded the Jewish Center, and the Jewish Center's leadership. The Jewish Center was (and is) a twelve-story building with impressive facilities; in addition to the sanctuary itself, there were club rooms, meeting rooms, a library, a gym, a swimming pool, in brief all the attractions which are now virtually taken for granted in contemporary centers and Ys. But this was the first of its kind, and it had been conceived by Mordecai Kaplan. The very idea of a Jewish center grew out of his new approach to the nature of Judaism.

He later developed this concept of Judaism in his landmark volume, *Judaism As a Civilization*. It called for a major emphasis upon the symbiotic relationship of the Jew and the Jewish people. The Jewish people exists to provide self-fulfillment for the Jew, and the Jew has a responsibility to enable the Jewish people to perform this function for all Jews. Self-fulfillment implies the satisfaction of all the needs which Jews experience as a result of their being Jews. One of the major needs which modern Jews have is to find wholesome companionship and satisfying activities for their leisure time.

Kaplan very early recognized that Jews might assimilate economically and politically without wishing to lose their identity as Jews socially and culturally. If Jews find the forces of absorption stronger than they are able to resist, the community should establish gathering places, centers, where they might strengthen their capacity to withstand the onslaught of the environment.

There was nothing in the center idea to which the Orthodox could object. On the contrary, if they were inclined to segregate themselves in self-defense against assimilation, the center was perfectly suited to that inclination. But what the leaders had not anticipated was Kaplan's passion for living (intellectually, of course) in two civilizations. That meant assimilating the latest and the best of current thought into his life and the lives of those he was called upon to serve, and that in turn meant that he was prepared to allow a free trade in the marketplace of ideas. It soon became apparent that heterodox views would be preached from the pulpit, and *that* the Orthodox were not prepared to tolerate.

But was that a "red herring?" I learned later that the successful manufacturers, who made up a good part of the leadership of the Center, were far more exercised over Kaplan's espousal of the workers' cause. These were the days before the Depression, before Roosevelt, before the New Deal. Attempts to unionize the workers met with stiff resistance from the bosses, and many of the bosses were members of the Jewish Center. Of course, no one will ever be able to say with certainty which was the major course of the dispute—the radical religious sermons or the radical social themes to which Kaplan addressed himself. Suffice it to say that at a historic and bitter meeting of the congregation in 1921, Kaplan won a majority of the votes but decided not to remain. He resigned, planning to devote himself exclusively to his teaching at the Seminary.

Soon, however, a group of 22 families approached him with the proposal that he organize a new congregation where he would have the freedom to preach and teach according to his conscience.

In January 1922, the new institution opened its doors in a private house converted into a synagogue. Now, five years later, it had moved to larger quarters (still on 86th Street), this time a former private school for girls occupying two townhouses scooped out to form an auditorium, with classrooms upstairs and room for a small library. The membership had grown to about one hundred, consisting of some of the families who had broken away from the Center and others living on the West Side who had heard of Kaplan and were interested in belonging to a progressive institution, but one which was not Reform.

When I began to attend services on a more or less regular basis, I had an opportunity to observe these people. Few of them were college-trained, but they considered themselves somehow intellectual. They read the latest books; they went to the theatre and the opera and in many ways thought of themselves as the cream of Jewish society of the East-European variety. The women in particular were ladies intent on culture, going to lectures on art and "music appreciation."

The question that puzzled me was whether they really understood what Kaplan was saying. They were certainly devoted to him, and they came forward generously whenever he called upon them to give to Jewish causes. They sensed that he was making important statements, and they were thrilled at the thought that they were present at the formulation of new theories. They were flattered that he tried new ideas out on them. Being his congregants raised their status above that of others. But the question remained: did they not lack the educational background which would qualify them to appreciate the daring new interpretations of tradition which he was formulating? In any event, I must pay tribute to the lay men and women who recognized, in some vague way, that they were creating opportunities for an earnest, gifted, and learned rabbi to grapple with the problem of Judaism in the contemporary world.

When Kaplan asked me to work with him at the SAJ, I asked him what the duties would be. I was to run the institution, including the school, the finances, and the budget. All this was to be done concurrently with my final year of study at the Seminary. The offer was more than I had ever hoped for, but even at a cursory glance more than I thought I could handle. I had never seen a budget. I had never directed a school. I had taught for a year as a freshman at the Shaare Zedek congregation. I knew nothing of administration. And—no mean consideration—I faced a battery of comprehensive examinations at JTS. I did not, however, reveal to Kaplan any of my misgivings. I swallowed hard and said I would think it over.

I cannot recall how I reached home that afternoon. I was blinded with pride, bursting with joy. Executive Director of the SAJ! It was ridiculous. Rabbi Kaplan was inviting me to undertake, and I was undertaking, a responsibility for which I was unprepared in absolutely every sense of the term. Only in retrospect do I understand to some extent his reasons for turning to me.

He had devoted much time to organizing the Society, planning membership meetings at various homes, consulting with members of the Board on all policy questions, having to spend hours and hours convincing the reluctant laity to accept even minor innovations in the liturgy, not to speak of the major reform he had carried out—namely, the introduction of the bat mitzvah ceremony. The Society had grown quickly for a while, but then it had reached a plateau. Further growth was difficult, and then came the Crash. Most of his followers were badly hurt, and money was scarce. The magazine had to be suspended.

In the meantime, he was making very slow progress with his major work. He had been at the manuscript for at least fifteen years, and he was still not yet fully satisfied with it. He needed more time to work on it, and the Society was becoming something of a burden. He needed someone to whom he could turn over the day-to-day responsibilities. A series of executive directors had all proved to be either inefficient or unwilling to stay on indefinitely in the role of administrator. He had offered the position to Milton Steinberg. Milton turned it down, expressing a strong desire to be on his own somewhere away from New York. He had offered the position to Henry Fisher, a classmate of Milton's, who had refused it for other reasons. Henry was an excellent student, an efficient administrator, and an eloquent speaker, but he suffered from a sense of social inferiority. He had come to America as a teenager and struggled all his life to support his widowed mother and siblings; he felt he had not had the chance to acquire the social graces which the SAJ would demand of him. I believe he underrated himself.

That was why Rabbi Kaplan approached me in the spring of 1930. The incumbent, David Pearlman, had decided to become a rabbi and was entering the Jewish Institute of Religion. The SAJ needed someone at once, and Rabbi Kaplan apparently feared that upon graduation I might be invited to a congregation which would offer me a larger salary than the SAJ was prepared to pay. He had mentioned the sum of $2500 for the year.

I assumed that the Board of Trustees was aware of this offer to me. Obviously I did not yet know how Rabbi Kaplan operated at the SAJ. My only concern was: would I be humiliated as I had been when I "led" the Junior League? The offer, of course, appealed to me greatly: I would be in a different kind of synagogue, designed for the thinking Jew. And I would be having daily contact with my teacher, from whom I was learning what I had been seeking for years.

My parents were overjoyed. But Grandpa was plunged into deep sorrow. What was going to happen to his grandson? Into what heresies would I be seduced if I became further enmeshed in the net that Kaplan was spreading out to ensnare me? For Grandpa, though he had read little of Kaplan's writing (there was as yet little to read), sensed that he was a dangerous influence. When Grandpa had advised me to go to the Seminary, he had done so because, as I have said, he believed that the best rabbinical positions were available to its graduates. He was willing to overlook the "fact" that the professors were "ignorant." But there was a tremendous difference between *amharatzut* (ignorance) and *epikursis* (heresy). Kaplan not only accepted biblical criticism. He arrogated to himself the right to violate Jewish law. He had allowed a girl to celebrate her becoming a bat mitzvah!

Beginning in the first year I had discussed my studies with Grandpa. Proud of my new learning, I had spoken of the various theories concerning the origin of the Bible. Grandpa was furious. What right did they have to teach such nonsense? I defended my teachers, smiling inwardly as I recalled how I had reacted to Dr. Wise the first time I had heard him speak on that subject. A hot argument ensued, continuing until my father intervened. He took me aside and pleaded with me not to upset Grandpa. After all, he was an old man, and he could get sick from getting too excited. Why not either agree with him for the sake of peace, or avoid discussions altogether?

In my zeal for truth I rejected the first suggestion and agreed to adopt the second. Thereafter we never talked about what I was studying at the Seminary. Incidentally, this man, old at 72, lived almost thirty years more. He died in 1956 at the age of 101½, leaving behind a manuscript in English on the *Authenticity of the Bible* that he requested, in his will, be published. It fell to my lot to edit the work, since I was the only member of the family qualified to do the job. It was a painful project, editing a work which presented a thesis I could not accept. So far as the two of us were concerned, Grandpa had had the last word.

Before going off to camp that summer for my third season at the Pocono Camp Club, I spent a few hours with Mr. Pearlman at the office of the SAJ. He showed me bank statements, budgets, bills to be paid, minutes of the Board meetings, records of the Hebrew school, and a host of other documents. My head began to whirl. What had I let myself in for? What had most of this to do with being a rabbi? If this was what a rabbi had to do, why were we not introduced to the subject at the Seminary? Many of us had notions about what the curriculum of the Seminary should have been, but we had completely overlooked the fact that additional courses of an academic nature would not have helped students face some of the down-to-earth problems which a congregational rabbi must confront.

Even at the SAJ, where I had thought Rabbi Kaplan needed only ask in order for his wishes to be granted, the procedure was demeaning and even humiliating. He invited me to attend a meeting of the Board in order formally to introduce me and to propose the plan which he had outlined to me. Since I had written for the *Review* and had on at least one occasion delivered a sermon from the SAJ pulpit, I was no stranger to most of them. But they felt awkward about being asked to ratify an offer which they had not approved in advance. Kaplan was embarrassed because he had not consulted them prior to speaking to me, and of course I was totally bewildered, not knowing what to say because I had not actually applied for the job. It was a mess.

But that was not all. After the interview I was asked to leave the room but not to leave, since they intended to report to me at once the decision of the Board. The meeting was being held in the Library room, separated by flimsy French doors from the adjoining room. Physically I was out of the Library; actually I could hear almost every word that was spoken, especially since the voices grew louder as the debate grew hotter. I looked for some other place to wait, but the only choice was the stairs leading to the lower floor. I felt that decency demanded I keep out of earshot, but even on the stairs I could hear several members of the Board angrily challenge Rabbi Kaplan's arbitrary and unilateral decision.

They asked good questions: how could so young a fellow run the institution? What experience did he have? Did not Rabbi Kaplan know that the SAJ was running a serious deficit? How could he offer $2500 to someone who was not even a graduate?

The only redeeming feature of that agonizing experience was Rabbi Kaplan's defense of me, which I really could not avoid hearing, for his powerful voice had risen to a crescendo. But even his unqualified recommendation was insufficient, for I gathered from other voices that there was still some grumbling about the whole affair. Finally, Kaplan did what I witnessed his doing on several occasions thereafter: he threatened to resign if he did not have his way. That did it. I was elected Executive Director of the SAJ, officially and finally.

One must understand the power of Rabbi Kaplan's threat. When he agreed to establish the SAJ, he insisted upon one provision—that he was not to receive a salary. After his two previous experiences he had come to the conclusion that the only way he could be assured complete freedom of the pulpit as a congregational rabbi was to serve without salary. The SAJ accepted these terms, pleading only the right to pay the premiums on an insurance policy. This arrangement placed a weapon in his hands which he used on rare occasions but with great effect. If he did not have his way, he threatened to resign. Unfortunately young rabbis do not as a rule have senior rabbis like Rabbi Kaplan to come to their defense. He did not always appreciate that fact, when he would criticize harshly a rabbi who confessed that he could not speak his mind freely, having a wife and family.

Once again, before returning to camp, arrangements for the High Holidays were made through the student body, and I was recommended to a large congregation in Boston (actually Roxbury). They were going to need a rabbi because their spiritual leader had gone on sabbatical to Palestine. Mishkan Tefilah was one of the largest congregations in New England, attracting more than a thousand worshipers for the Holidays.

It was certainly the largest congregation I had ever seen. The experience was heady. Addressing such an audience gave me a sense of power which could easily have convinced me that I spoke with more authority than my knowledge or my experience warranted. The temptation to pontificate was almost irresistible. In fact I did not resist. Before the Holy Days were over, I felt that I could handle a congregation like this. The response of the people was exhilarating; would I consider coming back for the Shavuot holidays, toward the end of the religious calendar?

Getting down to work required extraordinary discipline. Even then, at the comparatively early age of 24, I recognized the dangers of the rabbinate. Here I was, still wet behind the ears, preaching about some of the central issues of life based on my limited experience, which was centered almost exclusively in the classroom. Because I had donned a robe and wrapped myself in a large *tallit*, mature men and women looked up to me (literally and figuratively) to hear what I had to say. Rabbi Kaplan had remarked in class that the preacher stands "three feet above contradiction." In the synagogue there was no encouragement to ask questions, and certainly none to make statements. The laity were a captive audience, expected to pay respectful attention to what the "rabbi" (I was only a student) taught.

As I thought back upon my earlier days, when I first entertained the notion of becoming a rabbi, I realized that my original impulse resulted from an urge to get up in the pulpit and deliver a better talk than the one I was hearing. Was it conceivable that young fellows chose the rabbinate for the wrong reasons? I had indeed been very shy, almost self-effacing; perhaps like Walter Mitty, I unconsciously yearned to assert myself in public utterance, protected by my clerical status. If any remnant of self-disparagement remained, it would be submerged under the pomposity which characterized the rabbi. As a matter of fact, lay people considered pomposity entirely appropriate to a rabbi's manner of speech.

My experience in Roxbury unsettled me. Did I really want to accept the post which Rabbi Kaplan had offered me? Would I be willing to forego the opportunity if it arose to be at the head of a large and important congregation? The SAJ, with its one hundred and twenty-five families, seemed so pitifully small. And I was not at all certain that they really wanted me. Rabbi Kaplan had virtually forced me down their throats. At the SAJ they thought of me as a kid. At Mishkan Tefilah I was already honored as a rabbi.

My enthusiasm for the SAJ waned as the season progressed. I found that I was doing all sorts of menial tasks based on the material Pearlman had shown me—checking bills, checking on the attendance of the boys and girls of the school, trying to collect dues from delinquent members. My contact with the teachers, both of them, was pleasant since we had occasion to discuss curriculum. But I never had enough time for the pleasant occupations. Classes took up the entire morning and part of the afternoon. By the time I reached the office I had to hurry through the chores. Then I had to rush back home to do some preparation for my classes at the Seminary. For the first time I would be called upon to recite and would plead "not prepared." This happened even in Rabbi Kaplan's Midrash class. When he frowned, I felt like yelling, "Whose fault is it anyway? All the time I should have been studying I was swamped with the damn office details."

The members of the Board were none too sympathetic. Being inexperienced, I brought matters before them which I should have disposed of myself. On the other hand, I would occasionally make decisions and face their wrath or their ridicule because I had not consulted them. Some of them were reenforced in their prior prejudice that you could not rely on a *yeshivah bohur* to handle the business side of an organization. A student might be good at Talmud, but when it came to business, he was beyond his depth.

As they had promised, the Board of Mishkan Tefilah invited me to return for the Shavuot festival, but this time they informed me that their rabbi, Dr. Rubenowitz, had definitely decided to stay on in Eretz Yisrael and that they were looking for someone to take over the rabbinical duties of the congregation. They had interviewed other rabbis during the year and had come to the conclusion that they wanted me to come to them after graduation. Now I would have to make a decision: would I stay on at the SAJ or ask to be released so that I might accept Mishkan Tefilah's pulpit at $6000 a year!

I called Rabbi Kaplan and told him I had something of great importance to discuss with him. He said he had to visit someone in the hospital but that I could ride with him on the subway and we could talk about the matter en route. This did not seem the best place to talk about my future, but I was eager to inform him as soon as possible if I decided to leave the SAJ. The subway ride was for me a momentous one.

As we swayed with the train and shouted into one another's ear, I explained that I was faced with a vital decision. Apparently he had expected something of this sort and was prepared with his reply: of course it was entirely up to me, *but*, if I decided to accept Roxbury he would immediately resign from the SAJ and propose that it be liquidated. There seemed to be no future for it. The people were interested in the SAJ as just another shul. They had generated no enthusiasm for the idea of a center for the dissemination of his philosophy. Money was scarce, and the first flush of generosity had faded. The only hope for the SAJ was its capacity to attract a young man like me. If I opted for another congregation, he was ready to forget the whole project.

On the other hand, if I agreed to stay on at the SAJ (for $3000 a year), we would have an opportunity to work together. He did not specify what we would be working on, but he made it sound exciting and fulfilling.

I came home to discuss the problem with my parents. The prospect of my leaving New York appalled them. But I tried not to allow that consideration to influence me overmuch. I was already inclined to be cautious about embarking on a major move away from home, and I could not permit those feelings to overwhelm me.

The money involved was a minor factor. The best part of the Roxbury salary was the honor of having been offered so munificent an amount. Otherwise it would have made little difference in my lifestyle. The core of the issue was: where did I really want to function? In a large, prestigious but conventional congregation or at the small, innovative, experimental SAJ, where I would have the opportunity to work with Kaplan? Our

101

conversation on the subway had imposed a heavy responsibility. If Rabbi Kaplan meant what he said, I would be responsible for either the demise of the SAJ or its continuance. That was indeed a heavy burden to place on the shoulders of a fledgling rabbi.

I finally decided to remain with the SAJ.

The rest of my life was determined by that decision, one which I have not regretted for one moment.

In June 1931 I received my rabbinical diploma. This time the SAJ laity were less negative about my assuming the post of Assistant Leader. I assume that Rabbi Kaplan had let loose another of his thunderbolts.

6

Society for the Advancement of Judaism

That summer our family rented a house in Asbury Park, New Jersey. Myron had a job at an advertising firm, and I had been engaged by the SAJ. Father's business was just managing to keep its head above water, but we figured that renting a house would be cheaper than all of us, including Grandma, taking a vacation at one of the hotels.

The Kaplans took a place in West End, not far north along the shore. As a result, I visited Rabbi Kaplan often. We planned the year ahead. We traveled into New York by boat to attend an occasional funeral, but of course, not wanting to "waste time" just enjoying the ocean air, we worked on an introduction to the "Thirteen Wants" which he had formulated for the SAJ and which appeared in each issue of the SAJ Diary. We discussed his book. I had heard about it for all the years at the Seminary, but I had not been invited to read it in manuscript. That exciting and flattering opportunity came somewhat later that summer.

My curiosity was naturally at a fever pitch. Others, older colleagues in the rabbinate and in Jewish education, had been given glimpses of selected pages, but Rabbi Kaplan always warned that what they were reading was not the final version.

His continuous rewriting and editing led some of them to doubt that the book would ever appear. He was a perfectionist; he had been working on the book for decades, and he was over fifty years old.

One day, he surprised me by asking, "Would you like to read the manuscript of my book? And would you please suggest any changes you think ought to be made?" He handed me two fat loose-leaf binders, which I brought home to Asbury Park. I plunged right into the *magnum opus*.

Much of the material, it transpired, was already familiar to me. Pages were echoes of sermons I had heard at the synagogue or parts of lectures delivered in class at the Seminary. Since I had been so efffectively influenced by his thinking, I could not (nor would I dare) propose any basic changes. Kaplan had mentioned to me that Dr. Israel Chipkin, an educator, had been shocked by the proposal in the manuscript that Shabbat be moved to Sunday, in order to enable those who had to work on Saturday to observe Shabbat without financial sacrifice. What did I think? I said I agreed with Chipkin: the Reform movement had tried that, and it had failed.

Dr. Chipkin had also been shocked by Rabbi Kaplan's attitude toward eating at the homes of non-Jews and his liberal views concerning the position one should take toward intermarried couples. These sections did not seem out of order to me. But on the whole, my comments confined themselves to the use of certain words and phrases. Rabbi Kaplan generally conceded my points, frequently assuring me that I probably had a keener ear than he since English was my native language, while he had had to learn it as a second tongue. He would sometimes butcher a colloquial phrase, and I would call his attention to the more idiomatic expression.

The book, entitled *Judaism As a Civilization*, was eventually finished and entered in a contest for the best work on the future of Judaism in America. Julius Rosenwald (of Sears Roebuck fame) had offered a first prize of $10,000. In the opinion of the judges, Kaplan's book was superior to any of the others, but one of the judges had refused to give the total sum to Rabbi Kaplan for he could not condone the strong affirmation of Zionism in the work. Rabbi Kaplan told me that the dissenting judge was Judge Irving Lehman.

Having entered the ranks of Conservative rabbis, I was entitled to attend the convention of the Rabbinical Assembly, which took place that year in Long Branch, New Jersey, in the neighborhood of both Asbury Park and West End. There I observed for the first time the three-fold division of the Conservative rabbinate—the leftists, the rightists, and the centrists. Rabbi Kaplan was the unofficial leader of the leftist group, in which Milton Steinberg, Eugene Kohn, Solomon Goldman, and a small band of colleagues were to be found. On the right were people who seemed to me to be quite old, largely European-born but American-trained, corresponding in great measure to the "yeshivah" group in the student body; the center group consisted of virtually all the rest.

The issues, as I remember them, revolved around Jewish law and what could be done about it. Already at the beginning of the thirties the talmudic experts were struggling with the problem of the *agunah*, the deserted wife who is neither divorced nor widowed, just abandoned. How could she be released from her absent husband, or the husband who refused to give her a Jewish divorce (*get*)? The rightists were opposed to tampering with the Law. The leftists (who became more radical as time went on) were proposing ways of circumventing the Law; the centrists were eager to do something but were not prepared to take any action which might be criticized by the Orthodox.

At one session, Milton Steinberg, only three years out of the Seminary, took the floor and boldly proposed that the fundamental problem was that Conservative Judaism had not come to terms with the implications of its position. What was needed, he eloquently declared, was a platform for the movement, the formulation of a philosophy. Much of what I heard at that convention has long since receded from my memory, but the echoes of Milton's appeal reverberate still. Members of the Rabbinical Assembly will testify to the fact that the Conservative movement to this day has not adopted a platform. There were still three identifiable groups in the Assembly as late as the 1960's.

Today the leftist group has virtually collapsed; the center group has become more rightist; and the right is hardly distinguishable from the center.

I cannot honestly say that my first convention disillusioned me. I knew where I stood, and I knew that all the leftists were facing a long struggle. But with confidence in Rabbi Kaplan's assessment of the situation, I believed that in time the leftists would gain control of the movement. It was only a matter of time. When *the* book appeared, the opposition was bound to evaporate; there was no escaping the logical implications of Kaplan's conception of Judaism as an evolving civilization. Basic changes would come when the leaders, especially those who did not identify themselves with Orthodoxy, saw the light.

I was wrong, of course. But I knew I was wrong long before Dr. Kaplan was prepared to concede that attempting basic changes within the Conservative movement was doomed to failure. Until the sixties he continued to hope that not only Conservative but also Reform Judaism would reconstruct itself from within. For the time being there was nothing to be done except to try to get more leftists elected to the executive council. By 1933—two years later—I had become something of a politician. It was a new role for me, one for which I was totally bereft of talent. But we did manage to get Rabbi Kaplan elected president of the Rabbinical Assembly.

Rabbi William Greenfield was the instigator. From Waterbury, Connecticut and later Indianapolis, he was a master strategist. He might have gone far in politics, but he concentrated his talents on the Rabbinical Assembly. An ardent disciple of Rabbi Kaplan, and a sworn adversary of Louis Finkelstein (whom he regarded as an evil genius), he hatched the idea of nominating Mordecai Kaplan for the presidency of the RA. He attended, uninvited, the meetings of the nominating committee, and persuaded them to bring in Kaplan's name as a protest against the intransigency of the RA leadership and its collaboration with the Seminary authorities, who sought to block Kaplan at every turn. We all knew that Mordecai Kaplan would make a terrible president because he had no interest whatever in administration and if elected would very likely confine his radicalism to public utterances. He would not have the acumen to "pack" the committees—particularly the Law Committee.

But he and his henchmen—including me—wanted Kaplan's election for symbolic purposes. We wanted to demonstrate to the rest of the RA that when the chips were down Kaplan had more support than his detractors were ready to admit. The centrists and the rightists insisted that Kaplan represented only a handful of uncritical worshipers.

Unfortunately, the nominating committee was hopelessly divided until the morning of the election, which in those days took place the final afternoon of the convention. As usual, many of the rabbis had to leave to catch trains, and only a small group was left to do the voting. Of course word had leaked out that Kaplan was to be nominated, and the opposition was prepared to nominate a rival from the floor. We did not yet know who was to lead the opposition, nor who the alternative candidate was to be. Our talented campaign director was to meet his match: when Kaplan's name was read as the choice of the nominating committee, Rabbi Finkelstein asked for the floor. This was a bombshell, indeed. We could not have foreseen that a colleague on the faculty would openly oppose a senior faculty member. But in his usual clever manner, Dr. Finkelstein proceeded to make a good case for rejecting Kaplan.

Everyone knew, he said, that Dr. Kaplan was very busy with his teaching, with his congregation, and now with putting the final touches on his great book. If we imposed the burden of the presidency on him, we would be responsible for having impeded the progress of the professor's significant work. He understood our desire to honor our teacher, indeed *his* teacher, but we should not do him a disservice in the process. Therefore, added Dr. Finkelstein, he wished to nominate Dr. Jacob Kohn, a distinguished colleague and a friend of Dr. Kaplan, who, after all, stood for the same things that Kaplan stood for. . . .

There was just enough of a kernel of truth in Dr. Finkelstein's impassioned plea to give it plausability, but its intent was obvious. He was out to block Kaplan's election, and he was proposing a colleague who had moved out to Los Angeles (after our Temple Ansche Chesed could no longer afford to keep him) and who had not even paid his dues to the RA for a few years. In those days, Los Angeles was very far away. If elected, Kohn would simply delegate all authority to someone else—probably Dr. Finkelstein.

We proceeded to vote by secret ballot. The tension was almost unbearable, but Kaplan won by a very few votes because Greenfield had the temerity to stand up and with his accustomed *ḥutzpah* expose Dr. Finkelstein's strategem. It was obvious, he told the remnant of the convention, that Finkelstein and Kaplan were on opposite sides of every issue and that Kaplan's election would be a threat to Finkelstein's growing influence in the Seminary.

As his supporters knew full well, Kaplan's administration was to be uneventful. His followers had won a battle, but the war went on. Indeed, the war was intensified because the rightists had received an unmistakable signal: a revolt was brewing which might destabilize the Conservative movement. As long as Kaplan had admirers, as long as he was loved for his intellectual honesty, his passionate devotion to the Jewish people, his courage to challenge the idols of the Jewish marketplace, there was no danger to the establishment. But if he himself were goaded into action, the very foundations of the Conservative movement would be endangered.

Finkelstein and his followers were well aware of the basic issues. Kaplan was clearly determined to teach the radical notion that we Jews had come to the end of an era, the era of supernaturalism. Behind his overt demonstrations of traditional piety —his wearing of *tsitsis*, his *kashrut*, his observance of Shabbat, and all the rest—he was an iconoclast. He rejected the old concepts—personal God, chosen people, infallibility of the Torah and its interpreters, personal messiah, belief in resurrection. From Kaplan's perspective, all these were no longer tenable. A thorough reconstruction of the religion, the organization, and the way of life of the Jewish people were required if Judaism were to survive.

Why did they tolerate Kaplan's presence on the faculty? Actually, they were on the horns of a dilemma. On the one hand, he was very popular with the students. He raised considerable sums of money for the Seminary. One of the members of the SAJ, Israel Unterberg, had donated the funds for the Teachers Institute building. Kaplan had already resigned from the institution once, and only by popular demand was he persuaded to withdraw that resignation. They could not forget, either, that Schechter himself had chosen Kaplan to serve. On the other hand, the Seminary came in for constant criticism from the Orthodox and from the ignorant non-Orthodox, whose support the institution needed. In addition, he was virtually undermining the traditional Judaism to which the Seminary, the United Synagogue and the Rabbinical Assembly were officially committed.

Rabbi Kaplan had withdrawn his resignation when Dr. Cyrus Adler promised him academic freedom. That promise was kept. As long as Dr. Adler lived, Dr. Kaplan was never directly pressured to modify his views. But indirectly every opportunity was taken to attack him. For instance, it is difficult to recall a single convention of the Rabbinical Assembly when Professor Ginzberg did not rise to denigrate or ridicule Dr. Kaplan's teachings. Sometimes the attack came from an oblique angle. I remember a Hanukkah party at which Ginzberg remarked that long after John Dewey is forgotten, the Talmud will live on. It was obvious to everyone that for "John Dewey" one was to read "Mordecai Kaplan."

Superficially the members of the faculty maintained a civil relationship, visiting one another from time to time. But beneath the surface, the struggle went on for the "souls" of the students. As far back as I can recall, Dr. Kaplan was unhappy at the Seminary. On our frequent walks around the reservoir of Central Park, I would listen to his complaints about the way he was treated, in the first instance by the faculty who sought in their classes to undo whatever he hoped to accomplish in his classes; in the second instance (later on) by the students themselves who, in the new wave of piety which was spreading over them, would express themselves in the most disrespectful manner. I wondered how long he could endure this sort of mental torture. I wondered too why he was willing to take it.

At the end of Kaplan's first year as president of the Rabbinical Assembly, he asked to be relieved. He declined the usual second term. It took almost twenty years before a "Kaplanian" would again be elected to that office.

My preoccupation with the Conservative movement was only an avocation. My days were filled with the responsibilities of the SAJ. The most onerous duty was the bi-weekly sermon. In this respect I bore a lighter burden than most of my colleagues, who are expected to preach at least once a week, and sometimes twice. Rabbi Kaplan and I alternated. But even this schedule was hard to maintain, particularly if I wanted each talk to have substance and form. As I look back upon the years during which I had to turn out weekly discourses, I find it difficult to see how I managed. Under ordinary circumstances, to have something worthwhile to say week in week out, is an almost insuperable undertaking. To meet the standards required by one's teacher of homiletics who is sitting on the same platform and listening with critical attention imposes an almost unbearable burden. It is one thing to prepare a prize-winning talk once a year at school. It is quite another to maintain a standard high enough to justify the fact that the senior rabbi had bet his reputation for good judgment on my performance.

And performance it was, and is to this day for those who are in the active congregational rabbinate. Congregants sit back and criticize the sermon as though they were representing a newspaper on opening night. They either praise the rabbi to his face or give him a lousy review behind his back. At the SAJ I got a "mark" after each Shabbat talk. If Rabbi Kaplan thought little of my sermon he would say, "Shabbat shalom" in a noncommittal way. If he liked it, he would shake my hand a bit more vigorously. Remember, he did not believe in direct praise. If the sermon was terrible, he would quietly suggest that perhaps I might like to accompany him for a walk around the reservoir.

My father was no help. He and my mother attended services regularly, sat near the front, and beamed. No matter how well or how poorly I did, he would stand out in front of the building after services, and while greeting the congregants, would smile and ask (rhetorically, of course; he wanted only one answer): "Well, how did you like *that* sermon?" I could neither cure him of the habit nor impress upon him how embarrassing it was for me.

Changes have occurred in recent years. Rabbis are now more inclined to teach, to explain, to fill in the background of Torah readings, and even of the prayers themselves. They have become too self-conscious about preaching because they are not

110

so sure they know the answers to vexing questions. They still wax oratorical if the situation calls for the denunciation of terrorists' massacres or the Soviet Union's treatment of Jews. But on issues of a more personal nature, like sexual behavior, business ethics, ritual observance and the like, they prefer to serve as resource people, filling in the background so that people will be familiar with the various approaches to these problems. The safest theme is historical. So few Jews know anything about the history of their people that the rabbi can comfortably instruct, and congregations as a rule enjoy learning.

This type of discourse lends itself better to informal delivery. And since the listeners are genuinely interested in what they are hearing, they respond less like critics of a virtuoso performance and more like students in a classroom. The sanctuary is, for most adults, the ideal kind of classroom: they don't have to take notes (they are usually discouraged from writing), they do not have to prepare, they are not called upon to recite; there are no examinations. Unfortunately, from an educational point of view, these weekly lessons are the least effective, for the reasons mentioned and because there is no continuity, as a rule, between one session and another.

But back in the thirties, the new style had not yet developed, and each talk I gave had to have a point. "What's the *point?*" Kaplan would shout in class, terrifying everyone. "You must be able to summarize a talk in one sentence." So every other Shabbat I had to make a point.

One of the characteristics of the SAJ services which had attracted me was the introduction of new supplementary readings. Inserting such readings today is commonplace. Years ago it was an innovation. I enjoyed listening for the selections Rabbi Kaplan would introduce each week. I did not enjoy the practice quite so much, however, when I became responsible for supplying the new material. Each fortnight I would search through volume after volume of prayers and meditations, written for the most part by non-Jewish authors (mostly Protestant), seeking appropriate texts. In almost every instance it would be necessary for me to cross out the references to Jesus or Christ; it was remarkable, I thought, how useful these prayers were when denuded, as it were, of their theological references. Christians, I believe, could utilize Jewish sources more easily than Jews could pray from Christian texts. Christians were not usually offended by being reminded of their Jewish roots; Jews would have been deeply shocked if I had not eliminated the "Jesuses." Behind the different *sancta*, however, were we not all praying for the same blessings?

One of the more painful if infrequent duties of the rabbinate was officiating at funerals. I tried to avoid spending time with bereaved families because, apart from the sheer gloominess of the scene, this kept me from reading and studying—a luxury rabbis have little opportunity to indulge in. I nevertheless recognized that it was precisely on these occasions that I performed the most useful functions. No matter how far Jews drift from their Jewish folkways, they almost automatically revert to them when tragedy strikes. Ancient rituals spare them the need of improvising; the formula is at hand. They want to do the right thing, and the right thing usually means the traditional route.

The first step, of course, is to call the rabbi, if they "have" a rabbi. If not, the well-oiled machinery of the morticians goes into action. A rabbi is available through a pool of clergy who have contracted for this service. Why do they need a rabbi? According to Jewish tradition, anyone who knows the funeral ritual and can perform it is eligible. There are no priests in Judaism any more. Any competent Jew can lead worship services, conduct funerals, even perform weddings (if equipped with the knowledge of the laws). No doubt there is a vestige of magic involved in the felt need for a rabbi. It may be that most Jews are so ignorant of Jewish tradition that they do not realize that a licensed clergy is not required. In any event, the rabbi represents the Jewish community to most Jews. In times of crisis, Jews apparently need to come home to the Jewish people of which they are a part, however quiescent has been their membership in it.

Every religious leader knows, or learns, the right and proper words to say, the appropriate tone and posture. But sometimes an unexpected challenge arises for which one is totally unprepared. I remember occasions when a stricken widow would ask "Why?" Why did God take away her husband of thirty years, whom she knew from childhood, with whom she spent such happy years, who was the father of her four lovely children, who had so much to live for? . . . When I was young and not very wise, I tackled this immemorial problem of theodicy like a philosopher. I would actually engage in theological disputation with her. "Why," I would ask, "do you ask this question? Why don't you ask what you did to deserve such a fine husband and family? Why do you not question God's wisdom when you experience good fortune? Why only when death strikes?"

This approach was not only futile; it was cruel and irrelevant. What I did not understand was that the woman was simply giving vent to her sorrow, emitting a cry for help, for comfort and compassion. She was certainly not about to enter into a theological discussion. Later I learned better, and from then on I felt compensated for the time that these funerals would take, the meetings before and the visits after. To be sure, a trace of annoyance was left; what was I doing, wasting my time riding out to the cemetery with a family I hardly knew? My annoyance would be intensified when I observed that the immediate family would soon be talking about the people who had attended the service, noting those who had been absent, expressing pleasure about the presence of some special person, then gradually drifting to the news that morning on the radio, sometimes to the current sports scene. Did they really need me to comfort them when they seemed capable of returning so readily to their normal habits of conversation?

The answer would come quickly as we entered the cemetery grounds. At once, voices were hushed. The casual conversation ceased, and the realization of where they were and why they had come overcame them. I did not at first realize that all the small talk had been forced, artificial bravado, a pitiful attempt by each to distract the other. Attention quickly reverted to the rabbi, whom they needed to tell them what to do, where to stand, what to say.

I shall never forget the first funeral at which I had to officiate alone. A young woman had lost her husband quite suddenly. She was inconsolable. She cried and wrung her hands, and she almost collapsed when we reached the cemetery. When the body was finally lowered, she broke away from her relatives and literally attempted to throw herself into the grave with him. I thought I would not survive the ordeal. The sight was terrible enough; the thought left me a wreck: how utterly hopeless seemed her life, how bleak her future!

One day six months later, I received a phone call from the widow, the young woman who had nearly plunged herself into the grave. Somewhat bashfully she asked whether I could be free on a certain day to perform a wedding ceremony. She was to be married! In my naivete I had imagined that bereavement left a person totally undone for the rest of her/his life. I was not aware of the healing power of time.

It is true that some bereavements leave permanent scars and inextinguishable memories. The loss of a son or daughter is of that nature. Sometimes an individual does not remarry after losing a mate. But fortunately human resilience is greater than one might believe in the moment of crisis. What it meant for me was that I did not any longer allow myself to be totally prostrated by witnessing sorrow or by presiding over the rituals of mourning. I learned how to protect myself without becoming altogether callous in the presence of another's tragedy. At the age of 25, it is a valuable lesson to learn but one not easily mastered.

One of the peripheral problems surrounding the rabbi's role as pastor stems from the mourner's yearning to be reunited with the deceased. Will he/she go to heaven? Do we Jews believe in heaven and hell? Is there immortality? Will there be resurrection in the end of days? What does Judaism have to say about these ultimate questions? Rabbi Kaplan's insistence upon intellectual honesty made it virtually impossible for me to make any promises to the bereaved that I could not conscientiously defend. When questioned, he would launch into elaborate re-interpretations of ancient concepts which were more suitable for a seminar than for a house of mourning. It was hardly comforting to know that death is an integral part of life, or that true immortality consists in the enduring influences which one's life exerts upon survivors, or that one lives as long as those who loved him remember him.

The immediate and inevitable response would be that this was all well and good, but not a satisfactory substitute for conscious and purposeful living. Immortality means living forever. Otherwise it means nothing at all, at least nothing that can be of any comfort to the bereaved. At times like these the rabbi wishes either that he were back in the age of innocence so that he could say with conviction, "Yes, I believe the dead live on," or that he had gone into some other profession altogether.

Perhaps a third possibility is to tell the people what they want to hear, and to hell with intellectual honesty for the time being. There would be plenty of opportunity later, when the pain was not so acute, for philosophical distinctions. It may be that many rabbis do just that, but I have always found it difficult to revert deliberately to assertions of doctrine contrary to what I truly believe. In this respect I think I have been less than effective as a rabbi, or at least as the kind of rabbi most people seem to require.

The same difficulty assailed me when I had to visit congregants in the hospital. I was not really very good at this phase of my work. I resented having to spend hours holding someone's hand and pretending great solicitude. Very often the member of the congregation was hardly known to me at all. Congregants might come only on Yom Kippur but when ill expect the rabbi to pay a pastoral call. The real trouble comes when the patients ask the rabbi to pray for them.

The anti-supernaturalist stance I took when I opted for Kaplan's approach to Judaism became a source of conflict when a sick person pleaded for intervention with the Deity on his behalf. Does one say that God has more pressing problems than to inject Himself into your *personal* problem? Is it best to say that I don't believe in the kind of God who listens to prayer and then out of His infinite mercy provides a cure? Is it permissible to tell patients that if they came to shul more often, they might have deserved the health they now cry for?

The physicians are not helpful either. When they have done all they can for a patient and realize they are fighting a losing battle, they say, "Now you are in God's hands." Who needs this kind of specious theology from the doctor? (Insurance companies resort to similar metaphysical doctrines when they refer to "acts of God.")

During my first two years at the SAJ, I experienced many hours of doubt as to whether I had really made a wise decision. I was doing all the things I would have been doing at Mishkan Tefilah or any other conventional congregation. In some respects I was responsible for duties of which I would have been relieved in a large institution. The school, for example, would have been under the supervision of a principal. At the SAJ I was responsible for administering the school as well. Aside from having to learn on the job, I discovered that many of the sons and daughters of my well-to-do members were spoiled brats who behaved abominably. Perhaps they were no different in Roxbury, but that would have given the principal the headaches I now suffered. For instance, on one occasion when a teacher came weeping to me, complaining that the kids were fresh, I called them in to upbraid them, only to hear one of them say, "She should be grateful that we come at all. Otherwise she would have no job, and she would starve to death."

The so-called Women's Division was no different from most other sisterhoods. They would meet in the homes of members who had large living rooms and spend most of the time either telling one another of the bargains available in the Fifth Avenue department stores or quarrelling about whether the annual luncheon should serve fish or meat. The attendance was better when the meeting was at a home every woman wanted to see. They did not hesitate to investigate even the kitchen and the rooms where the meeting was not being held. I had to attend these meetings and wait patiently until they were ready to hear a five-minute talk on current Jewish events or a book review.

I heard a good deal about how the SAJ was different. But I was hard put to identify precisely how different and in what respect. Yes, bat mitzvah had been introduced. Rabbi Kaplan, ten years before when the SAJ began, called his daughter, Judith, to the *bimah* (informing her the night before just what she should read), and one by one other girls had followed. But the other innovations—the textual changes in the liturgy, the supplementary prayers—had little meaning for these ladies who believed that they were indeed unique among the daughters of Israel.

I was supposed to be working with Dr. Kaplan. As I recall, my main functions were to free him to finish his major book and to benefit from his critical analyses of my sermons. The SAJ had not been liquidated, but it was in the doldrums. It was just

116

about holding its own thanks to the staff (Cantor Moshe Nathanson, the secretary, the two teachers, and the superintendent), who, during 1932–1933, waited more than six months to receive their salaries. Many a time I was asked to travel downtown to visit various members who had not paid their dues and to extract at least some part of what they owed. Finally the Board appointed Mr. Bernard Semel their spokesman to the staff proposing a settlement. He was a businessman with a remarkable talent for telling Yiddish stories and for devotion to the cause of Jewish education. He told the staff that if we surrendered our claim to back salaries, we would be paid on time thereafter. I had no difficulty in accepting the proposition, since I lived at home and was responsible only for contributing my share to the family budget. Cantor Nathanson, with his customary genius for timing, had just become the father of twin girls, making a total of three children. How he managed I shall never know.

But in the depths of the Depression we had no choice. The only question which continued to trouble us was how we could be sure that the SAJ would be able to meet its obligations from that time forward. The question was answered, fortunately, by the Liebovitz family, Abe and Harry, who contributed $25,000 to the SAJ for the purpose of purchasing cemetery plots which the congregants were urged to buy from the SAJ. The property was in Mt. Hebron cemetery, and again Mr. Semel was appointed chief salesman. For years he was still being quoted as having said, "It's beautiful out there. People are dying to be buried there."

The SAJ had let me down. The exciting collaboration with Rabbi Kaplan had not materialized.

My personal life was faring no better. I had become so involved in my work that I did not generally provide for recreation in my leisure time. Before I realized it, Saturday nights had rolled around, and I had made no provision for them. I had maintained contact with some of the girls I had known at college, and I would call them at the last moment for a date. They were more tolerant of my casual behavior than I deserved. If they were free they accepted, even though the date meant nothing more than a walk or a soda. Was I unconsciously avoiding any more sustained relationships because, somewhere back of my mind, I had already chosen the one whom I would some day want to marry? Good question; the answer is yes.

She was Rabbi Kaplan's eldest daughter Judith. I had met her briefly one Saturday evening when we were gathering for a seminar. She was on her way out. As she later said, "I wouldn't be caught dead without a date on a Saturday evening." The glimpse of her that I did get, however, registered as love at first sight. That phrase sounds ridiculous, appropriate for movies and cheap novels. But I insist that such things happen. It did to me.

What was I hoping to find? First, of course, a Jewish woman, *Jewishly* Jewish, a characteristic lacking in several other young women whom I knew. She had to love music and be deeply involved in it. She had to be blonde and blue-eyed. She had to be "intellectual," that is, not self-consciously so but naturally intelligent and intellectually curious. And, if possible (such requirements!) she had to share an enthusiasm for the kind of Judaism to which I was planning to devote my life. It is thus no coincidence that I thought I had found her in the household of Rabbi Kaplan.

But at that stage in my emotional development, I was not ready. I could not handle it. My shyness, my belief that I was not physically attractive (remember the big nose and the ears that stuck out) paralyzed me. I stood by helplessly while she showed no sign of having noticed me. (I was wrong.) I should have known that the worst would happen: she married someone else, a man (from my thoroughly biased point of view) utterly unworthy. Naturally, I was asked to attend the wedding, a modest affair at the Kaplan home. As I walked back, after the reception, I experienced the beginning of what would today be diagnosed as a mild nervous breakdown.

During the following year I almost ceased to function. I suffered from attacks of vertigo. I slept an inordinate amount of time. The doctor said I had "hypoglycemia." Chemically he was undoubtedly right, but he missed the point. There was obviously a direct connection between the hypoglycemia and the shock of attending the wedding of a person whom I felt I had lost forever.

By an extraordinary effort of will I carried on. I confided in no one, and as far as I know neither my family nor the SAJ members suspected the truth. The only ones who sensed that I was in love with Judith were her cousin Rita and her husband Lionel.

This I infer from the fact that Lionel took me aside the night before I was to leave for a summer in Palestine (1933), and with a knowing smile informed me that Judith Kaplan was probably going to be divorced. I did not know that the marriage had soured quickly. Was he sure of his facts? And why did he think it necessary to whisper the news in my ear? I said, "Really," as calmly as I could.

7

Visiting Eretz Yisrael

For some time I was hoping to find someone who was interested in a trip to Eretz Yisrael so that we might travel together. But I knew no one who could afford such a junket; the Depression was still very widespread. Besides, in 1933 Zionism was virtually an esoteric doctrine. Ideologically very few were convinced of either its practicality or its desirability. For me, however, Zionism represented a completely new challenge. In one's own land, one did not have to fight the environment. There nobody asked, "Why be a Jew?" There one could achieve wholeness, integration. A new nation was being forged out of the remnants of a scattered people. There the prophetic spirit could once again flourish, the national genius reassert itself. . . . All the Zionist rhetoric which I had heard over the years began to make sense to me. The visions of people like Dr. Benderly were no longer far off in the heavens, but within reach. All one had to do was to go there, taste the reawakened energy of the Jewish renaissance, and merge into the new Hebrew people.

I spent twenty-one days getting there on a cruise. The Women's Division gave me a movie camera and projector. Others in the congregation brought me gifts to the boat. I sailed on an American Export Line cruise ship filled with school teachers, apparently the only ones in those days who had steady jobs.

To my surprise, I discovered that I could overcome my shyness. Perhaps it was the exhilarating experience of learning that I was not going to be seasick after all. Perhaps it was the sense of total detachment from my accustomed surroundings. Or my plunge into sociability may have been powered by the awesome prospect of spending three weeks on the ocean without talking to anybody.

One person with whom I struck up a conversation was Patricia Bowers, a slight, pretty girl with whom I was soon walking the decks. I had no idea who she was, nor did she know anything about me. So we made up a game of twenty questions. She was getting off at Gibraltar to meet her father who was working in Spain. He was none other than the American Ambassador, Claude Bowers. I believe she was equally stunned to discover she was talking to a rabbi!

Another couple consisted of a captain in the army, retired because of illness, traveling with his charming wife to visit her father, who was the minister of the American church in Geneva. The fact that we were both related to the religion business made my being a rabbi less exotic. I soon found myself lecturing to them about this new approach to Judaism in which I was involved. We spent many hours on deck exploring the implications of Kaplan's philosophy and probing the meaning of my devotion to a land where I had never been. Before they left the boat at Marseilles, they made me promise to visit them in Geneva. They wanted particularly for me to meet a young and wonderful clergyman named James Parkes, a dear friend of theirs who was working at the International Student Center there.

One of the gifts I received for the trip was a copy of *Old Wives' Tale* by Arnold Bennett. I mention this seemingly trivial fact because it symbolized for me the tug of war which began as soon as we left New York harbor. As a rabbi, as one traveling for the first time to Eretz Yisrael, I expected of myself a mounting excitement at the prospect of actually stepping on the soil of my ancient ancestors. But I became so absorbed in the novel that I could not tear myself away from it. At Marseilles, at Naples, and at Alexandria (where I visited with friends) I interrupted my reading, and was properly enthusiastic about my adventures in foreign parts. But when the boat left Alexandria and we were informed that the next morning we were to land at

Jaffa, I waited for my pulse to begin beating rapidly. Nothing happened. I took out *Old Wives' Tale* and immersed myself in its fascinating account.

What was the matter with me? Why was I not out on deck peering into the darkness for the first glimpse of the Holy Land? Why was I not silently humming *Hatikvah*? I thought back over the voyage: the thrill of watching lava move relentlessly down the slope of Vesuvius; the beauty of southern France, with its impressive ancient ruins; the awesome sight of the pyramids and the rocky ride atop a camel. I had responded to these and other sights, but only as a tourist. Now I was approaching Palestine not as a mere tourist but as a Jew coming home again. It was the fulfillment of a centuries-old dream for the Jewish people and an almost life-long dream for me.

And yet there I was, reaching for a novel, eager to stay on a bit longer in the world of England and France, where I surely did not belong, rather than to open my heart to the land where I did belong. I realized that this was not the first time I had experienced a deep schism within me. I thought back to those early days when the other kids would dance the hora and I stood on the sidelines. Was it because I really did not think they had earned the right to dance, not having worked and sweated and drained the swamps? Or was it because I could not wholehearted-identify myself with their total abandon? As they danced, it seemed to me they were turning their backs upon America. They were totally at one with Eretz Yisrael. In some respects, I thought, I understand the Zionist ideal better than they. I know more about Judaism. Yet I could not forget so completely that I was an American with deep roots in this land.

As I lay on my bed in the cabin, it came to me that my roots were not just in the United States. They reached down to the whole of Western civilization. I had not only been born in America. I was raised there, educated there. My entire being was fashioned by this country, its language and its ideals. On the other hand, this Western culture was strange to me. It spoke in the accents of Christianity, which had been and continued to be essentially hostile to Jews. Even when Christians were friendly, they expressed themselves in a strange way. For instance, the

Baptist professor with whom I had shared a table on the boat.

He was retired from a seminary in Chicago, and was on his way to Jerusalem to visit his son, who served as director of the YMCA. We talked of many things, and of course the new Hitler regime in Germany. He had learned that I was a rabbi and expected that I would be familiar, as he was, with the "Old Testament." Did I realize, he said, that Hitler on the one hand and the rebuilding of Palestine by the Jewish people on the other, were fulfillments of the prophecies to be found in the Book of Daniel? He was a good and gentle soul, but for him the suffering of the Jews—which was of course most unfortunate—was simply one ingredient in a theological pattern. He was far more interested in the Christian interpretation of *our* Bible than he was in the flesh and blood agony of fellow creatures.

Of course I expressed my reservations about his whole approach to Scripture. But I did so gently, cautiously, even fearfully, lest I destroy that delicate bond of good will upon which we Jews rely for our safety. Was this to be our permanent condition, refraining from commenting upon strong and unmistakable differences from good gentiles for fear of losing the freedom we now enjoy? Was this really being at home in the western world? Was this the price we would have to pay for Christian approval of the Zionist movement? The hell with that, I said to the empty cabin. On to Eretz Yisrael . . . But the defiant mood was short lived. Do I really belong in Palestine? Am I not also a curious visitor? Do I entertain serious intentions of settling there? And so on into the night.

The boat stood out about fifty yards from the shore of Jaffa. The gangplank had been lowered, and the Arab boatmen had begun to hover near it, prepared to take passengers to the shore. If you timed your jump right, you landed in the large rowboat, and someone threw your baggage after you. There was no port as yet in neighboring Tel Aviv. Indeed the future metropolis was then only a suburb of Jaffa.

I sat in the rowboat grabbing the sides with each hand. I glanced up to see the minarets of the many mosques, the droshkys lined up at the shore, and far to the left I had my first look at the all-Jewish village. The shouts I heard were by now familiar sounds; the porters at Alexandria had also yelled as they worked. Hearing them the first time I had thought they were engaged in a furious fight. Now I knew that these noises were normal.

I was beginning to get excited. Once I saw the actual landscape and realized that in a moment I would be setting foot in Eretz Yisrael, the debate of the previous night suddenly seemed unreal. How could I have had any doubts about the way I would feel? Now I was scampering up the stone steps, offering my passport to the British officials, and scanning the thin crowd for a glimpse of the distant relative with whom I was supposed to stay. She was on my grandma's side of the family. She had written us in Yiddish from time to time, keeping in touch with the family she had never seen and probably never expected to see. It had been arranged that I would have a room in her flat for the first few days, and I might even leave my stuff there if I went off on a trip.

It was not hard to find her. Actually, she found me. I was the only young American male to debark. I was obviously not the goyish Baptist professor with the gray hair. She addressed me in Hebrew, and to my great surprise I responded in Hebrew! We located the bags, and we were off behind a horse which seemed too tired to go anywhere. But there was no hurry. It was only half past seven in the morning, and there was a busy world to observe on both sides of the droshky.

I dropped my bags and had a glass of tea. She gave me a rundown on the various members of the family (they had gone off to work by then), and I described Grandma, my parents, my brother, and my Uncle Jake. Then she said I didn't have to stay and talk with her. She had housework to do, and I didn't come to Palestine to sit indoors. I was to go out and take a walk and get acquainted with Tel Aviv. But she warned me not to go marching around in the July sun. From noon to four, one should remain in the house. (I was truly astounded by her matter-of-fact treatment of me; I had worried that she might try to be a mother-away-from-home. I was relieved.)

No sooner had I begun my exploration than I noticed, to my shock and grief, a photograph of Cantor Rosenblatt, with a black border around the frame. He had apparently died a few days before my arrival, and later I learned that he had suffered a heart attack while singing for a film. Memories of Yom Kippur and the World Series! Memories of Grandma crying away while he prayed for *parnosseh*.

Tel Aviv in 1933 was indeed only a suburb of the older and larger Jaffa. And as I soon discovered hitchhiking up and down the coast, the Jewish settlements were few and far between, and each was a frontier village: Rehovot, Nes Ziona, and the rest, whose names were familiar to me from stories told by Grandpa from when he visited the country in 1889. Indeed, they were probably not much larger some forty years later. The total population of Jewish Palestine (the *yishuv*) was about 250,000 when I visited there: the first sprinkling of German Jews was arriving, but they did not add very much to the number.

I took the bus up to Jerusalem, checked in at Amdursky's (the hotel Grandpa had suggested, since they knew him), and marched directly to the old city, impatient to see the Wailing Wall. It was a complicated walk through narrow and darkened alleys, and when I caught sight of the Wall, suddenly, unexpectedly, I stood stock still. *This* was overwhelming. In the narrow passageway there were a few old men, some praying, others resting there in the deep shadows, and the British police were everywhere in evidence. I recalled that in 1929, only four years before, incidents at the Wall had triggered Arab riots and massacres in Hebron and other places. I missed having someone with me with whom to share this unforgettable moment and to philosophize.

Hitchhiking seemed to be the normal way to get around. I met another young American from Detroit, and we made our way north to Metullah.

Through the Emek I managed to get rides on the back seat of a doctor's motorcycle, almost losing my bag and the typewriter which my father had given me as a gift; actually, I almost fell off once or twice on the rough unpaved roads to Ein Harod and Tel Yoseph. In Haifa I looked up some American friends, who invited me to stay in their apartment, since they were about to leave for a week's vacation up in the Lebanese mountains.

Back in Jerusalem, I attended a concert conducted by Karl Salomon, one of the recent German arrivals, at the amphitheatre of the Hebrew University. I was so moved by the Hebrew version of an aria from Handel's "Israel in Egypt" that I borrowed a typewriter (I had finally left my own at the flat in Tel Aviv) and dashed off a review-article.

I brought it to the assistant editor of the *Palestine Post,* Ted Lurie, a cousin of one of my friends in the SAJ. He accepted it. Seeing my name in print in Jerusalem prompted me to impulsively ask Ted whether I could possibly get a job working for the *Post.* He said there would be no problem at all. Everyone was so eager for Americans to settle in Palestine that offers like this one were made in haste, an offer which I am sure Ted Lurie would regret on second thought.

Rabbi Albert Gordon, a former classmate at the Seminary, was on his honeymoon. I met him and Dorothy at the home of American friends we had in common, and we were pleased with the possibility of traveling together. The three of us would spend hours exploring the likelihood of settling in the Land. Apparently, some of the thoughts going through my head corresponded to ideas in theirs. We were among Jews concentrating upon the common task of building a nation. We were young; we had not yet established families. We were needed, everyone said, not as rabbis, to be sure, but in whatever capacity we could learn to function. For me, journalism sounded exciting. Perhaps I could become a foreign correspondent for some paper in the States, reporting developments to a public I understood.

Ordinarily I would not have suggested a visit to Henrietta Szold. I respected her greatly and was hesitant to impose upon her busy schedule, but Al and Dorothy had requested an opportunity to visit her at the Eden Hotel, where she resided when she was in Eretz Yisrael. They thought she would not object to their bringing me along. She, of course, knew and had worked with Mordecai Kaplan long before I had had any association with him. I felt I could with propriety crash this visit—if only to bring greetings from Rabbi Kaplan.

In the course of the visit both Al and I mentioned to Miss Szold that we were considering the possibility of settling. She took us completely by surprise by emphatically opposing this notion. By no means were we to abandon the United States. We were needed there. The *yishuv* could use young muscular men (we were young but otherwise unqualified); there was hard work, *schvartze arbeit, (melakhah sheḥorah)* to be done. They

126

did not need any more intellectuals, and certainly not more rabbis. When I timidly suggested that I might find work as a newspaper reporter, she scoffed. Why waste all that good education on journalism? There were hundreds of others who could do that job. Judaism in America needed to be strengthened; the future of Zionism and the *yishuv* depended upon a strong Jewish community. This was our true function; we should go back and get to work!

I could not blame Henrietta Szold for the fact that we did return to our respective congregations. I am inclined to think that if we had been serious about our intention to remain, we would not have asked anyone—not even Miss Szold—and even having asked her, we would not have been swayed by her immediate and emphatic reply. We were probably sending up trial balloons and playing with the thought of *aliyah*. I had made a commitment to the SAJ; I was still very much attached to my parents, and Ted Lurie's comment was not really a firm offer.

After six weeks I was on my way back to the States via Italy, Switzerland, and Paris. In Geneva I visited for a few days with the retired army officer and his wife whom I had met on the boat going to Palestine. Switzerland, especially Geneva, was delightful, and my brief encounter with Parkes was stimulating. He was working on a book dealing with the historical background of the break between the Church and the Synagogue and asked me for the names of some people to whom he could show the work he had done. I promised to introduce him to Professor Alexander Marx, my former teacher.

Later that year Dr. Parkes did come to New York, and I had the pleasure of bringing the two together. James Parkes became a distinguished figure in the kind of theological literature that is historically authentic and friendly to the Jewish people. He died in the summer of 1981.

In Paris I found a letter from my father containing an article published in *Opinion*, a monthly edited by Stephen Wise. The article was written by Ludwig Lewisohn in reply to something I had written in a previous issue. At my father's urging, I called Lewisohn (it took a lot of courage for me to do this kind of thing) and asked whether he would allow me to visit him. Apparently he remembered my piece and encouraged me to come to his home. For me this was a thrilling adventure. I had read his *Island Within*, one of the influential Anglo-Jewish novels of my college years. I had also dipped into his critical history of American literature. In a way he had become a sort of idol, representing the distinguished intellectual who had made it in the larger world, who had rediscovered his Jewish identity through anti-Semitism (described in *Upstream*), and had been totally reconverted to Judaism.

My quarrel with him centered in his overreaction to his years of alienation. From almost total assimilation he had swung to the notion of "once a Jew always a Jew." There is some mystic bond which is never broken, even in the case of Jews who have had no contact with Jewish tradition. It all bordered on a kind of racism which, in the summer of 1933 seemed to me to bear with it the germs of dangerous doctrine.

His red-headed wife stuck her head into the room just to say hello. I gathered from his remarks that this second wife, being Jewish, was far more satisfactory; the first, being gentile, had been cold. I had already suspected that the *Island Within* was autobiographical; now this impression was confirmed.

We spent only a few moments on the article in *Opinion*. The rest of the rather lengthy visit was devoted to his eloquent description of the revolution which he had experienced when he returned to Judaism. I was already outlining in my mind an article I would write when I returned, a portrait of the *baal teshuvah*, the repentant sinner. One of his comments has remained with me over the years. It was his reference to *Creative Experience in America*, his major work on American literature, which he described as a potboiler, written just to make a few dollars! He was no longer interested in goyishe books.

The other event in Paris was my discovery, through the Paris *Herald*, that the family Lamport was staying in Paris. Sam Lamport and his wife May were important figures in the SAJ. They were founders of the Society, and she was chairperson of the Women's Division (practically a permanent position). Their two daughters, Sara and Felicia, were with them. The girls had been in one of my young people's groups at the SAJ. On an impulse I called them at the hotel, and Sam, not being a particularly gentle or refined character but a very successful businessman, said, "Hell, Rabbi, don't let an opportunity like this go by. How often do we have a chance to visit with our spiritual leader (ha ha) socially? We'll expect you in an hour."

Sam Lamport was the kind of man whom it was useless to resist. In an hour I was there, ushered into a palatial suite at the best hotel in Paris. They were all about to go golfing. I was not —and am not now—a golfer, but I shlepped along. Sam ordered the porters about like slaves, to the embarrassment of his daughters, who thought he was loud and vulgar. May, who was quite deaf, was oblivious to the brash speech. What made the visit memorable, however, was May's asking me whether I knew that Rabbi Kaplan's daughter Judith had gone off to Reno for a divorce.

The next day I sailed back to the United States. I had been away almost thirteen weeks. I had undergone spiritual crises. I had decided to settle in Palestine; I had decided *not* to settle in Palestine. I had made up my mind that the rabbinate would be *precisely* what I wanted, so long as Judith Kaplan would have me. On the way back, I met several young women returning from a summer abroad. When we got better acquainted, they inevitably learned that I was a rabbi, and I found myself going through the same old routine—why be Jewish, why religion, why be a rabbi, should there not be one universal religion, isn't religion a divisive force, how can an intelligent fellow believe all that stuff?

I could not wait to get back, so that I could launch my campaign to win the blonde with the blue eyes and the charming personality.

8

Judith and Judaism
As a Civilization

In the fall of 1933, the Depression was unrelieved, but I found people a bit more hopeful. Roosevelt had launched his program for recovery, and while the results were hardly perceptible, a new mood had set in. The fact that Hitler had also launched his program did not dim their spirits. They had no way of knowing what lay in store for the Jews, or for the world at large. Roosevelt was trying to warn the nation of the dangers of an impending war, but domestic problems came first, and at home economic recovery was the immediate goal.

I was dismayed to discover how hostile many of our members were to Roosevelt's program. They thought of themselves as middle-class capitalists. Yet they were as insecure as many millions of workers who found in the President some reason for not flying into the arms of the leftists. Strangely, the most affluent of the members of the Society were strong supporters of Roosevelt. They probably sensed, and properly, that he was saving capitalism from its severest critics.

Like many of my generation, I had been attracted to Marxist solutions. I might well have joined the communists if they had not so egregiously misread both Zionism and (Jewish) religion. Their opposition to Zionism was based on the dogma that it was a form of imperialism, designed to enable the British to preserve their power in the Middle East. While the British may indeed have thought in terms of their imperial interests, their behavior toward the Zionist movement revealed that they considered the movement to establish a Jewish homeland to be in direct conflict with those interests. I thought that if the communists were as wrong about everything else as they were about Zionism (and I had just seen Zionism in action), then they were dead wrong about everything else.

Their denunciation of religion, too, seemed to me to be entirely misdirected, certainly when it came to Jewish religion. While many radical Jewish groups had turned their backs on traditional Judaism, they nevertheless displayed the kind of passion for social justice which could only have been generated by their Jewish civilization. True, tradition had made them passive rather than active, and they had had to break with tradition even to become Zionists. But to think of organized Jewish religion as a retrogressive force appeared absurd to me. I knew religious Jews; I believe they would have made zealous communists (as I almost became) if Marx had not shown himself to be such a self-hating Jew, such an anti-Semite.

Kaplan helped me greatly to understand the difference between socialism and communism; socialism seemed to be a civilized form of protest against the evils of the *status quo*. And I had seen in Palestine the pioneering work of the early *ḥalutzim*, who were propelled by socialist ideals to form cooperatives and communal settlements. But unfortunately I was very naive politically, like many others I guess. I could not distinguish a healthy socialism from a cruel and oppressive one.

My visit to Italy had given me an opportunity to see fascism under Mussolini. Of course I saw the trains running on time. The tenth anniversary of Mussolini's march on Rome had attracted tens of thousands, myself among them, and I was tremendously impressed with the exhibition and the literature which was handed out. Naturally, I knew nothing of the multitudes who were languishing in jails, or of those who were tortured for their political views.

I believed that it was possible to introduce socialism without sacrificing civil rights. True, the Soviet Union provided none of the guarantees of our American Constitution, but I believed that this was a temporary situation, to be remedied as soon as the transition period was over. In brief, educated but simple-minded people like me were ready to write off the American system, which had obviously failed, but we were willing to give Roosevelt a chance to prove us wrong.

As for my private life, my goal was kept clearly in mind. I would wait a decent interval before launching my campaign. In the meantime I seized every opportunity to make myself conspicuous in the Kaplan family circle. The camera which the Women's Division had given me had produced several reels of movies for home showing and I presented an evening of these films to the congregation. Judith, who was teaching at the Center Academy in Brooklyn, came to see the pictures and asked whether I would show them to the children at the school. I agreed, and this gave me a chance to ride back and forth with her on the subway.

But soon a major opportunity arose. One of the cousins of the Kaplans was Harold Bernstein, who still nursed dreams of being another Larry Hart (of Rodgers and Hart). He suggested that we collaborate on a musical show, to be put on by the younger people of the SAJ. It would involve them in a form of synagogue activity, and maybe some money could be raised for the benefit of the Society. He asked Judith to work with him on the music, and he proposed that they get me to do the book. With words and music accounted for, all they needed was a plot. It would deal in some way with life in a shul. And of course it had to be funny.

The prospect of working on a show with them was a boon. I no longer needed to concoct excuses to see Judith, to take her out. Of course money was very scarce; this was the most inexpensive date one could imagine. We began meeting at the home of the Bernsteins one evening a week. I am not certain to this day whether the whole project was not intended to do what it actually accomplished. But my courtship began.

After working on the script or the lyrics for an evening, we would take a walk or I would walk her home. During rehearsals, it became almost routine for Judith and me to leave together. No privacy could be achieved while crowds were milling around, so these strolls back to the house gave us some precious moments alone. However, once we came back to the apartment, we might as well have said goodnight and forgotten about spending any time with one another, for Mordecai Kaplan was still up, working at his desk. When he heard us arrive, he immediately called me to say that he had something important to discuss and that Judith should come along too.

No matter how late we returned—and we tried coming later and later—he was up and at work, poised to intercept us and invite us to have a discussion. While these hours spent around his desk were among the most frustrating imaginable, they were also some of the most precious. This unlikely trio, seriously talking Judaism in the middle of the night, was certainly unique.

Working on the musical show, Judith had confirmed my deepest intuitions concerning her charm, her humor, and her intelligence. Sitting around the desk with her father added a special dimension: she possessed keen insights, revealing a philosophical mind along with a passionate love for everything Jewish. While I would surely have preferred being alone with her these final hours, I was thrilled by the phenomenon of so close-knit a bond which tied all three together.

That spring the show went on. It was called *Punch and Judaism*. It ran for one night at the 92nd Street Y, and it made $1000 for the congregation. It was a hit, even though the amateurs did not enunciate their words (*our* words) clearly enough. Much of the cleverness of the lyrics was lost.

At a party following the performance, everyone (we later learned) expected Judith and me to announce our engagement. But I was not about to fall into that cliché. The moment was not going to be shared with any musical, no matter how much fun we had doing it. When others were present I acted as though nothing was going on. Of course, I fooled nobody: they had been watching us, spying on us, reporting to one another whether they saw us taking a walk in the park. Fortunately we did find the right moment one Sunday afternoon after having attended a wedding. We sat on a bench on Riverside Drive, and suddenly it was done. (Judith has frequently repeated the canard that she was drunk and didn't know what she was doing—except that she also confessed coming along to a wedding where she had no business being, on the assumption that I would be there.)

Manny was disgusted; he said I had sold out by marrying the boss's daughter, like a true bourgeois. I really do not know whether he meant this seriously; but I was never to find out. He was killed shortly thereafter in a plane accident.

––––––––––––––––––––

The publication of *Judaism As a Civilization* was an obbligato to this major theme. The book had been with us right along. Whenever we came back late at night, we would find Kaplan struggling over proofs, even page proofs, correcting, improving, constantly perfecting. One night Judith lost her temper (which she inherited from her father), and shouted at him, "You and your God-damned perfectionism!" I was shocked, and for a moment the glow of my burgeoning love was dimmed. In my home, no one ever raised his or her voice. Words like "damn" were strictly forbidden. Besides, neither Myron nor I would ever talk that way to one of our parents, whatever we might think.

But I soon learned that this kind of flareup was not unusual in the Kaplan household. On Friday night the whole family came together for dinner. Judith was tense because she refrained from smoking on Shabbat in the presence of her father. Some remark by one or another of the daughters would ignite an argument, and before long Rabbi Kaplan was shouting, they were all shouting back, and Lena was begging her daughters not to upset their father. She could not bear to see this happening. "I'll jump out of the window," she would cry. "I'll plunge a knife into my heart." The storm was soon over, and this family was back to their warm loving selves. I stood aghast. I had never seen such happenings, and I could not understand how they quickly recovered after some of the words that had been spoken—or yelled.

In any event, we were all relieved when the book finally

appeared in May of 1934. The following month Judith and I were married.

The SAJ was filled to capacity; as someone remarked, like Yom Kippur, but more cheerful. Many came even without an invitation. They were not going to miss this exciting affair. (Rabbi marries the boss's daughter!) I had promised Dr. Finkelstein that he would participate in my marriage ceremony, if and when. Kaplan insisted that promises must be kept; so, in spite of the strained relations between Finkelstein and me, I asked him to be part of the ceremony. Rabbi Phineas Israeli, Rabbi Kaplan's brother-in-law, was the second rabbi and Kaplan himself the third. Cantor Moshe Nathanson chanted the benedictions.

Neither Judith nor I enjoyed this wedding. It was beastly hot; there was no air-conditioning. I was dressed in a cutaway and a high hat (borrowed from one of our trustees). In a word, we were uncomfortable, overwhelmed by the crowds and, as an extra dividend, we never got near the refreshments.

Two days later we sailed for Palestine. I had been there only one year earlier, but I looked forward to guiding Judith through the country. As most married couples probably know by now, honeymoons are highly overrated pastimes. What we needed most was to rest somewhere, to follow a leisurely schedule. Instead, we undertook this strenuous trip.

One memorable event, however, cannot go unrecorded. In July of 1934, Chaim Nachman Bialik, the revered national poet, died in Vienna following an operation. His death shocked every Jew in Palestine. Posters appeared on all billboards—"*Nafla ateret roshenu*" (the crown has fallen from our heads). Judith and I went down to Tel Aviv for the funeral. It was an unforgettable scene.

The entire country came to a halt. Schools were closed. Buses brought people from all over, for work had ceased totally. In a burst of ingenuity, I found a house in which a Dr. Zwisohn lived. It was on Allenby Road, where the funeral procession was to take place. I recalled that my parents had known such a person, and I inquired of him whether we might view the procession from his window facing the avenue. He looked a bit skeptical, but apparently he was sufficiently impressed with our respectable appearance. So he made room for us at one of the windows facing the street.

My movie camera was at the ready, and though the sun beat down on the lens (shaded by a newspaper in Judith's hand), I filmed the impressive event. Years later I had the film made into a videotape, and we view it from time to time. Our younger friends are amused by our youthful looks, not appreciating, I fear, the historic value of the footage showing the funeral.

We returned after having spent six weeks in Palestine (and all the money of our wedding gifts). We settled into an apartment in the same building as the Kaplans' (285 Central Park West), which we were able to get for $40 a month. Judith resumed her teaching at the Center Academy, and I returned to the routines of the SAJ.

The major change in our lives consisted of the appearance of the book. When it appeared the previous May, we did not realize that the major burden of distributing it would fall on us; Macmillan did little in this regard. None of us had had any experience in this kind of work, so we had to improvise. Fliers were printed and sent out to rabbis and educators, Zionist leaders, lay heads of religious bodies. Since those who were already in the field had heard of the forthcoming appearance of this long-awaited volume, the sales were encouraging. We had the feeling that there would be a steady demand for the work over a long period of time.

Soon synagogues and centers began to schedule symposia and discussion sessions around *Judaism As a Civilization*, and suddenly I found myself in a new role! Regarded as Rabbi Kaplan's closest disciple and colleague, I was invited to explain the work to audiences. Rabbi Kaplan too was invited by interested groups, but he did not accept all the invitations. He was already back at his desk, planning future publications. He urged me to represent him. Thus, in a sense my real career began. It consisted in interpreting Kaplan to the people.

My first responsibility was, of course, to the members of the SAJ. For the first time, they said, they were beginning to understand what their Leader had been preaching from the pulpit these many years. They reminded me of the Yiddish folk tale about the *maggid* who attracted large crowds each time he spoke, and when someone asked the little old lady what he had said, she replied, "I couldn't understand a word, but did he give a wonderful *drasha.*"

I soon realized that teaching the book directly from the text was almost impossible. Even though the lay people were above average by virtue of their interest in the subject and their desire to hear it expounded, they were nevertheless unfamiliar with many of the philosophical concepts used in developing the central idea of the work. Clearly, a popularization of *Judaism As a Civilization* was needed. In the summer of 1936, I wrote *Creative Judaism.* Behrman House published this first effort of mine at an extended piece of writing.

But even before undertaking this task, I discussed with Rabbi Kaplan the need for a magazine which would take the basic ideas of the book and apply them to the current scene. The old *SAJ Review* had passed out of existence, as I noted, when the great Depression struck. The time had come when its successor had to be established, even though the economic situation was only slightly improved.

We brought the matter up before the Board of Trustees of the SAJ. It was obvious that they were in no mood to undertake financial responsibility for a journal at that junction in the life of the Society. Yes, some of them thought the idea was good (in general); they were loath to say "no" to Rabbi Kaplan. But "now" was not the time. I record with gratitude the earnest plea of Harry Liebowitz that we be allowed to proceed with the project. He moved that the facilities of the office be made available and that the magazine be officially published by the SAJ, with the understanding that it should not be included as an expense in the budget of the SAJ.

Harry Liebowitz was one of two brothers who had developed a very successful shirt business. Though unschooled in any formal sense, they were deeply interested in cultural and religious matters. They were not altogether unfamiliar with major trends in the theater, the opera, Jewish education, and Zionism. They sensed that in Mordecai Kaplan they had a leader whose courage and imagination deserved their full support. Indeed,

Harry's older brother Abe and his wife had been largely responsible for urging Kaplan to organize the SAJ in the first place.

Harry's eloquence was just barely adequate, however. His motion passed by one vote. I shall remember that meeting long after I have forgotten most others.

The original budget was to be $900 a year. We were going to publish 20 times a year, on a bi-weekly basis for 40 weeks. Subscription was to be $1.00. Each issue was to run 16 pages. The format was to be based on *The Standard*, the organ of the Ethical Culture Society. Much of this was decided between us, even before we knew who was going to comprise the Editorial Board.

In the late fall of 1934, Rabbi Kaplan and I sat down and made a list of the people who we thought might be willing to join such a Board. We were looking for rabbis and educators who had, at one time or another, expressed their general sympathy for Kaplan's approach to the problems of Jewish life. Invitations were sent out for a meeting at the home of Rabbi Kaplan, and the following accepted the invitation to join the Board: Rabbi Ben Zion Bokser, a classmate of mine at the Seminary, was radical in politics, traditional in his Jewish observance, and liberal in his religious thinking. Rabbi Israel Goldstein was one of the graduates of the Seminary most critical of the Conservative movement for its failure to come to grips with the problem of *halakhah*. Endowed with great energy and executive talent, he became the president of many major Jewish organizations. Rabbi Leon Lang had served the SAJ as executive director while a student and considered himself a disciple of Kaplan. Rabbi Eugene Kohn was also a Conservative rabbi devoted to Kaplan's approach and one who (subsequently) identified himself totally with the movement as a staff member of the Reconstructionist Foundation (founded five years later, in 1940). Rabbi Milton Steinberg has been mentioned more than once in this chronicle. He was then serving the Park Avenue Synagogue.

Rabbi Barnett Brickner was a Reform rabbi who was also a Zionist—a combination which made him potentially a Reconstructionist. He served the Euclid Avenue Temple in Cleveland. Dr. Alexander Dushkin was a leading educator, from his earliest days close to Kaplan. Dr. Jacob Golub was in the same category, a gifted writer of textbooks and an effective youth leader. Rabbi Edward Israel (who died suddenly at a very early age) was a Reform rabbi who later became a high official in the Union of American Hebrew Congregations. Dr. Max Kadushin was one of Kaplan's earliest disciples, Hillel director, rabbi, scholar, and indeed a *ben bayit*, one who came frequently to the Kaplan home.

The main business at the first meeting was devoted to giving the baby a name. Kaplan proposed "Reconstructionist." Most of the others found this too long, and not clearly reflective of the Jewish character of the magazine-to-be, perhaps even subject to misunderstanding (such as Reconstructionism after the Civil War). However, Milton Steinberg strongly urged that we adopt this name, and the group agreed.

On January 11, 1935, Shevat 7, 5695, the first issue of the *Reconstructionist* appeared. The circulation stayed below one thousand the first year. Basically, we solicited the same people to whom we had sent the fliers about the book. (SAJ members received their copies free, as a way of thanking the Society for allowing us to use its facilities.) Our one and only secretary at the SAJ, Hannah Machlowitz, handled all the work involved, keeping records, paying bills, sending out the magazine with the aid of a hand-operated Addressograph machine. I did the proofreading, the dummying, and the correspondence with writers. At the beginning we relied heavily on the Editorial Board for articles and book reviews. I also worked with Kaplan on the writing of the editorials.

From the very start we met regularly as a Board to discuss the editorial section of the journal. Suggestions for topics were placed on the table, and when we had decided which had priority, we proceeded to hammer out an approach. Rabbi Kaplan always insisted that I preside at these meetings because he wanted to feel free to participate in the debates. The major thrust of our editorial concern was social justice. The efforts of Roosevelt to save the system elicited the scorn and the anger of our friends who were already either communists or radical socialists. Reformers were considered worse than reactionaries because they were trying to prop up a system which was essentially evil.

We were inclined to favor labor and labor Zionism. In

American terms this meant showing a strong sympathy for the unionization of the workers—often irritating some of our lay-people, who were paying for the magazine. I recall that Ben Bernstein, when he was chairman of the SAJ Board, made sure that we inserted a statement in the magazine to the effect that the editorials represent the views of the editors *only*. The statement is still there. One editorial was called, "Is God a Capitalist?" It provoked the harshest criticism of all. For us, the system was wrong: we were convinced that producing for profit was the villain; one should produce for use. The economy should be planned. We were not going as far as the communists. We did not approve of everything the Russians did, but at the same time we were suspicious of those who found fault with the USSR. We assumed they were fascists in disguise, or at least social fascists, whatever that meant.

In Palestine affairs the same spirit prevailed. We were all for the *kibbutz* and the cooperative. Jabotinsky was for us the equivalent of Mussolini, military-minded, more concerned with national independence than with social justice. While we were unhappy about British politics, we felt, with Weizmann, that the British could eventually be trusted to carry out their promises. On the other hand, we were opposed to the *Hashomer Hatzair*, which was heavily committed to Marxism and preached the bi-national state. We believed that there were no Arabs with whom to carry out any such plan. Judah Magnes and Henrietta Szold and several others of Brith Shalom also advocated bi-nationalism, but we thought them unrealistic.

As socialism was our panacea for all social ills, it followed that social organization was our answer to the internal problems of Jewish life. If philanthropy placed its emphases upon hospitals and non-sectarian centers, if education languished, if individual Jews disgraced the Jewish people by their unethical behavior, it was all due to the fact that we did not have the right kind of social organization. The idea of the democratic organic Jewish community was stressed repeatedly in our editorials.

Our unique approach to religion was reflected in many articles and reviews. Rabbis Kaplan, Eugene Kohn, and Milton Steinberg contributed richly to the elucidation of our Reconstructionist understanding of the nature and role of religion. Since we represented the philosophy of Judaism as a civilization, we gave the appropriate space to all aspects of the Jewish experience: education, the arts, and scholarship.

After graduating from the Seminary, I did little studying. What I read in magazines and books was random. Most of the time I was looking for material I could use in preaching or adult education. More and more I felt that what I had acquired at the Seminary did not qualify me in any sense to be a scholar. Rabbi Kaplan had on several occasions commented about some of the lacunae in my knowledge. The courses at JTS had introduced me to a variety of subjects; I was expected, like all the young rabbis, to go on from there on my own, but like most of them I did not. In addition, Rabbi Kaplan urged me to study Talmud. He would remark that if I were to participate with him in the reconstruction of Judaism, I would have to know more than I did about what it was I was reconstructing. Frankly, he would say, *gemara* is a waste of time, but you have to know that stuff so that you can establish your authority. Apparently this had been his experience: until he received Orthodox *semikhah*, any critical comment he made about the tradition was discounted. With a full-fledged rabbinical degree, he could afford to preach the necessity of moving beyond the rabbinic heritage.

By and large I read what interested me at a given moment. The discipline of study—especially in rabbinics—never attracted me. What was worse, I was easily distracted from any commitment made to myself to follow through with a fixed program.

In the spring of 1935, having become involved in the production of the new magazine, *Reconstructionist*, I decided that my journalism would be better served if I could make of myself an expert in Jewish studies. What I uttered from the pulpit of the SAJ drew upon the store of learning I had acquired at the Seminary and Columbia. The sermons were limited in their reliance upon sources. With Dr. Kaplan sitting there on the pulpit listening to every word and virtually giving me a grade after each effort, I was careful not to make glaring errors. But if I hoped to put my ideas into writing, I thought I had better enrich the store. Thus arose the idea of studying for a Doctor of Hebrew Letters at the Seminary.

I had a theme which I thought might force me to study the rabbinic sources. At the same time it would enable me to document a thesis which Dr. Kaplan had said was important in support of our Reconstructionist theory: traditional Judaism was basically otherworldly, like Christianity (with variations), and the Judaism of today and tomorrow will have to be changed into (he used his favorite phrase, "transposed into the key of") this-worldliness. Those who invariably defended traditional Judaism against any and all criticism usually insisted that traditional Judaism had always been this-worldly (unlike Christianity). Dr. Kaplan was sure they were merely blinded by their loyalty. They were not facing the facts; they were reading back into the past what they wanted to see there.

My thesis, then, was to demonstrate that other-worldliness had played a vital role in the thinking of our forebears. I became excited about the prospect of pursuing a higher degree. I would be compelling myself to adhere to a strict regimen of study and at the same time performing a service to Reconstructionist thinking. I was taken aback, however, when I discussed my subject with Prof. Louis Ginzberg. He told me that I was far from ready to choose a subject, that I was going to have to undertake a great deal of preliminary reading which the DHL program required, beginning that summer (1935) with *Dor Dor V'dorshav*, a lengthy history of Jewish tradition by Isaac Hirsch Weiss.

That summer the plan was for Judy to take the music job at Camp Cejwin, while I would devote myself entirely to plowing through Weiss. Mr. Schoolman, the director of the camp, was especially considerate of my needs. He set aside a tent which was not being used. There I placed my books on a desk. I had no other duties but to sit and study Torah. I felt very old-fashioned: my wife was working, and I was sitting and learning. But, of course, it didn't work out that way at all. First, it was very hot in the tent; second, the insects drove me mad. Third, the going was slow. Fourth, I needed some exercise, so I found myself playing tennis for an hour or so each morning. I got into discussions about Spain and the Loyalists, about collective security and isolationism and the New Deal. And finally I was tempted to abandon Weiss altogether when I was roped into a performance of Gilbert and Sullivan's *Patience.*

When the summer was over, I did not even suffer a guilty conscience. I had been bored—pure and simple—by the lonely task of poring over a Hebrew text which I had been assigned simply as a prerequisite for getting down to what had really interested me. I believe that Prof. Ginzberg was testing me to see whether I was indeed a serious student.

But I was still determined to move on to graduate study, and that fall I decided to go back to Columbia to study under Professor Salo Baron for a Ph.D. This time my thesis was to be in the field of modern Jewish history, specifically the role of Jews in labor movements and socialism, and the implications for the development of Labor Zionism. I had taken courses with Salo Baron from virtually the first semester he taught at Columbia, and I believed that he could direct my studies better than anyone else then at Columbia. There were no other Jewish studies offered, except the Semitic languages which Professor Gottheil taught, and they did not interest me.

My choice of the Labor Zionist movement and its history had been sparked by my two visits to Palestine in '33 and '34. I don't understand, in retrospect, why I was so slow to make the necessary connections, but the fact is that I was preoccupied with radical movements and obsessed with Zionism. Conventional thinking established an adversarial relationship between the two. The socialists (and of course the communists) were violently anti-Zionist, while the Zionists considered any movement for the improvement of diaspora life to be a diversion from the main issue, which is the solution of the Jewish problem. My growing awareness of people like Hayim Greenberg produced what seemed to me to be the obvious synthesis: socialist Zionism. It had not been obvious to me until it struck me with the force of a revelation.

In December 1934, when the *Jewish Frontier* began to appear, it published an article of mine solicited by Greenberg outlining the essential differences between the Histadrut and the Revisionists, the former concerned with establishing the cooperative society, the latter determined to achieve political independence.

My sympathies were, of course, with the Histadrut. Writing about Labor Zionism helped me to formulate more clearly whatever views I had by then developed and whetted my appetite for a knowledge of the origins and background of the movement. Shlomo Bardin's book, *Pioneer Youth in Palestine*, which had been his doctoral thesis at Teachers College, stimulated my curiosity as well.

My experience with Baron proved to be no more successful than the earlier attempt to pursue a DHL at the Seminary. This time my problem was Baron's insistence that I would have to study Russian and master it sufficiently to be able to read the writings of the late nineteenth century and early twentieth century Russian revolutionaries who had had so great an influence upon the early leaders of *Poale Zion*. For me this was out of the question. I knew it would take me several years to learn that outlandish language, and I was not about to spend that much time laying the groundwork for beginning to dig into the sources.

However I still was attracted to Baron and Columbia, and I came up with an alternative proposal which he welcomed, namely, to write a history of the Conservative movement. A friend and contemporary, Beryl Levy, had been working on a study of the Reform movement, and Baron believed that my thesis would constitute an appropriate comparison study to his. Since I was convinced that Reconstructionism was based primarily upon providing an alternative to the Conservative movement into which I had been graduated, the idea seemed ideal until, in his usual thoroughgoing manner, Baron outlined for me what I would have to read in the German language journals going back to the 1840's, when Zechariah Frankel broke with the original Reformers and laid the foundations of what was to become the Conservative movement in the United States.

My German was not very strong. I had taken two years of the language at Columbia, but that had been almost a decade before. In the interval I had made little use of German, and when I examined the ponderous articles in the *Wissenschaft* literature my heart sank. Professor Baron was undoubtedly correct in insisting that any thesis on this subject required careful study of the German sources, but I simply could not reconcile myself to this sort of discipline, considering the fact that, other considerations aside, I was responsible for running a congregation and had taken on the major part of the magazine project.

Perhaps the overriding factor in my ability to give attention to further study at this moment was the crisis that had arisen in our family. On Pesaḥ of 1936, Judith gave birth to a baby boy. The event sent us into paroxysms of joy. But after a year it became apparent that something was wrong. The pediatrician, an old friend of the family (who had actually taken care of Judith herself) was an excellent doctor, but had no explanation for the fact that Ethan had stopped growing mentally. What followed was a frantic search for an answer. Little was known at that time, apparently, about retardation, but whatever expert opinions we could obtain led to the same sad conclusion: an accident of some sort had occurred, and while he seemed perfect physically (and very beautiful), his mind would remain on the level he had attained at six months.

Fortunately, we were already having another child. Lightning did not strike twice in the same place. Our little girl, Miriam Rachel, born in late 1938, quickly developed a startling precocity. But her quick intelligence made our dilemma all the more difficult. Did we tell her about her little brother, who by this time was being boarded out at a special home? Pictures of Ethan were on display at the Kaplans' home, and she noticed them; and she sensed that the little boy was part of our family. Yet she also sensed that she was not to ask questions.

How does one handle this kind of situation? Perhaps at a later time, when we were wiser and when good advice was more available, we would have done better. But we dealt with this crisis poorly. Miriam ultimately learned the whole story, and so did her little sister, born in 1945. But the Kaplans were unaware that anything was wrong, and when they left for a two-year stay in Palestine (1937–1939), they were totally ignorant of what was happening.

As for Judith and me, the pain was real, but fortunately we were equipped with a theology which enabled us to maintain our equilibrium. We had replaced the notion of God as a Personal Being who rewards and punishes with our conception of God as the Power that makes for salvation (to use the Kaplanian phrase). It never occurred to us to ask: Why did God do this to us? What did we do to deserve this? We recognized that accidents happen, and by their very nature they are random. Some good did come out of the entire episode: I, as a rabbi, was better equipped to deal with similar tragedies in the lives of those I served. Religious faith need not be sacrificed when (as Rabbi Kushner put it in his book) "bad things happen to good people." I tried to convey this idea to bereaved men and women many times thereafter.

9

On My Own

Rabbi Kaplan went off to Palestine in 1937 at the invitation of the Hebrew University to teach the Principles of Education. Lena of course went along. She left with mixed feelings. Proud of the recognition accorded her husband, she did not relish being away from her family for two years. Nor did she relish the thought that riots were taking place in Palestine, and she would worry herself sick every time Rabbi Kaplan would have to take the trip down from Mt. Scopus, with snipers lurking everywhere.

These two years were very difficult indeed. Aside from the ongoing worry about our child, we were worried about the Kaplans in riot-torn Palestine. In addition, I was in a constant panic lest I muff the opportunity to prove myself when called upon to lead the SAJ alone. In addition, the magazine, which was only a little over two years old, was as unsteady on its legs as an octogenarian. As long as Rabbi Kaplan was around, he had the older generation in the palms of his hands, and if we needed a few hundred dollars to meet the deficit, he asked for it and got it. They were reluctant, but they were even more deferential. I was afraid that during his absence they would rebel, and I would be left with a journal which would die of cash starvation.

The magazine depended upon the SAJ because we went to the same people for support of both. If I made a mess of the congregation, the magazine was surely doomed. If I made a mess of the magazine, I would never be able to face Rabbi Kaplan again. And he was 6000 miles away, unable to defend me if I found myself under attack. I was thirty-one, and I had never been confronted with the challenge of facing up to the *baale-batim* (lay leaders). Those close to my age, with whom I got along very well, were not yet old enough to carry the heavy burden of both the congregation and the magazine. I guess I was most worried about Joe Levy.

Joe Levy had been a moving spirit among the founders of the SAJ. He was short, powerful, inclined to act like a little Napoleon, and both self-educated and self-made. Surely it was of Joe Levy that the *bon mot* must have first been uttered: he was a self-made man, and he worshipped his maker. He owned and ran, single-handed, a chain of clothing stores—totaling, I believe, sixty-seven, at the height of his career; Crawford Clothes was Joe Levy. He boasted of the fact that as a young man he had attended classes at Cooper Union. On the basis of that exposure to the academic world, he considered himself cultured. He recognized, however, how tempted cultured people were to walk with their heads in the clouds. He was proud of his practical good sense, and he did not hesitate to advise me on how to conduct myself as the Acting Leader of the SAJ. He would take me aside from time to time and suggest that I might omit some of the prayers and readings which I introduced from non-Jewish and non-liturgical sources. I once tried to make the point that we Jews are united by bonds of history, destiny, and culture, rather than by a uniform theological position. I made the "impractical" blunder of suggesting that theologically I had more in common with John Haynes Holmes than with a well-known Orthodox rabbi. After services, he took me by the arm and said he was walking me home.

We paced back and forth in front of our apartment house on 82nd Street for half an hour. He urged me to avoid such inflammatory remarks in the future. My defense (which I thought was pretty clever) was that I was merely expounding what Dr. Kaplan would have said in a similar situation. I guess it was all right for Dr. Kaplan to say such things. He was older and more authoritative. But a young fellow like me had to be more careful.

The discussion ended in a stalemate, but I was deeply affected by the sense of his power and my own vulnerability. He reminded me more than once that he was not personally a Reconstructionist. Nevertheless he admired Dr. Kaplan and would do anything to help him. I was not so sure he would go out of his way to help *me.*

No one could have known how worried I was because I maintained a calm exterior. But every Shabbat morning was an ordeal. At times I thought I would not be able to go through with the service and the sermon. My throat would go dry. I felt dizzy. Panic seized me. How I managed to come through without letting on even to Judith that I was having the equivalent of an emotional crisis, I still do not know.

I must attribute some part of my courage and determination to the people who were on the Editorial Board. I recall dreams, actually nightmares, in which I held the magazine in my hands and saw nothing but one blank page after another. Jokingly I mentioned these noctural visions to my colleagues. It was Dr. Samuel Dinin, then dean of the Teachers Institute and a devoted disciple of Dr. Kaplan, who made a motion that "it was the sense of the Board that we should not worry." It was passed unanimously, but my vote should not have been counted. I worried that not enough material would come in, that we would not be able to pay the printer, that the SAJ would reverse its earlier decision to allow us to place on the front page "Published by the Society for the Advancement of Judaism."

It was clear that unless we took some steps to invigorate the program we would falter seriously. With unwonted courage and energy we proceeded to do something about it. Our discussions culminated in the decision to call a conference of our friends, a weekend seminar to deal with the future of Reconstructionism, to assess how far we had come, and to spell out plans for future activity.

Cejwin Camp was selected as the site. Mr. Albert Schoolman, its director, was a close friend (and member, with his family, of the SAJ), eager to be of help. We chose the Labor Day weekend since by then the regular summer camp activities were over, and we invited Simon Shetzer and Milton Steinberg to deliver papers.

Shetzer was then president of the Jewish Community Council of Detroit, and had been influential in establishing what we believed would become the model for future organic communities. I was to report on the progress of Reconstructionism.

The weekend was successful in several ways. First the attendance was surprisingly large—some sixty people came. Second, the enthusiasm was most encouraging. What impressed us most was the fact that for the first time these people were coming together in the absence of Mordecai Kaplan; we saw it as a harbinger of self-reliance.

My report, published in the *Reconstructionist* of November 18, 1938 (Vol. IV, no. 14) was filled with optimism. Within four years after the publication of *Judaism As a Civilization*, we had made many friends throughout the country; the magazine had come into being, and had spread to libraries, Hillel Foundations, community centers, and private homes. New books had appeared: Kaplan's *Judaism in Transition* and *The Meaning of God in Modern Jewish Religion*; Samuel Dinin, Milton Steinberg, Eugene Kohn had added to our list of works expounding the basic ideas of Reconstructionism. The spoken word had brought the message to many communities. And the logic of events had advanced many of our ideas of community, education, and the arts.

But the essential problem was: where do we go from here? I wrote:

> It has always been our hope that Reconstructionism would not merely become another faction to add to the already over-multiplied factions in Judaism, and for the last two years we have wrestled with the problem of how we can effectively propagandize Reconstructionism without suffering from the limitations of organization. We have not elected officers; we have no specific membership dues, nor membership privileges. As a matter of fact, since the publication of Dr. Kaplan's book, we have not had a meeting or convention which approached the nature of an organizational function until this one which we are now attending; and even here I think the most careful observer would be hard

put to it to identify who is president, who is secretary, and who is treasurer, and who are members and who are not. Even if you pay your dollar registration, you are not expected to assume any obligation, and if you have not paid your dollar and you attend our sessions, you are in as good standing as anybody else. You see, it is a paradox. . . .

Other speakers on the program included Ben Zion Bokser, Bernard G. Richards, Abraham Duker, Michael Alper, and Louis Kraft, acting director of the Jewish Welfare Board. They discussed various aspects of the problem of Jewish communal life and social action. But it was Milton Steinberg who addressed the issues which were closest to our concerns at the moment, namely, the future program of the movement. (In my address I remarked, "The movement, if we can call it a movement. . . .") The following questions were on the agenda:

1. How can our periodical be improved?

2. What projects should Reconstructionism engage in during the coming year in addition to publishing the *Reconstructionist*?

3. How can the Editorial Board of the *Reconstructionist* be helpful to local groups in carrying on Reconstructionist activities in their respective communities?

4. How shall Reconstructionism be organized and financed in order to make possible the wider scope of activities projected?

The discussions produced the following decisions:

1. That an effort be made to employ the services of a competent person to give his entire time to furthering the literary projects suggested in the discussion (such as a book of supplementary prayers for home devotion, a new *haggadah*, a literature evaluating Jewish religious observance out of which might grow a normative code of Jewish ritual practice, popular pamphlets and tracts explaining the principles of Reconstructionism in simple terms, and

syllabi and courses for Reconstructionist study groups).

2. That efforts be made to raise a fund for a Reconstructionist Fellowship to serve this purpose. (This suggestion resulted in the engagement of Rabbi Eugene Kohn. Details are related in the pages below.)

3. That an effort be made to organize in the various communities in the country groups of Friends of the *Reconstructionist* who would solicit contributions to this fund and subscriptions to the *Reconstructionist*, and who would organize whatever local activities may be helpful in giving effect to the Reconstructionist program of Jewish life.

4. The organization of an administrative committee of laymen, representing, to begin with, congregations whose rabbis are on the Editorial Board of the *Reconstructionist*, to collaborate with the Editorial Board by administering the financial affairs of the movement (sic).

The great enthusiasm which the proceedings of the weekend had generated was only partly affected by the news, heard on radio, that a crisis in Europe was taking place. The meeting of Chamberlain and Hitler in Munich was resulting in "peace-in-our-time." Some of us were relieved. We cherished the notion that Hitler's limited objectives were putting off war for an indefinite period. (Others were not so confident or so naive.) I believed that any peace, no matter how unsatisfactory, was better than war, no matter how restricted. Most of all we were relieved that the Kaplans, who were in Palestine, were in no immediate danger.

One of the results of our Reconstructionist Summer Institute was the awarding to Rabbi Eugene Kohn of our first (and last) Fellowship. Milton Steinberg persuaded a philanthropist, who insisted upon anonymity, to contribute the sum of $2500 for the preparation of a volume of supplementary prayers and readings for the High Holidays, badly needed to make the traditional service more meaningful. Thus was produced our first liturgical work, *Shir Hadash*. It was published by Behrman's Jewish Book House in the fall of 1939. It served as a source of enrichment of the traditional *maḥzor* at the SAJ and many other congregations until it was finally incorporated into the *High Holiday Prayerbook*, published in 1948 by the Jewish Reconstructionist Foundation.

The establishment of the Foundation was the second step in the implementation of the proposals made at the 1938 Institute. By the time the Kaplans returned to the United States in the fall of 1939, it had become apparent that the SAJ Board was no longer in the mood to remain the official publisher of the magazine. It was also apparent that if the journal was to survive, support for it would have to come from beyond any one congregation. Already the year before, this fact was recognized, but nothing was done to enlist wider support. No one had been engaged to devote his full time to organization; surely the SAJ was not in a position to subsidize such a project. In fact, as I have noted, the Society wanted to unburden itself of the magazine.

Thus, in 1940, Rabbi Steinberg and I brought together a small committee of lay people from his congregation, the Park Avenue Synagogue, and the SAJ, to establish what I thought should be called a Foundation. Ford had one, Carnegie had one, Rockefeller had one; why not the Reconstructionists?

The idea was to make possible scholarships and fellowships for creative personalities, to add literary and artistic content to our Jewish lives. In addition, we hoped that funds would also be made available to spread the word, to send out speakers to Jewish groups throughout the land, to help them understand what Reconstructionism was proposing for the renewal of Jewish life. The Foundation would, we hoped, contribute toward further judaizing the Reform movement, liberalizing the Conservative movement, and perhaps religionizing the secular movements. Our role as gadfly and inspiration would be enhanced by such a Foundation.

Suffice it to say that the Jewish Reconstructionist Foundation did not become that kind of foundation, for it began with no funds. As important as some of the incorporators were (people like Simon Rifkind, later a federal judge), their major contribution to the cause was their willingness to place their names on the original articles of incorporation. We looked forward to generous gifts from the members of the Park Avenue Synagogue, but little materialized from that source because Milton was extremely reluctant about asking people for money. We were convinced that his influence was so great that he could get anything he asked for, but he did not want to use that influence on a personal basis, and was not so sure that he could succeed if he tried. Milton believed that his function was to preach and to teach. Administrative functions he left to others, and that included the way money was raised and how it was spent.

The burden of support remained on the shoulders of the same loyal SAJ group as before. Changing the auspices of the magazine from the SAJ to the JRF was of little help. If anything, it only confused many people who for years continued to refer to the SAJ as the institutional headquarters of Reconstructionism. They were not entirely to blame because the Foundation was housed in the SAJ building, and I spent as much time upstairs (JRF) as I did downstairs (SAJ).

The closest we ever came to extending the SAJ to include another congregation was the abortive attempt to merge with the Park Avenue Synagogue. Committees were actually appointed, and a first step was taken with the creation of a joint high school program. There were no more than fifteen boys and girls involved, most of them from the SAJ. In order to avoid political friction, we agreed to meet alternately at the Park Avenue building and at the SAJ. The high school was short lived, mainly because we encountered the same basic impediment to cooperation which exists in virtually all congregational activities: the synagogue is supported by its members. Loyalty to a congregation must not be weakened in any way, lest that support be withdrawn or reduced. The rabbi and lay leaders must constantly remind the members that they are getting service for the dues they pay and the contributions they offer. Any activity which is conducted jointly with another congregation is likely, in the minds of the leadership, to lure member families away from the congregation—perhaps to the other cooperating institution. Hence, cooperation between and among synagogues continues to be a rare phenomenon.

Kaplan frequently remarked that congregations are like private clubs existing for the benefit of their members. The major purpose to be kept in mind is to keep the club together. Any circumstance which might tend to cause members to withdraw shifts the burden of support onto fewer shoulders, and is therefore undesirable from the viewpoint of the organization and its supporters.

In recent years sheer practical considerations have compelled some congregations to join efforts; either the individual congregation does not have enough individuals to make a particular activity worthwhile, or a larger congregation will initiate an activity that threatens to draw members away from a smaller one, and a shotgun marriage is effected between the two.

On the other hand, while Rabbi Kaplan was undoubtedly correct in calling the congregation a private club, there is no gainsaying its vital role in the lives of those Jews who take it seriously. Surely, the congregation is no substitute for the organized community, but by the same token, the community cannot take the place of the congregation. As I witnessed the participation of our members in the activities of the SAJ, I recognized that only the congregation provides them with the services of a rabbi. They would talk about "my rabbi," implying someone to whom to turn when confronted with any kind of Jewish or personal question. It may be a matter of ascertaining some fact about Jewish history or about the proper way to observe a holiday.

Most important, however, the rabbi is available when personal problems arise: illness, bereavement, or conflict within the family. In my student days, we were not prepared to undertake this aspect of our responsibilities. Today seminaries spend considerable time introducing future rabbis to the world of pastoral care. They must learn not only how to handle difficult situations, but also how to resist getting involved in those situations which call for expert training. Somehow the fact that we bear the title of rabbi still seems enough to qualify us as counsellors in many eyes. Perhaps people take more seriously than they are willing to admit the notion that rabbis have a direct line to God, the source of all wisdom. If rabbis are indeed wise, they should walk with infinite care the narrow ridge between confessing their human frailties and preserving the authority which many lay people so desperately hope the rabbi possesses.

I began to assume this part of my rabbinical responsibility quite early because while most of the members of the SAJ revered and loved Dr. Kaplan, they felt it was an imposition on his time to bring their petty (?) troubles to him. He had "more important" things to do. In addition, I believe that they suspected he would perceive their problems in ethical rather than psychological terms. That is, he would be less sympathetic to their weaknesses. A person of iron will himself, he assumed that with the application of will, every problem could be solved, especially when the will was put to the service of the *right*. I believe they usually considered me more human, more *sympatico*. As a result, even those of the older generation who reminded me often that Kaplan was their rabbi, not I, would find their way to my study with their problems.

The problems usually dealt with the family: difficulties with teenage children, friction between mothers-in-law and daughters-in-law, sons or daughters going out with non-Jewish peers leading (God forbid) to intermarriage. As I think back on the many times I was consulted, I have come to at least one conclusion: troubles generally flowed from the presence of money, rather than from the absence of money.

One day, a woman came crying to me. She could not manage to get her daughter-in-law to be civil to her, let alone love her. "I have tried everything," she said. "Whatever I get for my daughter, I get for her. I bought my daughter a new house in Westport; I bought one for her too. A mink coat for my daughter; a mink coat for her. But nothing helps. She is still cold to me, cold like ice." I tried to point out to her that people do not love others because of what others give them. This only stresses their dependence; they are expected to be grateful. Most people do not like to have to say thank you. We love those in whom we have invested care and love. This was hard for her to understand, and at her age I could not change her lifelong habits of thinking.

When parents complained about their children, I usually assured them (with absolutely no evidence to back up my assurance) that the kids would turn out fine. Parents had to be patient and have faith in their own progeny. Most of the time this worked; at least temporarily, the parents worried less, and that by itself was an alleviating factor in their relationships to their problem children.

I did not hesitate at times to turn the tables on the parents and blame them for some of the problems they complained about. I always arranged to do some teaching, particularly in the confirmation classes for teenagers between 13 and 15, and I met informally with the older teenage groups at various homes. Listening to their conversations is probably the best way to learn what goes on in their respective families. One can almost hear verbatim the words and phrases of their parents, and the hierarchy of values comes through very clearly.

Hence, when parents would visit with me, I would shock them by telling them as much as I dared to reveal about them. This gave me the opportunity to explain to them that their children's scale of values had come directly from their homes. Of course, peer influence was not to be overlooked, but basically these boys and girls were the products of their parents.

The emphasis in Reconstructionism upon the organic Jewish community was always intended to offer an alternative to the system of autonomous competing and essentially private congregations. While these congregations organize along so-called denominational lines, they are, by and large, not representative of ideologies. Those who join congregations do so for a variety of reasons: the rabbi is popular, the building is not too far from home, and the children can get to religious school without carpooling, the cantor has a pleasant voice, it is not too Reform, or too traditional. Rarely does a family, before joining a congregation, carefully investigate the theology, ritual, or the liturgy of the institution. The congregation, for its part, rarely if ever requires of prospective members that they subscribe to the basic principles upon which the congregation has been established.

As a result, Jewish religious and educational life is badly organized. The children attend a variety of private religious schools, none of which is strong enough to provide the staff or the equipment to do an effective job. The public religious school does not exist in most places, for there is no organized "public," as there is in a municipality or state. In other words, there is no *community*. In a few cities the community exists at least to the extent of providing communal education. Those parents who have genuine concern about the sort of concepts of God or Torah or Israel that their children ought to be taught supplement the communal schools either at home or in carefully selected Sunday schools or summer camps, or in non-congregational youth clubs or movements.

To the extent that the SAJ and the Park Avenue Synagogue shared most—if not all—the views expounded by Dr. Kaplan, a half-hearted attempt was made to bring the two congregations together. The experiment failed because the good intentions of the leaders of both groups could not overcome the obstacles built into the very nature of congregations.

10

The War On
Two Fronts

I had almost resigned myself to abandoning the whole idea of a Ph.D. when my friend, Henry Rosenthal, suggested that I go back to Columbia to work on a dissertation in the philosophy department, as he had done. Henry had been granted permission to write an unconventional essay, representing not so much research (although research was involved) as original thinking. Professor Herbert Schneider was his mentor, working within the philosophy department but specializing in the field of religion. There was not yet a separate department of religion; the courses in religion were a segment of the philosophy program. Henry thought this might be more to my liking.

Indeed it was. Schneider welcomed me back warmly. I had taken virtually all the courses he had taught when I was an undergraduate. He had followed my career, at least sufficiently well to know that I had spent four years at the Seminary. Since I had been a philosophy major, he generously proposed that I might be exempted from the language exam, that I did not need to stop for a Masters degree, and that I could fulfill the course requirements by simply taking 18 credits in the form of two years of seminar with him.

I discussed the project with Dr. Kaplan, who felt that this

159

was a fine opportunity to apply the principle of polarity to the question of religious tolerance. Polarity was one of his favorite concepts. He had come upon it through his reading of Morris Raphael Cohen, and he felt that it had important implications for the relations of minority groups to larger American society. After some exciting sessions with Schneider, the overall plan of the dissertation began to take shape in my mind. The work was finally completed in 1940; I defended the thesis in the spring of 1941.

I shall never forget the ordeal of the defense. Virtually the entire philosophy faculty was present—including Friess, Edman, Nagel, Randall—with Dr. Van Deusen of Union Theological Seminary and Lynd from Teachers College supplying the theologian and the sociologist. Van Deusen gave me the hardest time because, as a firm believer in missionizing, he took strong exception to my view that from the point of view of *The Ethics of Tolerance*, (the title of the work) missionizing is unethical. I had developed the idea that any truth to be valid must be of universal validity and therefore universally applicable. If a religion represented a truth which is authentic, there is no reason that it cannot be incorporated into another religion. Therefore it is a fallacy to believe, for example, that one must change one's religion (or civilization) in order to accept a truth about the ethical life or human nature.

I received the Ph.D. degree in June 1941. Dr. Schneider thought my thesis might be attractive to a general publisher. But after rejection by Morrow, we gave up and placed it with Kings Crown Press, a subsidiary of Columbia University Press which specialized in doctoral dissertations. Copies went to a few important people. John Dewey said he was looking forward to reading it; whether he ever did or not remains a mystery. But Thomas Mann did read it and said he found it quite valuable.

There was considerable rejoicing in the family, naturally. My friends in the SAJ considered the event worthy of notice, using it as an occasion to honor me; it was also the tenth anniversary of my graduation from the Seminary.

That summer, we shared a house in Deal, N.J. with the Kaplans, as we had done the summer before, and I had the opportunity to observe at close range the star to whom I had hitched my wagon. His way of life was fascinating, if calculated to give anyone like myself an inferiority complex. His dedication to study, reading, writing and *thinking* without letup was stupefying. He followed a strict routine from which he never deviated. Upon arising he would put on his *tefillin* and spend several minutes reading, either from a *siddur* or from some other book, in English or Hebrew. After breakfast, he would take a brisk walk. He said he sometimes got his best ideas while walking. When he returned he would open a bridge table, take it out on the lawn with several books, and proceed to work. It seemed that he did not lift his eyes until lunch time. Immediately after lunch he took a nap for forty-five minutes. Then he would return to the table for more work until his second walk, which took place before dinner. After dinner he went back to work.

His idea of relaxation was to vary the work; that summer, it consisted of persuading me to write interpretive versions of the Psalms. We would do about two a day. I would draw up a rough draft after our discussions, and then he would work with me on its final form. I cherished, as I always did, the chance to think something through with him and to put it into appropriate language; I also welcomed the opportunity to do something which would convince him that his son-in-law and colleague was not just a lazy bum.

I was able to enjoy the activities for which I had little time during the year. Judith and I would play the piano, four hands. We would go swimming with our little girl. I played tennis frequently, and I had the capacity to sit and stare into space, without feeling guilty—except when Kaplan was in that space, working as though he were trying to meet a deadline. In fact, that was what he was usually doing: he had no time for this or that, like going to the movies, unless some serious idea could be extracted from the plot; or reading a novel, unless it made a point which would illustrate some other point he was making in his journal. This was indeed a serious man.

But not just serious in general; serious about Judaism and the future of the Jewish people. He brought to bear upon this theme the full power of his mind and his erudition. Everything he read was translated into the key of Judaism. Once in a while he would say to me that he envied my ability to play. As a boy he had never been allowed to play on the street; his mother would call him back to their flat and remind him that he had to study.

Once he asked me whether I would teach him how to drive a car. I have no idea where he thought he was going, but I was willing to give it a try, though I was a bit apprehensive about teaching in our Ford without dual controls. We tried it twice. He gave up, but the experiment was not without some implications for Judaism: it is not enough to know how to drive, one must understand what the destination is. So it was not a total loss.

I was giving serious thought to where we were going as Reconstructionists. The fact is that I was not happy with the way we were functioning. After almost two years, the Foundation had achieved nothing of importance. Yes, we had worked on a new *haggadah,* but that had nothing to do with the Foundation.

Eugene Kohn, Rabbi Kaplan and I had prepared an experimental version of the *haggadah* for the SAJ, which we tried out on Pesah, 1940, and the final form of the English text I prepared under the very careful scrutiny of Dena Behrman, whose taste and skill in editing I greatly admired. The Behrmans had published the book that year. We would have preferred issuing it through a Press of our own, but we had no money. In retrospect, the lack of a small sum to publish the *New Haggadah* denied us the opportunity to make a great deal of money, for the book was a bestseller (and remained so for decades).

But its appearance precipitated a crisis. While the American Jewish public gave the *New Haggadah* a splendid reception, the faculty of the Seminary was furious. A letter signed by every member of the faculty was sent to Kaplan protesting the publication of a liturgical text which violated *halakhic* regulations. For instance, some parts of the *Hallel* were omitted; some lines from one of the psalms were also deleted. In addition, a mistake was made in a footnote concerning one of the rabbis of the tannaitic period. Finally, most shocking of all, the book read from left to right. (The last was a binder's error; it was corrected in the very next printing.)

I had always known that Kaplan's views were not popular

with other members of the faculty, but I was truly amazed by the content and the tone of this round-robin letter. Rabbi Kaplan had, after all, been one of the original faculty chosen by the "sainted" Dr. Schechter more than three decades before. I was grieved that these colleagues did not have the decency to speak to Rabbi Kaplan about the book face to face, calling his attention to some of their objections. (I was somewhat relieved when Dr. Robert Gordis wrote a personal letter, indicating that, as a member of the faculty, he was compelled to sign the faculty letter against his better judgment.)

As usual, Dr. Kaplan was reticent about his feelings. He would go no further than to remark that Dr. Gordis had shown true friendship in writing his letter of apology. But knowing Rabbi Kaplan as I did, I was certain the attack on him hurt him deeply. In one way, it was the culmination of years of petty but persistent persecution. In another way it was the beginning of a campaign to discredit him altogether.

Apparently, what shook up the faculty was the fact that for the first time, Dr. Kaplan and his associates *published* and in effect put their stamp of approval on a prayer text intended for distribution outside the confines of the Society for the Advancement of Judaism. What Dr. Kaplan did in his own congregation was tolerable, if reprehensible, but the moment the heresies were broadcast, the zealots for tradition felt compelled to take action.

One final reference to criticisms from other sources. I believe the man whose objections to portions of the text disturbed me most was Maurice Samuel. I was and will ever remain a devoted admirer of Maurice Samuel, and perhaps that is why I took his criticisms seriously. He felt that we had knuckled under to the adherents of the good will movement by deleting from the text the verse *"Shefokh hamatekha al hagoyim,"* "Pour out Thy wrath upon the nations which know Thee not." He insisted that at that moment when the world was called upon to resist and destroy Nazism, the quotation from the Psalms was all the more needed. He made no apologies for calling upon God to pour out His wrath upon Hitler and his murderers.

Our omission of the Ten Plagues annoyed Samuel almost as much. What was wrong with perpetuating the folk custom of pouring out a drop of wine with the mention of each plague? In fact, there was much to be said in favor of it because in the Midrash the Sages had specifically ordained that the cup of joy must be less than full since the Israelites' emancipation had been accomplished at the expense of God's (Egyptian) creatures.

But Kaplan had argued that if the *haggadah* was to be edifying, and if our purpose was to engage the attention of young people, we should omit all texts which smacked of cruelty and vengeance. I can truly testify that he never reckoned with possible gentile reactions. Knuckling under was a stance he resolutely eschewed.

That summer revealed the full extent of Rabbi Kaplan's alienation from the faculty of the Seminary, or, to put it more precisely, the full extent of their embarrassment at being associated with him in the same institution. Whether the publication of the *New Haggadah* precipitated the action, I do not know. However, I strongly suspect that the whole matter would not have come to a head at that particular time if the book had not appeared that spring.

One day, Rabbi Kaplan was asked to come to a meeting in New York to meet with members of the faculty to expound his philosophy. My first impression was that at last the faculty had decided to conduct a sort of seminar in which each member would outline what he believed the Seminary stood for, what Conservative Judaism was all about, how better to bridge the gap between the esoteric world of scholarly research and the vast audience addressed each week by the graduates of that institution.

Of course, the summons was nothing of the kind. It did not take long to relate it to the publication of the *New Haggadah* and the letter which Dr. Kaplan had received from the faculty. It dawned on us that there was to be some sort of examination to determine whether Dr. Kaplan was indeed qualified by doctrine to remain a member of the faculty. The thought was incredible, but it would not yield to any alternative that we could think of. We would have to wait and see.

And see we did! I shall never forget driving to the station to meet the train on which Dr. Kaplan was to return from Manhattan on one of the first of the hot humid summer days after that lengthy session at the Seminary. He apparently arrived sooner than I had expected, and not seeing anyone to meet him started to walk back. I was shocked and grieved to see this man, his head bent, walking slowly (not his usual gait) and almost mournfully. He looked like a beaten person. Obviously, they had put him through the wringer.

He did not go into great detail. Why? I believe that he was still seeking a reasonable basis for their action. Perhaps they really wished to know just what he was teaching the students. After all, the Seminary did not intrude into each professor's classes, and if they had not studied with care what he had written in *Judaism As a Civilization*, or *Judaism in Transition* or *The Meaning of God in Modern Jewish Religion*—if they were not regular or even occasional readers of the *Reconstructionist* magazine, how were they to know the nature of his ideas about God, the Jewish people, and the Torah? Were they to rely upon gossip?

At this point I believe I expressed myself with greater emphasis than ever before. I tried to open his eyes to what was going on: this was an Inquisition. They had had enough of his heresies, and they were seeking a good excuse for expelling him. The little pin pricks to which Professor Ginzberg had resorted up to that time were now to be replaced by a fullscale campaign to get him out. I begged him to resign, to withdraw before they took any such step. In fact, the episode impelled me to sit down and write a memorandum addressed to him, in which I set forth what I believed was right and wrong about the way we were going about spreading the word.

I do not have a copy of that memo, but I know that Kaplan read it carefully and put it in his files. I hope that when the archives are combed carefully one of these days soon, the memo will show up. But I recall quite clearly what I said:

From the earliest days Dr. Kaplan was attempting to direct the Seminary leadership and the influential members of the Rabbinical Assembly to break with the Orthodoxy in which all of them were raised. If the Conservative movement was to achieve a character of its own, if it was to become more than a cosmetically treated version of tradition, it would have to take a stand which grew out of the scientific scholarship to which all of them had been exposed, both Jewish and general. In those days the essential differences between the Seminary and the Yeshivah had been that the Seminary encouraged scientific scholarship (*Judische Wissenschaft*) and the Yeshivah banned it. But the paradox was that the Seminary merely studied. It did not act upon the implications of that new knowledge. If the positive historical school demonstrated that Judaism had evolved over the centuries, how could one resist further evolution?

The attempt to reform Conservative Judaism from within had failed. Under the leadership of Cyrus Adler, and now (1941) Louis Finkelstein, there was no indication of any possibility that a new approach would be adopted. I therefore appealed to Dr. Kaplan to withdraw from the Conservative movement and start a movement of his own. The only other option was to join the Reform movement, which in 1937 had adopted a set of principles more closely approximating what Dr. Kaplan was teaching. As a matter of fact, Dr. Kaplan would often refer to the visit which Dr. Felix Levy had paid to his home with the draft of the Columbus Platform, as it came to be called, hoping to obtain Dr. Kaplan's *haskamah*, his stamp of approval.

But that option too seemed to me (and of course to Dr. Kaplan) far-fetched. Large numbers of Reform rabbis had voted for it reluctantly, or at best were giving it an interpretation which could never satisfy one who called for a maximum program of Judaism, an organic Jewish community, a vigorous support of Zionism. . . . The American Council for Judaism had actually emerged out of the Reform movement, and its founder, Elmer Berger, had not then been repudiated. The time had come, I believed, for a fourth group to be created, a group that would draw to it all these left-wing Conservatives and right-wing Reformists, leaving the right-wing Conservatives to rejoin the ranks of the Orthodox.

If we Reconstructionists were not willing to take this drastic step, then we should stop acting as though we were indeed a separate group. If we undertook to publish a *haggadah*, we should declare to the Jewish world that this was intended only for the members of one congregation. If we were to think in

166

terms of a Shabbat Prayerbook or any other liturgical text, we should make it clear that we were doing no more than what some members of the Rabbinical Assembly had done—edit a *siddur* or *maḥzor* for internal use only. Our major efforts should be directed to missionizing for our points of view through the magazine and other writings, attempting to get each denomination to make those changes which would bring them more in line with our conception of Judaism.

We had to make a choice. One could not play in a baseball game and act as umpire at the same time. As things stood we were neither fish nor fowl. We could look forward to nothing but frustration. If we were a school of thought, we had to behave like academics and stay above the battle. On the other hand, if we were or hoped to become a movement, we had to take the kind of action which is needed if a movement is to begin.

Rabbi Kaplan was apparently not moved by my memorandum. He always respected me and gave serious thought to what I had to say. This time too he promised to think about what I had written and give it careful consideration. But I was not sanguine about the results of such consideration. The episode at the Seminary did not shake his loyalty to that institution. The star chamber proceedings did not move him from the course which he had chosen, to teach and write and propagandize, and to refrain from taking any action that might be interpreted as divisive.

What would have happened if the policy of persecution had been maintained at a high pitch over a period of months will always remain a mystery, but shortly thereafter a new policy was introduced. It is my belief that this new policy was proposed by Prof. Moshe Davis and accepted by those responsible for directing the course of the institution. The new policy dictated that JTS had more to lose than to gain by exacerbating the relations between Rabbi Kaplan and the faculty. Persecution would neither lead to changes in Rabbi Kaplan's philosophy, nor in his determination to teach it. To expel him would create a scandal, and besides, Cyrus Adler had indeed promised Rabbi Kaplan academic freedom, which by implication meant permanent tenure.

How much wiser to embrace Rabbi Kaplan and to exploit

him in order to demonstrate to the world that JTS was the embodiment of pluralism and democracy! Here were Prof. Ginzberg and Prof. Kaplan sitting down together under the same roof. This would fulfill the high requirements of a true university, and, incidentally, would alienate neither the friends of Ginzberg's traditionalism, nor the adherents of Kaplan's heterodoxy.

There is no other way that I can explain the sudden reversal, the emergence of a new and unprecedented mood. But whether my theory is correct or some different hypothesis would better account for the change, the fact remains that a radical transformation of mood did occur, and Rabbi Kaplan's loyalty to JTS became stronger than ever. My memorandum may have shaken him for a while. But it was totally ineffectual. The timing was wrong. 1941 was much too early to hope for a new direction in Reconstructionism.

My decision, in the fall of 1941, to enlist in the chaplaincy was surely the result of many impulses. I had wearied of the attempt to convince Rabbi Kaplan that we ought to strike out for ourselves as a movement. I was annoyed that the SAJ still insisted that I remain as Associate Leader, instead of promoting me, as Rabbi Kaplan had urged, to the senior position, allowing him to retire as Emeritus. But perhaps most influential of all was the genuine patriotic upsurge which I experienced at that stage in the tragic direction of the war in Europe. While Roosevelt had not said so in so many words, any careful observer of events knew that he was preparing the nation to enter the conflict. Conscription had been introduced, and he was using every possible device to supply the British and their allies with materiel. The armed services were calling for more and more chaplains.

The system called for one chaplain for every thousand soldiers under arms. This meant that a quota of Jewish chaplains had to be filled, and at that point many places remained unfilled. I made up my mind that my duty lay there. Of course, I had to discuss the matter with Judith. As usual, she supported me, albeit reluctantly. It would be no fun for her to raise our little Miriam alone. I also felt I had to confer with Rabbi Kaplan, not to get his permission exactly, but to think through with him what was to be done about the SAJ and the magazine.

"Déjà vu" is the only way to describe the impact of his response on me. Ten years before, when the question arose as to whether I was to accept his offer to join him at the SAJ or take the post in Boston, he had said it was up to me—but if I chose Boston he would liquidate the SAJ. This time he said that if the chaplaincy was my choice, we would wind up the magazine and the Foundation. There was no one else who could or would take over that responsibility.

In the mood I was in at that point I refused to worry about what would happen. I proceeded to apply.

The Jewish Welfare Board was given the responsibility (as the nondenominational Jewish service organization) of setting up the certification process. The board which the JWB established consisted of representatives of all three major groups then in the religious community. Every candidate had to be certified by this board. Its job was to ascertain whether the candidate was a graduate of a recognized seminary, and to give each candidate an interview. Generally, the interview was confined to determining whether the rabbi was prepared to undertake all the duties of the chaplain—especially the duty of conducting services which would be acceptable to every soldier, regardless of religious background or preference.

When I came for the interview, I was asked the usual questions. But then a strange question came from one of the Orthodox rabbis, Herbert Goldstein. He said, "Do you believe in God?" I was ready to answer that question, in my own way, but Milton Steinberg, a member of the board, immediately shouted, "Ira, don't answer that question." Considerable confusion followed. This question had never before been asked of any candidate, and many voices were raised simultaneously on one side of Milton's position and the other. The chairman then asked me to leave the room, so that the issue could be resolved.

Once again I found myself standing on the outside, pacing up and down, while within a group of people was deciding my fate. I was amused. I was not shocked by the question as Milton had been. In fact I had more or less anticipated the question, and I was eager to use the occasion to make a statement before the representatives of the three groups on the question of the need to find room within Judaism for multiple theologies. Perhaps this was not exactly the proper place, but on the other hand, this was a place and a time when decisions were being made. Theological discussions generally have no practical consequences, but this time a credo might be decisive indeed.

After about ten minutes, the door opened and Joseph Lookstein, an Orthodox rabbi, emerged. He was a short, rotund man with a moon face, good natured and affable, but he was clearly embarrassed. He said, "Ira, I asked specifically for the opportunity to inform you that the board has certified you. I also wish to apologize for my colleague." So—it was a tempest in a teapot. In fact, two tempests in two teapots, because when I went for my physical examination, I was turned down: poor eyesight and insufficient natural teeth.

The magazine was not liquidated, nor was the Foundation. I was partly relieved that I would after all remain at home with my family, but I was also a bit envious of my colleagues who had good sight and enough teeth, who would be having the kind of experiences that might never again be possible.

Back in the civilian life which I had never left, I became restive. I did not find fulfillment in the routines of synagogue activity, and not sufficient satisfaction in the responsibilities of the magazine. It is not surprising therefore that I looked at the so-called secular areas of Jewish life for creative work. I never did regard those areas as inimical to religion; my orientation to Judaism as a civilization enabled me to recognize that, whatever labels they bore, those who chose the secular world were redirecting their spiritual energies into fields which sought expression outside the synagogue. Anti-clericalism still played a part in their ideology; but I soon discovered that being a rabbi was no crime in their eyes if the particular cleric they were working with was a *mensh*, that is, was ready to acknowledge that one could be Jewish and idealistic without attending services.

The Labor Zionist movement attracted me particularly because it sought to combine the goals of Zionism with the ideals of prophetic Judaism. The personalities which the Labor Zionists attracted were also very much to my liking. I was especially attracted to Hayim Greenberg, a remarkable man of spirit and culture. He was a philosopher, a mystic, a socialist, a literateur, an endless talker and tea-drinker and cigarette smoker. As editor of the *Jewish Frontier*, he filled its pages with wise observations of people, of political movements, of literature. He always symbolized for me that unique combination of sophisticated Jewish learning and deeply moral political views.

Another personality, so different and so strangely similar, was a Quaker woman, Dr. Rachel Davis DuBois, a pioneer in the work of intercultural education. Her Workshop for Cultural Democracy was a struggling little organization, but it attracted some distinguished individuals, like Dr. E.C. Lindeman and Dr. W.E.B. DuBois (no relation, though his presence on our board got Rachel into trouble with the McCarthy investigators). I became a sort of Jewish consultant to the group and arranged for several Workshop sessions at the SAJ itself.

Throughout the 40s, Judith and I created cantatas, beginning with *What Is Torah?* We did five in all. I wrote the text, and Judith composed the music. They were written for Confirmation exercises at the SAJ. We needed desperately to find alternatives to the puerile stuff which usually served. (Our fifth cantata, *Thy Children Shall Return*, we did on commission from Hadassah for the 25th anniversary celebration of Youth Aliyah.)

I also accepted the invitation of Hadassah to serve on their National Advisory Committee on Education. They enlisted a number of very distinguished scholars and educators; Dr. Shalom Spiegel served as chairman. Unfortunately, he soon became ill. I was asked to replace him. The Hadassah organization is extraordinary in many ways, but in this particular instance they followed a more conventional pattern—they spent many hours in consultation with experts and then proceeded to design their own program. But out of this fascinating experience came the idea which led to the publication of *Great Ages and Ideas of the Jewish People*. I persuaded Leo W. Schwarz to accept the editorship, and I think he did an excellent job.

Writing occupied some of my spare time. Articles appeared in the *Jewish Social Service Quarterly*, the *Hebrew Union College Monthly*, *Hadassah* magazine, *Jewish Social Studies* and the

Jewish Frontier. But most of my writing went into the *Reconstructionist* magazine and special columns which we had begun to circulate to the Anglo-Jewish press through the Seven Arts Feature Syndicate. We made these articles available without charge to any newspapers which chose to print them. This was part of our program for disseminating Reconstructionist philosophy to the laity. Various members of our Editorial Board participated.

Another medium for the spreading of the "gospel" was pamphlets. The Foundation issued a series of such pamphlets, beginning with Milton Steinberg's *To Be or Not To Be a Jew.* Many thousands of these pamphlets were distributed through the armed forces during the War. The Jewish Welfare Board was responsible for this facet of their program of meeting the needs of Jewish soldiers. In this connection I recall an incident which reflects the state of Reconstructionism at that time.

In order to obtain the official endorsement of the Jewish Welfare Board for any materials to be sent to members of the armed forces, we had to go through the central office in New York. Rabbi Philip Bernstein was in charge. I came with my friend Leopold Sneider. When I introduced him to Rabbi Bernstein, the rabbi quipped, "What? A fourth man? I thought Reconstructionism consisted of only Rabbi Kaplan, Rabbi Eugene Kohn, and yourself." He was not entirely wrong; there were a few others, but not many. (To such a degree were the three of us linked that the wits were wont to describe the Reconstructionist trinity as the father, the son-in-law and the holy ghostwriter. The last designation came from Eugene Kohn's role of occasionally taking Rabbi Kaplan's rough notes and translating them into polished prose. Then they were edited into their final form by Rabbi Kaplan.)

The war years, 1941–1945, are blurred in my memory. I try to recall what we were thinking, how we were feeling, but somehow what comes to mind is simply the impression that we plodded along, doing the job, hoping for a quick end to the conflict, which we knew would be long and painful. Our personal contribution to the war effort was insignificant. We attended courses in first aid and learned how to put a bandage on an arm or a leg.

Anyone injured in a bombing raid would have had little chance of survival as a result of those ministrations. And we surrendered our car, although as a clergyman I would have been entitled to a "B" sticker, which meant I could buy gas necessary to my work. I did not need a car in New York anyway. Our sacrifices, obviously, did not deserve much praise.

As I reread volumes of the *Reconstructionist* during those years, I find that except for an occasional article or editorial, we went about our business as though the most important long-term issues were the most urgent ones. Single-mindedly we deplored the failure of the Jewish people to form unified and democratic communities. We urged greater emphasis upon communal rather than congregational education, bemoaned the fact that intellectuals were alienated from their Jewish heritage, fought against any sign of the recrudescence of Orthodox theologizing, and the like.

Here and there we took note of the plight of European Jews, expressing our grief over the extermination of entire communities (hoping that the reports were false, dreading to learn that they might be even worse than what they contained). We wrote about the problems of winning the peace long before peace was on the horizon. The record is not a disgraceful one, but it is not a brilliant one either. We raised money; we joined in protests and demonstrations. But in retrospect what we American Jews did was pitifully weak in light of what we now believe we should and could have done.

The summers of 1942 and 1943 were spent at Camp Tabor, a camp for boys and girls with a colony on the site for adults. The owners, Rabbi and Mrs. Jacob Grossman, attracted to the adult colony some parents of the campers, but most were rabbis and their wives, Conservative rabbis in particular. Every morning several of us would go for either a three-mile or a five-mile walk, and we would engage in some lively conversation. I have the distinct impression that the topics discussed were either *kashrut* or the observance of Shabbat. Once in a while for my benefit, we would get into a hot argument about the chosen people or the broad theme of *halakhah*. This did not seem strange to me at the time, although I find it hard to believe that I was not at times revolted by the self-absorption of all of us spiritual leaders. Perhaps it was the summer atmosphere, the beautiful countryside, the relaxed mood, the sense of detachment. Perhaps they too wondered why the rest of us were not impelled to devote more of our time and attention to the events on the other side of the world.

The fact remains that we were not too different from the rest of the American people. Broadway continued to produce shows. Movies were filmed and shown. Although military uniforms were ever present, and no theater performance began without the singing of the Star Spangled Banner, this country was not undergoing hardships, nor were its citizens preoccupied with the war except for parents and families of soldiers at the front. On the contrary, in many instances people were making more money than ever before.

The Zionist movement flourished, even though it was split over the issue of Jewish statehood after the war. One need only consult any reliable history of Zionism to learn that we all sensed the coming of a climactic moment when the guns would be silenced and the Jewish people would be free to move ahead without delay to the fulfillment of the immemorial dream. The Arab leaders had opted for Hitler. That was one of the major factors, we believed, that would facilitate the establishment of the State. With Ben-Gurion we declared that although the infamous White Paper had restricted Jewish immigration and had even anticipated a total suspension of Jewish immigration after five years, the Jews would fight the war as though that document did not exist and fight the White Paper even though it had been issued by an ally.

On the day of the Normandy Beach landing, we crowded the SAJ praying for victory and for peace as though we had not already repudiated the supernaturalism on which the prayers were based. On VE Day we rejoiced with restraint. Roosevelt had left us, and we were bereft. In addition, the war against the Japanese had yet to be concluded. The atom bomb explosion thrilled and terrified us, long before we were aware of the full extent of the human tragedy involved. VJ Day, and it was over. And Truman at once terminated the rationing of gas!

The two major issues we faced were our future relations with the Russians and the fate of Palestine. Though they were our allies, we feared and suspected the Russians, but we also condemned those who began to talk almost immediately about fighting the USSR. The liberation of the death camps resolved all questions about the need for creating a self-governing state which would assure, as nothing else could, the uninterrupted flow of Jews to the Land of Israel. But on what conditions? The Arabs had sworn enmity, not only to the Zionists but to all Jews who supported them. Partition had already been proposed, but Zionists were divided. The bi-nationalists urged a partnership with the Arabs. Those who opposed them (like ourselves) could not conceive with whom such a partnership could be set up.

Thus, the word "reconstruction," while acquiring new and exciting meaning, diverted attention away from the USA and its internal affairs. It connoted Palestine, Europe, DP's, and the raising of funds for the physical revival of the Jewish people, its revival politically, militarily, economically, everywhere but right here at home. And "reconstruction" did not include the religious and cultural.

Our attention was riveted on events abroad—in Germany and at the UN until the end of 1947, when the UN voted for the establishment of a Jewish State in Palestine, through the early stages of the war launched against the Jews there, both before the Declaration and after it. Emptying the camps, bringing the survivors to the Land, helping to arm the Haganah, taking positions on one or another side of the Jabotinsky–Ben Hecht Revisionists, celebrating, mourning, and campaigning, we poured our energies into the immediate and urgent issues. It was clearly no time for debating naturalism versus supernaturalism, or the revision of this or that text in the prayerbook or the *mahzor*. When I stop to consider that we did actually publish the *Shabbat Prayerbook* in 1945, and that it caused some waves, I am astonished. Did we really have room left in our minds for such things?

The attempt to broaden the base of support for Reconstructionism in 1938 at the Cejwin conference led to the establishment of the Friends of Reconstructionism, largely from the membership of the SAJ and the Park Avenue Synagogue. But this was dissolved when the Foundation was established. Reconstructionist fellowships were started in 1943; a major chapter in

Chicago was led by Rabbi Solomon Goldman. The fellowships were more successful than any of the previous efforts to add numbers to the list of sympathizers and supporters. With Rabbi Jack Cohen leading these efforts, groups were started in Baltimore, Arlington, Alexandria, Philadelphia, Brooklyn, Los Angeles, Oakland, Orlando, Milwaukee, and Kansas City. This is indeed an impressive list, but one must now draw hasty conclusions from it. These fellowships consisted of a few people who received the magazine and presumably discussed it at their meetings (frequency unknown). They were not offered any services, like programming, or even regular visits from the main office. It is not surprising that they soon faded.

A Youth Fellowship was started in 1946, but it too did not flourish.

The major strength of Reconstructionism resided in its publications program. After the *New Haggadah* appeared in 1941, Rabbi Kaplan felt that we ought to proceed with a *Shabbat Prayerbook*. He invited Milton Steinberg and Eugene Kohn to join us as an editorial board of four. Our meetings took place at fairly regular intervals at Rabbi Kaplan's home. Our method was to discuss which of the controversial issues, theologically, needed to be dealt with. We agreed that there were four possible approaches: keep the text intact, change the wording to make it compatible with our outlook, retain the text but add an interpretive version along with the literal translation, or delete the passage altogether.

The debates were exciting and stimulating. When we had exhausted an issue, we voted. Frequently we achieved unanimity. But when the group was divided, and even when three of us voted against Rabbi Kaplan's preference, he won. In the final analysis, we deferred to him. Milton was unhappy about the elimination of the *Musaf Amidah* (additional standing prayer), but he did not press the point. When his congregation adopted the book, he inserted material which he felt we had mistakenly dropped.

The *Shabbat Prayerbook* did not appear until 1945. For three years the SAJ experimented with it, using a loose-leaf binder containing mimeographed pages in Hebrew and English. I shall never forget the hours I spent over the Hebrew typewriter putting down the Hebrew text, and then the additional hours (and eyesight) spent on inserting the vocalization on the stencils. The SAJ members deserve a special word of tribute for their patience and tolerance during this trying time. It was not easy for them to generate a spiritual ambience while holding a loose-leaf notebook in their hands. Nor was it easy for me to frequently add and pull out pages while we tried this and that supplementary reading.

When the book appeared, a storm broke out. At a special meeting of the Agudas Horabbonim, the association of Orthodox rabbis (consisting largely of those born and trained abroad), the decree of excommunication was issued against Rabbi Kaplan, and a copy of the *siddur* was burned. This unpleasant event took place at the McAlpin Hotel in New York. The newspapers were full of it the next day. The repercussions were varied. On the one hand, we got more publicity out of the book burning than we would ever have been able to obtain in the normal course of events. Second, the first printing of the *Prayerbook* sold out within a few weeks. Third, virtually every segment of the Jewish community was aroused against the Orthodox rabbis. Letters poured in; resolutions were forwarded to us; editorials denounced the burning of the book, perpetrated shortly after the Nazis had burned those books which did not reflect their views.

While the Seminary faculty did not excommunicate Rabbi Kaplan, three of their number took the trouble to publish an article in *Hadoar*, the Hebrew language weekly, taking strong exception to Rabbi Kaplan's views as reflected in the *siddur*. In fact, thereafter Prof. Saul Lieberman refused to sit next to Rabbi Kaplan at faculty meetings; he took the *herem* seriously. (It may be of some interest to note that at Rabbi Kaplan's 95th birthday party, which Judith and I and Judith's sister Naomi arranged in Jerusalem, Professor Lieberman came and did sit next to Rabbi Kaplan, chatting amiably.)

I mention the *Hadoar* episode mainly to underscore my skepticism regarding the willingness of the Conservative movement to recognize as legitimate any overt expression of dissidence. One might ask how the reaction of several members of the faculty could represent the entire Conservative movement. The answer, unfortunately, is to be found in the relationship between the Seminary and the rest of the movement. The faculty are basically Orthodox in their approach to Judaism in general and *halakhah* in particular. No one can hope to be accepted into the faculty with a rank comparable to those already on it who does not adhere to the rules and regulations of *halakhah*.

I knew Shalom Spiegel when he was on the faculty of the Jewish Institute of Religion. He was by no means an observant Jew by Seminary standards, and this was not surprising since he had been an active member of Hashomer Hatzair prior to his coming to the United States. But when Professor Israel Davidson died and Dr. Spiegel was appointed to succeed him, he changed overnight. The *kippah* never left his head, and he was punctilious about Shabbat and *kashrut* and reciting grace after every meal. There are two possibilities. Either he saw the light in time to get the appointment, or he was given to understand that the appointment could not be made unless he saw the light. I believe that of these two distasteful alternatives, the latter is closer to the truth.

Another example, with a different twist: Salo W. Baron, the distinguished Jewish historian, was added to the faculty even though he was not strictly observant and did not pretend to be. However, Professor Finkelstein pointed out to me that he was merely "Adjunct." Similarly, Martin Buber, when he came at the invitation of the Seminary to serve on the faculty, was Adjunct because he observed only those mitzvot which "spoke to him." And, of course, he was married to a non-Jew.

In short, the standards imposed by the faculty on their own members and on the students of the JTS are Orthodox, and for years the synagogue under the auspices of the JTS was Orthodox (with men and women separate). The institution, however, considers itself the fountainhead of the Conservative movement, to the puzzlement of its alumni and many others. This dual and somewhat self-contradictory role accounts for the tension which exists between the Rabbinical Assembly and the Seminary. The rabbis are expected to perform their duties out in the field as Conservative rabbis, but they respect their teachers and the scholarship which their teachers represent. They feel that they themselves do not possess that scholarship in sufficient depth. Therefore the rabbis are loath to advocate any measure which might run into the opposition of the faculty.

For these reasons I believed that I could expect little from my colleagues of the RA, and getting involved further in RA affairs provided many painful proofs that my intuition was correct. For example, the RA had long hoped to produce its own liturgy for Shabbat and Festivals. When our prayerbook appeared, the pressure to proceed was increased. In order, however, that this new book represent all the shades of opinion within the RA, two Reconstructionists were put on the committee—Milton Steinberg and I.

By this time Milton was quite ill and accepted the assignment with the understanding that he would not attend the meetings but would submit memoranda on individual issues in the liturgy. Operating still on the assumption that the RA would take cognizance of different viewpoints, I agreed to serve too. To my dismay but not surprise, the committee outvoted me (and Milton) on every issue. We voted on the chosen people; on resurrection; the doctrine of reward and punishment (as reflected in the second paragraph after the *Shema*); on sacrifices. On many issues the vote was two against the majority. On some it was just I versus the majority. I did not remain long on the committee, for I saw that I was there for window dressing. I knew that I could not possibly prevail on any matter which required the kind of modification of text which I believed to be necessary for clarity and intellectual honesty.

By the end of the decade a group of Reform and Conservative rabbis was organized into a Reconstructionist Rabbinical Fellowship; its major achievement was the publication of a "Program for Jewish Life Today," a statement that was endorsed by 250 educators, social workers, and laypeople, and 285 rabbis. As always, Reconstructionism received the blessing of spiritual and intellectual leaders—who then went back to business as usual. This was entirely understandable since we at the Foundation had prepared no program for them to adopt.

We too went back to our business as usual. We proceeded to work on a *High Holiday Prayerbook*. Rabbi Kaplan again invited Eugene Kohn, Milton Steinberg, and me to form an editorial committee. Milton turned it down. First, he had suffered a heart attack and was not physically able to attend our meetings, but more important, he had major reservations about our radical departures from tradition, as displayed in our Shabbat *siddur*. Even if his health had permitted, he would not have joined the committee.

We adopted the same procedure, and by the summer of 1947 we were hard at work correcting galleys. It was most pleasant doing this tedious job in the open air, under a tree. With the Kaplans, we rented a house in Hunter, N.Y., from Irving and Pauline Mack (of the Borgenicht family). Judith and Miriam and I were now accompanied by our newest child, little Ann Nechamah. It turned out to be a very productive summer. In addition to correcting galleys, Rabbi Kaplan and I collaborated on a book dealing with the problem of cultural pluralism. I had been inspired by my association with Rachel DuBois, and when the Seminary announced a contest for the best book on that subject, I felt we ought to give it a try. We would sit down and talk over the ideas, and I would write them out. The book was completed that summer. Unfortunately it won second place, and we never tried to get it published. But we were satisfied that we had done a good job. (There is no explanation for the fact that we were content to leave it at that. I sometimes think the book would have been a genuine contribution. Sections of it later provided me with material for individual articles.)

That summer we also acquired a little cottage higher up the mountain which became our summer residence for the next twenty years.

The *High Holiday Prayerbook* appeared in 1948. But the year 1948 was, of course, memorable for more than the publication of a new liturgical work. I refer to the establishment of the State of Israel. I shall long remember the Saturday in November 1947 when the UN General Assembly voted in favor of partition. We prayed very hard for a favorable result of the voting that morning. On the Shabbat immediately following the declaration of independence the following May, we witnessed a highly emotional congregation filling the entire synagogue, eager to participate in some symbolic action which would reflect the pent-up hopes and anxieties of the preceding years, as well as the overwhelming joy of that moment.

We recited the *Hallel* and marched with all the Torah scrolls around the sanctuary, like on Simḥat Torah, singing and chanting for all we were worth. It was at moments of this kind that we experienced the central role of the congregation in our lives. There we shared sorrows and joys, personal and communal, with like-minded men and women who understood what their rabbis were trying to express. Religion actually functioned at these moments, exemplifying Rabbi Kaplan's general principle that, in order to have religion in common, one must have other things in common besides religion. I do not believe that I could have been as exalted anywhere else, that morning in May 1948, for it was with these people that I shared other things besides religion.

11

Sabbatical in Israel

The establishment of the State of Israel rekindled my enthusiasm for Zionism. The idea of a reconstituted Jewish nation in the Land of Zionism had saved me for Jewish life. It was exciting because it seemed to be the logical culmination of the whole drama of Jewish history. Zionism made the Bible come to life, it made Jewish experience meaningful. I could not understand the Jews' stubborn clinging to their identity other than as the need to make sense of their suffering. Homelessness was the key to the whole puzzle. Jews were strangers everywhere. Only when Jews returned to their home could their lot be different. What a dramatic moment in history this was, when the Jews could close the chapter of homelessness and begin a new one on the site of their entrance onto the stage of history!

That is why I was virtually transported by the lectures of Dr. Benderly; that is why, in 1933, when no one I knew had the urge to visit Palestine, I was driven to go there. And why the following year, on our honeymoon, we spent the summer in Palestine. And that is why there always remained a vestige of a sense of unfinished business with respect to Eretz Yisrael: should I not go back and settle there? Was this not the logic of it all— assuming that I was caught up in the total Jewish experience in my own life? And were not the reasons I came back twice actually rationalizations? Granted that the Jews of America needed me: was it true that my usefulness in the USA was greater than in Palestine? I could not erase from my memory the repeated question which the Jews in Palestine asked me (and us): have you come to stay? There was a wistful quality in their voices. They seemed to be asking and pleading at the same time.

I knew, of course, that the *yishuv* did not need the services of an American rabbi. But surely I could serve in another capacity, perhaps as a journalist or teacher. Or I could have retrained myself for some other function. More than once I regretted that I did not accept the offer—really the challenge—of Ted Lurie who thought I should work for the *Palestine Post*. When the going got rough in America, when I became thoroughly disgusted with the ever-recurrent question of why be a Jew, I would be tempted to drop the rabbinate and go on *aliyah*. Whenever my efforts to interest intelligent people in Jewish life and learning met with either scorn or indifference, I would ask myself why I was trying so hard to swim against the tide. As I have mentioned, often during the summers, away from the routine of rabbinical duties, I would pause to take notice of the way most Jews were living. They seemed to get along pretty well without an active involvement in Judaism, and I would ask myself: who needs me and who needs Judaism? Why am I foisting my personal *meshugas* on these nice people, whose lack of interest in Torah or Jewish observance is not really self-hate, but due only to the fact that their personal affairs and American life fill up their days?

Such questions frightened me. I had the feeling that if I let myself go, I too could get caught up in the day-by-day culture of the American people and before long become exactly like the Jews I would ordinarily be criticizing. But on the other hand, there would be a difference: given my education, and the years of my professional activity, I could never return to a bland acceptance of the fact that I was Jewish and let it go at that. I knew that I would always be torn between my Jewish and my American selves. Therefore the only road to take was the one which led to Palestine. There I would be whole again.

But would I? Would I not for the rest of my life remain an American, a first generation immigrant like my grandmother from Kovno, who lived in the United States for sixty-five years and never became an American? I would be identified as a newcomer by my unidiomatic Hebrew, by my shallow roots in the mores and habits of the *yishuv*, by a hundred and one American responses to daily stimuli. To be sure, virtually everyone in Palestine was an immigrant, but most of them came directly from Eastern Europe. The intervening generation, during which I became American, would stamp me as different, a member of a strange and new minority.

I would enjoy one distinction that separated me from the Yemenites and the newly arriving German Jews; I would be an immigrant who *chose* to come. I would not be a refugee. That would give me some special status, but it would also create problems which the refugees did not have. I could always return to the USA. This escape hatch, this freedom to give up if life became too difficult, would make my adjustment to the Land all the more difficult. *Ein bereira*, there is no choice, was the most reliable ally one could have in the struggle to adjust to a new and hard life. I would have a *bereira*. War, poverty, deprivation, all the ills to which life is heir in a pioneering country, would transform the USA, in my mind, into a paradise, and I would forget the heartaches of striving to make Jewish Jews out of Jews.

And so the debate went on, year after year. Not that I did anything about it. To be sure, plans were hatched, from time to time, but never reached the stage of action. For example, a group initiated by our friend Katya Delakova, the dancer, was organized for the purpose of planning a *moshav* consisting of Americans. Isaac and Rebecca Imber once took steps to bring together a similar group. But the groups were very much like ourselves—ambivalent. They thought they wanted to settle. They thought they ought to settle. They also liked living in the United States, although at times they felt guilty about liking it.

The closest we got, I think, was our experience at Cream Ridge, New Jersey during the summer of 1944. The war was on, and the government was encouraging Americans to plant victory gardens to increase the food supply. In Cream Ridge, a *hakhsharah* farm (training farm) was maintained by Habonim, the youth movement of the Labor Zionists. Under the leadership of Yosef Israeli, a *shaliah* stuck in America on account of the war, a project was launched to bring 25 American Jewish teenagers to the farm to assist the young men and women who were in training for *aliyah* but were also stuck because the British were restricting immigration. The idea was to increase the productivity of the farm and at the same time expose the teenagers to a *kibbutz* experience and some intensive education in Zionism. A similar farm existed not far off in Hightstown, run by Hashomer Hatzair under the leadership of Moshe Furmansky. While the two groups were politically at odds, Yosef and Moshe were good friends, and they worked together to rally young Americans to the cause. Judith and I were invited to come to Cream Ridge as the educational staff, she to do the music, I to lead discussions (*siḥot*). There was one other member of the staff, Ettie Skidell, who was a sort of camp mother.

This was the happiest summer we ever experienced. When it was over, we did not want to go home. We were convinced that settling in Eretz was the only genuine choice for an intelligent and sensitive Jew, and that life in the United States, and particularly in a big city, was stultifying, deadening. The friends we made were going to be friends for life. In a word, that summer of 1944 remains to this day a memorable one but a constant rebuke, a reminder of a dream unfulfilled.

This was our first intimate taste of a different kind of life, and we responded to it like eager youngsters. The people were somehow exciting, unlike most Americans we knew. Moshe was a genuine intellectual. We would argue by the hour, on religion, on the future shape of the Jewish homeland, on communism, on the "evils of capitalism." We disagreed on most questions, but that was irrelevant. His European education, his enthusiasm for ideas, his willingness to act out what he believed in, the fact that he believed in something at all—passionately, eloquently—set him apart from virtually everyone we had ever met. And he had humor and charm.

Yosef was older, perhaps a bit wiser, but very similar. He loved to talk about everything, by the hour. He was fascinated by life in America, and he saw and understood the dilemma of many American Jews like ourselves. Leah, his wife, was a lovely product of Riga (as was Yosef), who at an early age knew that her destiny was to be a *kibbutznik* in Eretz. She was a worker, but she was also a sensitive wife and mother who found in Judith a companion with whom to shmoos about *veibish* (wifely) things: cooking, the children, the problems of growing up. She was warm and understanding and, like Yosef, sympathetic to those American Jews who found life in the United States comfortable. (Alas, Yosef died of cancer. We visited them in Afikim in 1968, and he was already showing signs of succumbing to the disease. Leah still lives in the kibbutz.)

The program was invigorating: we worked at our assigned tasks from 8:30 to 12. After lunch we had a rest period, then we resumed until 3:30. Thereafter we showered and met as a group for our daily class-discussion. Dinner was at six o'clock, and then we had an evening program, either a town-meeting to discuss the program, rules, and regulations, or Judith would have the group singing or listening to records, or rehearsing a program for a future occasion, like Tisha B'Av. By 9:30 the kids were so exhausted that they went to bed without resisting. Indeed, at one of the town-meetings, they voted an earlier bedtime than had been planned.

Knowing something about the Labor Zionist attitude toward religion and rabbis I was somewhat apprehensive when I came. Should I tell them at once that I was a rabbi, or should I first work to be accepted and then reveal the awful truth? The decision was taken out of my hands. Yosef had already made known to the *ḥevrah* that I was a rabbi, and as expected, this was an obstacle which had to be overcome. Fortunately, we proved ourselves worthy of acceptance, and a warm and loving relationship was established. I think I became one of that small group of American rabbis who are *persona grata* with the secular Zionists. My success was confirmed when, in the fall, we were back at Cream Ridge for the wedding of Mendy Mendelson. He had urged me to officiate. It was a beautiful wedding. The *ḥuppah* consisted of two large tree branches overlapping above our heads. And when "Rem" (Remez, who later became the first chief of the Israeli air force and ambassador to Great Britain) was to be married, I was invited to officiate.

When we were packing to leave, Miriam asked, "Why can't we stay here all the time?" A good question. My answer was feeble—I have to go back to my office in New York. What do you do there, she asked, that you can't do here? I was stumped.

When it came to telling her—or myself—what I did in New York, I discovered that my work was somehow unreal, not like cleaning the chicken house, or picking tomatoes, or removing the vines from the asparagus plants.

Most of the *ḥevrah* made it to Eretz. The women got certificates; the men for the most part came in through *Aliyah Bet*, the illegal immigration. Some were caught and sent to Cyprus. A few changed their minds and never reached Israel, except as tourists. A few of the *ḥevrah* were killed in the fighting of 1948. Moshe Furmansky was killed in the fighting very early. He was cut down saving the chicken house at Mishmar Haemek. The Israelis returned to their *kibbutz*, Afikim. The Skidells finally made it to Kfar Blum. And we went back to 93rd Street in New York.

It was the memory of the summer of '44 that revived the impulse to visit Israel for a protracted stay. If the real thing was anything like what we had experienced at Cream Ridge, perhaps we might at last make a decision to go on *aliyah*. The SAJ granted me my first (and only) sabbatical.

The SAJ gave us a heart-warming farewell as we prepared to board the LaGuardia for Haifa. It had been one of the American Export Line boats (the kind I traveled on in 1933). Later it was transformed into a troop ship. Now it was used for passenger travel in the Mediterranean. Our plan was to go directly to Afikim at the invitation of Yosef Israeli. We thought we would put the children into school there, do our share of work, and from time to time get into our Ford (which we had shipped ahead and see the country after a lapse of almost sixteen years).

We arrived on January 3, 1950. From the first, the breaks seemed to be against us. When we reached Haifa, a refugee boat was unloading, and we were stuck within sight of the city for six hours. Finally, we landed on the pier, which apparently was not yet prepared to handle several hundred persons and their luggage. The chaos was unbelievable. Trunks strewn on all parts of the pier. There was no one who offered to help. The children were getting more and more restless, and we were all exhausted. Finally, a man sent by Yosef to see to our luggage and to us came along. After much searching he found us. One by one he found our six trunks. We were all loaded into a large taxi (the trunks to follow) and brought to a hotel. It was about 10 o'clock by that time.

But the day was not yet over. Discouraging news awaited us: we could not proceed to the *kibbutz* for a day or two because illness had broken out among the newly arrived immigrants. The rains had caused flooding, and the *kibbutz* was not ready for us. The hotel itself was run by the Histadrut, and hence not especially luxurious. In fact, it was rather depressing.

The next day we encountered further problems. The car had not arrived, and we would have to make our way to Afikim by bus. How long would we have to stay in Haifa? Nobody seemed to know. How long until the car arrived? No one knew. With plenty of leisure on our hands, we explored Haifa, and we engaged a car to show us the surrounding area. This was refreshing, but we were eager to get settled, and we had no notion of when that would happen.

Finally a break! Word came from the agent that the car had been unloaded and that I was to come to the pier to claim it. I found my way to the agent's office and in a combination of Hebrew, English, and Yiddish made myself understood. Unfortunately I understood him only too well. There were complications. No tourist was permitted to bring a car into the country without posting a bond to guarantee that he would ship it out again as soon as he left. I made my way to the Anglo-Palestine Bank in the city, where a Mr. Nathanson, brother of the cantor of the SAJ, was manager. He received me warmly, offering a cup of Turkish coffee. I had never drunk Turkish coffee, so I tipped the cup and swallowed the whole in one gulp. I found to my dismay that I had also poured a half a cup of mud down my throat along with the liquid.

The bond amounted to $1500, almost all the travelers checks I had with me. Of course, I would get it all back eventually, but what to do in the meantime? Besides, the bond was only the first step. I had to register the number of the car. Back at the pier I looked for the number and could not find it. The agent looked; a few workers came by and looked. No one could find it. Finally, someone, speaking with great authority, said the number was under the floor, and proceeded to borrow a hammer and screw driver to remove the floor. Suddenly it was lunch time, and off he went, leaving the tools and the dismantled floor.

I recount these events, which are still vivid in my memory after more than thirty years, because they constituted my first impression of what it would mean to live in Israel—at least at that stage in its evolution. A few days later we got word that the coast was clear. We were to board a bus to Tiberias and change to another which ran right by the kibbutz; we were to leave the trunks for pickup later. We took along all we could, and on a chilly January day, we left the hotel, looking for all the world like immigrants ourselves, and landed in Afikim. Yosef met us, full of apologies for circumstances that were really beyond his control. But the car—it was still on the pier. I would have to go back and get it later.

We were put into one of the heated rooms next to the infants' house. The warmth was welcome; the cries and shrieks of the babies at night were not. There were obviously not enough *matepelot* to take care of the needs of all the infants quickly enough to spare them—and us—the wailing and the crying. Then our younger daughter, Ann, developed an ear infection, so another reason was added to keep us in quarantine.

Finally, we were introduced to our room at the far end of the *kibbutz*. It was a large *kibbutz*, with more than one thousand members and dozens of others who were not yet elected to membership. Most came from Latvia. Some of the more recent arrivals were displaced persons from the camps. We knew very few people, apart from Yosef and Leah. I had hoped to perform some service for which I was trained, perhaps teaching. Judith also would have preferred some activity relating to music. But since we were to be temporary visitors, we could not be entrusted with any work which would have required long-term commitment.

The result: I was assigned to work in the plywood factory, Judith in the *mahsan* (a combination laundry and repair center for clothes, and the place where members came to acquire whatever they needed by way of clothing). My job was to work a *mehaberet*, a machine which glued irregular parts of wood to one another in order to make up one standard size sheet. Judith was given the job of darning socks—an occupation for which she was singularly unequipped, never having once darned a sock in her life.

My work was boring and fatiguing. I reached the factory at 6 in the morning, having eaten only a glass of hot tea and some bread. Work continued until 7:30, when we broke for breakfast; back to work until noon; back at work by one, quitting at 3:30. The hours were long; standing on one's feet on the cold, hard floor was torture. There was no variety to spark interest in what I was doing. What saved me from going altogether mad was my partner at the table, a middle-aged Viennese lawyer who had fled to China. There he became a prosperous insurance manager. He had a home in the country and servants, and had married a Chinese-born Russian-Jewish nurse. When the communists took over, they fled. This time he was determined never to migrate again, and he came to Afikim to join his brother. We had much to talk about. He wanted to know more about America, having been introduced to American civilization through *Time* magazine. I was fascinated by his odyssey.

Our conversations made the day pass tolerably well. After work we returned to our respective rooms to tidy up and spend time with the children. Judith, in the meantime, was having a problem with Ann. Not having ever been away to nursery school, she was naturally unhappy at the *gan* (kindergarten) and refused to stay there unless Judith spent the day with her. So Judith darned socks and stockings, acting as a part-time nursery school assistant. Sometimes she could not get away from the *maḥsan*, and Ann would abandon the *gan* and go look for her mommy. The kibbutz was large, and often she got lost trying to find our room. Since it was winter and rain had left large gobs of mud on all the paths, she was a pathetic figure in her long, floppy boots. All in all, not a spectacle to gladden the hearts of her parents. Sleeping time presented other problems. Since she could not yet communicate with her peers, she was particularly lonesome at bedtime. One of us had to sit by her until sleep overcame her.

Miriam adjusted better, but she too was beset with problems. She was bored to death. In addition, her clothes were not identical to those of the other children in the fifth grade, and they taunted her about that.

And it was cold. In the Jordan Valley, much below sea level, one would expect the winters to be more like Florida than like Wisconsin. Perhaps it felt like the latter because we were not prepared for what turned out to be a most unusual winter. It actually snowed. There must have been two to three inches of snow, which delighted both the adults, who had not seen snow since they had left their native Latvia, and the excited children. But it left their poor hands and feet frozen. The houses were designed to catch every breeze in the sweltering valley, and thus every flake of snow that might drop in.

We tried very hard to maintain a stiff upper lip, but as the weeks went by, we found we were less and less convinced that this experience was either enlightening or doing anyone any good. Judith's patches and my splinters were hardly adding to the growth of the country. We felt that we had learned enough about life in the kibbutz and decided to return to Jerusalem, where we would have a new and different kind of experience.

Driving through the Emek resembled nothing so much as a trek through New England in the winter. White snow everywhere, with the additional hazard of losing track of where the road ended. If we did not fall into a ditch on our way across and up to Jerusalem, it was a miracle. Tel Aviv was none too warm but certainly was a welcome change. After two days at the seaside, we moved on to Jerusalem, to the pension of Madame Ruppin in Rehavia. The house was warm! The "high tea" was delightful. We relaxed, preparing to spend the remaining months at this quiet, comfortable house when trouble began again.

Without recounting the details, let it be recorded simply that Miriam came down with polio, and for several days we were not sure how she would emerge from the attack. The weeks that followed were filled with supervised exercises, rehabilitation, and scrupulous attention to the task of keeping the families in New York in ignorance of the whole episode. The letters were masterpieces of fiction. We borrowed money from friends, lest the emergency become apparent from our sudden need for funds. We would have to return home sooner than we had planned.

We agreed that Judith and the girls would leave, and give me a chance to spend a few weeks in Israel on my own.

With Miriam again able to move about with some sense of security, we arranged a final fling—Pesaḥ in Tiberias with our dear friends Lee and Frances Sneider. Accommodations were difficult to get, but we settled for two crowded rooms in the house of a Sephardic family, with meals at the hotel. But the final fling was almost ruined by the sudden illness of Ann, who showed all the signs of having picked up the polio from Miriam. With gratitude and relief we learned that it was *only* the measles. We shall never forget Dr. Nelken's congratulatory outburst, "Mazal tov. Your daughter has the measles!"

One more mishap before Judith and the girls left for home. In Haifa, before sailing, Ann came down with a violent case of dysentery. It seemed for a day or two that they might not be able to travel with a sick child. Fortunately, her fever broke, and while she was too weak to walk up the gangplank (I carried her on my shoulders), I deposited three grateful passengers on the LaGuardia. And thus the grand experiment ended.

At that point I think I would have been risking my life if I had uttered one word about the possibility of settling in Israel. What I feared most was that our daughters might be so scarred by the experience that they might never again wish even to visit the Land.

(On March 20 a cable arrived at the pension. Dr. Dushkin and Bertha Schoolman intercepted it, and when I came in they told me to sit down. I was to receive a shock. Milton Steinberg had died.)

In the weeks that followed, I tried to make the most of my experience, but in the absence of Judith and the family the following six weeks were neither productive nor particularly pleasant. I flew back by way of London. I visited William Frankel, the editor of the *Jewish Chronicle*, who was kind enough to drive me around to interesting places. The gas rationing had been lifted just in time. I sailed home on the Queen Mary.

The question of *aliyah* was tabled indefinitely.

12

Last Years
at the SAJ

We were happy enough to be back in the States in
the summer of 1950. But, as we returned to "normal," I experienced again a spiritual letdown. The promise which seemed to
inhere in the pulpit of the SAJ had not materialized. Working
with Dr. Kaplan was still a privilege, but it was no longer a
novelty. A new and different kind of stimulation came, to my
surprise, from a totally unexpected source. In the fall of 1950 I
received an invitation to serve for one semester (winter 1951) as
Visiting Professor of Homiletics at the Seminary.

The chair was no longer occupied by Dr. Kaplan. He had
asked for, and been granted, a change in the designation of his
course. It was now Philosophies of Religion. His new responsibility, in fact, described more accurately the nature of his
teaching. Homiletics (the art of preaching) was, for many years,
simply a euphemism for an introduction to the "functional approach" to the Bible, and for testing new ideas as they emerged
from his lifelong project of formulating a philosophy of Judaism
for twentieth century America. Half the time was given over to
student sermons and their criticism by fellow students and

Kaplan, but time was spent not on how to preach, but on what to preach.

Since the change, the spring semester of the homiletics course had been assigned to various alumni of the Seminary who were assumed to be competent to handle it, but Rabbi Israel Levinthal presided over each fall semester. I had at no time considered myself as a likely candidate. In light of the faculty's attitude toward Kaplan, I assumed that I was *persona non grata.* Since I am, I suppose, an incorrigible optimist, the invitation to join the faculty even for one semester suggested to me that perhaps a new policy was being introduced, a major change in light of the blast against the *Shabbat Prayerbook* which had appeared a few years earlier in the *Hadoar.* Perhaps JTS was actually going to implement what Dr. Kaplan had proposed for the Conservative movement.

His proposal was that the Conservative movement openly and unmistakably declare that it is a coalition of three major trends in Judaism: the right, the center, and the left. Each would be free to promulgate its own philosophy and program within a framework which would be acceptable to all three. Dr. Kaplan wanted the leaders to acknowledge publicly what they knew to be the fact—that the Rabbinical Assembly was divided into three factions and that one of the reasons it was inhibited from making basic changes or assuring strong ideological positions was that the leaders were extremely concerned about keeping the group together. Knowing full well that the leftists would not defect, no matter how disgruntled they might be, the Rabbinical Assembly tilted always toward the right, appeasing the traditionalists and at the same time avoiding too strong a confrontation with the Orthodox. The center group might be swayed once in a while toward a liberal position, but as a rule this group tended to cling to the status quo.

Within the Rabbinical Assembly the existence of these three groups was tacitly conceded. The Committee on Law and Standards, for example, always included members of all three wings. Nobody outside the rabbinic leadership knew about this because the deliberations of the Committee were never made public. All they knew was that most decisions included a majority view and a minority view, with local rabbis free to follow whichever view they found more agreeable.

What Dr. Kaplan had suggested was that a public statement be made to the effect that each wing of the movement is considered equally legitimate. This would enable Jews to understand better the constituency of the movement, and it would symbolize, indeed actually reflect, the acceptance of the idea of pluralism within Jewish life. Those who passionately defended the concept of cultural pluralism as a rationale for the Jews' insistence upon retaining and even fostering their individuality within the larger American civilization should not hesitate to apply the same approach to Jewish life itself.

Optimism does not die easily, so it endured in spite of the fact that the semester ended without any perceptible change in the attitude of the establishment toward the left wing. I came and went, and that was the sum total of my experience as a member of the faculty, or rather as a visiting professor. As I look back, I put that isolated appointment in the same category as the advice which I assume Moshe Davis gave when persecution of Dr. Kaplan ceased. The leaders could point to my assignment to teach homiletics for one semester as a demonstration of tolerance. A wide chasm separated tolerance from genuine pluralism.

A third incident illustrated the new spirit of tolerance. I had been elected vice president of the Rabbinical Assembly upon our return to the States from Israel.

Once before my friends on the left had decided that I should be elected to a high office in the Rabbinical Assembly.

I cannot say that I actively campaigned, but I did attend conventions diligently and serve on committees. I was elected treasurer, which involved virtually no duties but gave me a chance to participate in the work of the Executive Council on which treasurers always served. Later on in 1946, I was proposed by Rabbi William Greenfield to the Nominating Committee as a possible nominee for vice president.

To my great surprise the Nominating Committee accepted his proposal and was about to bring in my name as their candidate for vice president when word got out (I believe deliberately in order to test the waters), and a storm broke loose. Rabbi

195

Greenfield took me aside and informed me that several members of the Assembly had threatened that if I were nominated, I would be challenged from the floor, and a rival candidate would be nominated. In the contest, said Bill, I would not win because I would be attacked for my lack of strict observance. In those days I was a smoker, and apparently I had been smoking on a Friday evening, and someone had reported the violation to a member of the RA. In any case it was the better part of valor to withdraw my name voluntarily.

As my self-appointed campaign manager, Rabbi Greenfield had initiated this move with my approval. He now sought my approval to cancel the whole effort. But I was tempted to make an issue of this threat. In fact, I was hoping that a contest would ensue so that I could engage my rival and those who would have nominated him in a public debate regarding the hypocritical position of the Rabbinical Assembly with respect to ritual observance. I knew that there were distinguished members of the Assembly who did not adhere to the rule against smoking on Shabbat but who were honored by the RA and the Seminary itself for unworthy reasons, like their influence with big donors. I was really eager to strike out at all those who posed as liberals but who were intimidated by their (I believe) unwarranted fear of reprisal from the Placement Committee. Even if I lost the election, it would be worth the opportunity to lash out at Dr. Kaplan's critics.

But this was not to be. Rabbi Greenfield and a few other friendly colleagues persuaded me that the time was not ripe, that the RA would be split, and that any likelihood of my being elected in the future would be ruined. So I withdrew. But the episode reenforced my conviction that the only way Dr. Kaplan's disciples could express themselves freely was to organize themselves into a new group altogether. This view, however, was not shared by Dr. Kaplan, who still hoped to effect changes from within.

In 1952 I became president. At the crucial moment in 1950, when the Nominating Committee brought in my name as candidate for the vice presidency, no voice was raised against me. The opposition had evaporated. Why? Some cynics suggested that this was because I had stopped smoking. No one could now accuse me of lighting up on Shabbat. I believe that my unopposed election reflected a new policy, as did Kaplan's restoration to favor and my semester of teaching.

It succeeded in keeping me within the movement and loyal to it. It did not, however, influence me to revise significantly my skepticism regarding what might or might not be achieved within the system. The two years of my incumbency as president confirmed me in that skepticism. I plunged into my work with zest. I introduced the practice of sending out a monthly letter to all the rabbis. I encouraged the organization of regional groups. With Rabbi Leon Lang stepping down from the editorship of *Conservative Judaism*, I proposed that we publish an annual like the HUC Annual. (I believed that the rabbis would more readily write for a volume than for a quarterly, and Rabbi Lang had complained that contributions were hard to come by.)

There was need for a journal but of another kind, one which would address itself specifically to the problems and needs of the rabbi. Believing as I did that American rabbis of all denominations faced virtually the same situation, one magazine, sponsored by all three groups, seemed the ideal plan. I met with the leaders of the Orthodox and Reform groups. I was discouraged by the Orthodox, while the Reform people warmly endorsed the idea. However, when I brought the matter to the Executive Council and suggested that the Rabbinical Assembly proceed with the Central Conference of American Rabbis alone since the Orthodox would not cooperate, I was turned down. As a result, the *CCAR Journal* (later a quarterly called *Reform Judaism*) came into being. The RA did approve one part of my plan. We were to suspend the quarterly and issue a volume. The first would be an overview of the Conservative movement from its beginnings to 1952–3, and the following volumes would represent the current thinking (and scholarship) of the rabbis. I appointed Rabbi Mordecai Waxman as editor.

Unfortunately, his work took five years, and *Tradition and Change*, as it came to be called, came out years after my administration. The result was that the whole plan was scrapped. Not another volume was prepared, and the magazine was revived. I am pleased that subsequent editors did not have the same difficulties which plagued Rabbi Lang, but I regret that the idea of an annual volume was dropped altogether.

Another effort to bring together the three groups, or at least as many as would consent to cooperate, centered on the establishment of a Jewish Museum. I could not see any connection between art and religious denominations; I thought a museum should be co-sponsored by all three groups. I brought the matter to Dr. Finklestein. He contended that the idea was not practical. Joint administration was unwieldy. So the Jewish Museum to this day is a project of JTS, but Yeshiva University now has a museum, and Hebrew Union College has one in Los Angeles.

A third effort was equally successful. Plans were projected for the establishment of a cantorial school. Hebrew Union College already had one, and I was honored to serve on its board at the invitation of Dr. Franzblau. I knew that the School of Sacred Music was genuinely pluralistic even to the point of encouraging those who had principles about the *kippah* to wear it while those who opposed went bare-headed. More important, the music of both the tradition and Reform were taught, and graduates were qualified to serve *any* congregation. I therefore requested a meeting in my office at the SAJ between Dr. Franzblau and Cantor Putterman of the Park Avenue Synagogue, to explore the possibility of a joint venture.

It was a stormy session. Several times, one or another of the cantors stalked out of the room, only to be physically brought back. Suffice it to say that I was again thwarted in my attempt to foster cooperative action and lower the barriers which separated one denomination from another. There are now three schools for cantors.

13

The Chicago Years

As my administration was about to enter its second year (summer of 1953), I received a call from Rabbi Wolfe Kelman, who had been brought in by my predecessor, Rabbi Max Davidson, as Executive Director of the RA. Kelman asked whether I would be interested in a pulpit in Chicago. The synagogue was Anshe Emet, a very large and prestigious congregation led for twenty-five years by Rabbi Solomon Goldman. After Rabbi Goldman's death, the congregation spent considerable time and effort drawing up a panel of rabbis whom they would consider for the position. The list consisted of Robert Gordis, Morris Adler, Jacob Agus, and me.

I subsequently learned (on how good authority I cannot say) that Gordis would not consider going to Chicago unless he was assured a teaching position at one of the universities there. Rabbi Adler was too conservative for Anshe Emet, which had the reputation of being liberal and innovative. Rabbi Agus was apparently not to their liking.

While I had been growing restive at the SAJ, I had no serious intention of ever going elsewhere. After all, this had been my first and only position. To my knowledge no one in the leadership or otherwise had ever expressed the desire to change rabbis. My family was in New York, and so was Judith's. Nevertheless, it was exciting to be asked to come to a synagogue which had been served by Solomon Goldman, a distinguished scholar, orator, Zionist leader, and respected communal personality. It was additionally challenging to be asked to follow a personality as strong as he. Goldman had always identified himself with Kaplan's views and had considered himself a Reconstructionist. He even organized a short-lived rabbinical fellowship of Reconstructionists in Chicago, which had raised the prospect of reaching out successfully to the Middle West, an area which we had hardly penetrated.

A comittee consisting of three couples led by Judge Harry Fisher interviewed me in a hotel room downtown in New York and urged me to consider becoming the rabbi of Anshe Emet. I had been reluctant to attend the interview, but I confess I was flattered by the invitation. Once there I warned them that they might be making a mistake. I was not the Goldman type of orator to whom they had become accustomed. I was not the scholar of whom they were so proud. Most of all, I was a committed Reconstructionist, and while Rabbi Goldman had been sympathetic, he had not energetically attempted to convert the congregation to that philosophy.

The judge undertook to speak for the group and eloquently refuted each of my points of resistance. A different style of speaking was in fact needed today since the old oratory was going out of style. Scholarship was to be honored, but a congregational rabbi could not properly serve his people if his major concern was research. And as for Reconstructionism—this was *precisely* why they wanted me. Goldman revered Kaplan and always spoke with the utmost fervor about his ideas.

I told them I would give the matter thought and would be in touch with them. Judith was not enthusiastic. Somehow she visualized Chicago as parochial and backward. To be sure, there were universities and museums and a good orchestra, but she was concerned that the people we would have to deal with would compare unfavorably with the sophisticated and knowledgeable congregants of the SAJ. However, she was willing to suspend judgment until we visited Chicago. In the meantime I was to bring the offer to the attention of the SAJ leadership. If at this juncture they were to attempt to persuade me to remain by offering generous support to the Reconstructionist Foundation and a salary which might rise above the level which I had been receiving, we would stay on in New York.

I therefore asked Maurice Linder, the Chairman of the Board, to permit me to see him privately at his office. We met, and I informed him of the offer which had come to me. He was clearly shocked, but after a few minutes of conversation he expressed the belief that I would be doing myself and my family a real service by accepting the offer. The SAJ could never hope to provide the salary I was to receive, and it was unlikely that the SAJ in its current position would be able to increase to any considerable extent its support for the *Reconstructionist*. People had always complained that they were being taxed twice, once for the congregation and once for the Foundation. They could not add to that burden.

It should be mentioned here that the West Side of Manhattan was beginning to decline at that time; many members were moving to the East Side, and only some of them maintained their membership after the move. The SAJ stayed at approximately 300 families. Proposals that we sell the building and follow the trend eastward had met with no support. I am sure Mr. Linder was thinking of my welfare when he urged me to give serious consideration to the change.

If he had been the only one to take that position, I would have brushed aside his well intentioned advice. But to my dismay other members of the Board agreed with him. This was a wonderful opportunity for me. The SAJ had not supported our efforts as they deserved. Perhaps Chicago would open up a whole new territory for the movement. Rumor had it that there were many wealthy members of Anshe Emet. Perhaps this was indeed the opportune moment for Reconstructionism's invasion of the Middle West.

Rabbi Jack Cohen, my younger colleague and friend who had been serving as educational director of the SAJ and part-time director for the Foundation, had been wanting for some time to make a change. His first choice was *aliyah* to Israel, and short of that, a pulpit of his own. In his usual sweet and ethical way, he informed me that if I went to Chicago, he would be a candidate for the position of rabbi at the SAJ. If I remained, he would seek a post elsewhere. He felt, properly, that the time had come for him to be on his own.

Dr. Kaplan was understandably ambivalent. He was most reluctant for us to leave, but he too saw an opportunity in Chicago which might accrue to the benefit of Reconstructionism in general and to me personally. Much to my surprise, my parents reacted in a similar vein. They were so impressed with the new position and the salary that went with it that they overcame their potential loneliness and advised us to grasp the opportunity.

By this time I was convinced that a new and bright chapter was about to begin, not only for me and my career, but for Reconstructionism. I was thinking mainly in terms of a wider base of financial support and the conquest of a large congregation for our philosophy. Judith and I traveled to Chicago to spend the Shabbat which coincided with New Year 1954. We were wined and dined, and I preached from the pulpit. I met the major *baale-batim*. We talked money and apartments and schools for the children—and the die was cast.

I had never been the rabbi of a large congregation. Serving 1400 families was a new and frightening experience. How did one get to know the members? How could one possibly perform the pastoral duties of so large a group, when funerals, unveilings, bar mitzvahs, weddings, and hospital duties threatened to occupy all the time of the rabbi? How did one supervise an executive staff of a dozen men and women? How did one give attention to a day school, a Hebrew school and a Sunday school? Most important for me, how did one move the enormous weight of a tradition which had been operating for a quarter of a century under a rabbi like Goldman whose reputation had been international and whose memory was revered by the membership as though his philosophy and program were infallible?

This last consideration was actually the first to be encountered. It happened immediately, during the first High Holiday season. Assuming as I did that they had selected me not only in spite of my Reconstructionism but (according to Judge Fisher) because of it, I wasted no time in acquainting the members of the Board with our Reconstructionist High Holiday prayerbook. I arranged for each member to receive a copy, browse through it, consult, and compare with the Adler *maḥzor* still in use at Anshe Emet. I thus hoped to introduce a sample of the sort of liturgy which we had devised. After the holidays I would meet with them and listen to their reactions.

To my amazement and dismay, the reaction came almost at once. It was channeled through the Goldman family. How did I dare to break my word? Had I not agreed that I would not push Reconstructionism? How could I have had the poor taste to criticize Rabbi Goldman (indirectly, to be sure) by proposing the use of a book which he in his wisdom had never seen fit to recommend? I did not understand what was happening. Indeed I regarded my little experiment as having been only a mistake in strategy. Perhaps I had not waited a decent interval.

But I was wrong. No matter how hard I tried to deny the fact, I had to face the shocking truth that Judge Fisher had actually told the Board that I had agreed to resign from the Editorial Board, that I had left my Reconstructionism behind, and that I was satisfied to keep Anshe Emet a Conservative congregation. This I did not discover until almost a year had gone by. It was told to me by friends whose loyalty I had earned in the early months of my stay. What a tragic comedy, indeed! I had rationalized my acceptance of the post on the ground that I was being given a golden opportunity to expand Reconstructionism, and now I learned that I had been deceived!

As soon as I felt confident enough to do so, I spoke up at a meeting of the Board. I denied that I had ever made such a promise, and I made it clear that I intended to pursue my goal energetically. Naturally, I explained, after many years of another's leadership, I would have to go slowly and pedagogically; but I made no secret of the fact that I wished to convert the congregation to Reconstructionism, and to its *financial support*.

My first objective was to adopt the Reconstructionist *haggadah* at a public *seder*. Rabbi Goldman had opposed public *sedarim*; he believed the family should observe the *seder* together. I agreed. On the first night the *seder* should be at home. But many families observed a second night, and still others have no families or do not know how to conduct a *seder* and need a community *seder* in order to observe the tradition at all. I was warned that few people would respond, but I persisted, and we had a very successful community *seder* with the *New Haggadah.*

My next goal was to adopt the *Shabbat Prayerbook.* This took longer, since it would be replacing a *siddur* which Rabbi Goldman had edited. His book contained supplementary readings which he had selected, but the text of the liturgy was unchanged. After many conferences, the decision was made, and our Shabbat book was introduced. The last bit of resistance came from the cantor, who was most cooperative but quite set in his ways. His music and the changes we had made in the text did not entirely coincide. In addition I urged the liturgical adoption of the *havarah,* the Israeli accent (which, by the way, was taught in the schools of the congregation).

Accommodations were made, and *mirabile dictu,* the roof did not cave in. Members did not resign, and the congregation remained intact! Heartened by these victories, I proceeded to agitate for the elimination of the Sunday school. We conducted a Hebrew school and a day school. But the Sunday school offered an easy way out for parents who did not take Jewish education seriously. Every rabbi and Jewish educator and many parents, recognized that one could do little in two or three hours a week. The Reform movement had taken over the idea of the Sunday school from the Protestants on the assumption that all young Jews needed to know about Judaism was its central message— that there is one God and that all humanity is one. The few rituals which Reform Jews observed at that point could easily be covered in this minimal program. But those who purported to take Judaism more seriously, those who were not prepared to dispense with the study of Hebrew or with traditional prayers, should certainly have faced up to the truth that Sunday school is nothing more than a futile gesture.

I could not believe that Rabbi Goldman would have objected because he had been an ardent exponent of maximal education. What surprised me was that he had not ever attempted to do away with it. This was a more serious problem. As friends pointed out to me, people attending the synagogue pay no attention to what they are saying. Many of them cannot read Hebrew, and if we put a totally different book before them, they would not know the difference. But the Sunday school?

This represented hundreds of families who would not be

associated with the congregation if the Sunday school were abolished, they said. I disagreed. I was sure that if we took the step, the few families we lost could easily be replaced. Those who demanded Sunday school could find schools elsewhere. The issue was debated at the Parent Teacher Organization, at the school board and finally the Board of Directors, and I won. As predicted, about fourteen families withdrew—no great loss to membership but a moral victory for education.

It is absurd to include the next issue among those already mentioned, but one has to know the heart of a sisterhood to understand that tampering with its traditional fashion show was tantamount to desecrating a holy object. I argued that fashion shows are immoral. They stimulate people's worst aspects—their vanity, their envy, and their inordinate preoccupation with themselves. In this matter I strongly doubted I would win, but after much persuasion, I was granted the opportunity to substitute for the fashion show a cultural afternoon (or as one of the ladies put it, a "so-called" cultural program). We invited Robert Starer, the composer-pianist, to present a program. While the Sisterhood women felt somewhat deprived, they too managed to survive the deprivation, and some even agreed that music is more appropriate for a synagogue than parading models.

Some of the problems I had anticipated did not materialize. I did not understand in advance that in a congregation of 5000 souls, only about five hundred are active and that the rabbi was not expected to worry about or get to know the other 4500. (This did not mean that he was not from time to time greeted downtown with the comment, "Don't you know me, rabbi? I belong to your synagogue!") As for pastoral work, I visited only those who participated in synagogue activities and those who were seriously ill. I simply had no time to hold the hands of indifferent members who were not so sick anyway. For this I was criticized, but I felt I had no alternative.

Despite the busy schedule, I managed to get involved in the business of the Chicago Board of Rabbis. Before I left I became vice president. The Zionist organization, which had been quiescent for some years, began to revive during my stay, and I was asked to serve on various committees. The local paper, the *Sentinel*, edited by a member of the congregation, carried guest editorials by me from time to time, when the editor-publisher was moved to invite me. He had wanted me to write a weekly column, but I begged off, and I am grateful that I did not undertake so arduous a task.

In New York I had been virtually anonymous. In Chicago I became a public figure. This was due, in part, to my position as head of a large congregation. In part, it was attributable to the size of the city of Chicago. The Jewish community of 300,000 was miniscule compared to the two and a half million Jews in New York. After a while one came to know the important Jews of the community, and this was not good for me. My family noted that I was beginning to sound pompous, giving voice to my opinions in a self-important way. After frequent radio and television appearances, I began to believe my own publicity.

Surely a rabbi derives satisfaction from this notion of his own importance. But I never ceased to experience a distinct loneliness and longing for the intellectual stimulation of New York. To my great disappointment my Conservative colleagues preferred to talk, when we got together, about the current rate of funeral fees rather than about the issues I was accustomed to explore with the members of the Editorial Board. I tried an experiment—organizing a Chicago Editorial Board which would be responsible for at least one issue of the *Reconstructionist* magazine per year. With much effort I brought together a few colleagues whom I respected and who would be willing to be identified with the *Reconstructionist*. The experiment was almost a total failure. One issue of the magazine was published in May 1955 (Vol. XXI, no. 5). There were no others.

Strangely, I found that I had more in common with my Reform colleagues than with the Conservatives. David Polish and Jacob Weinstein talked my language, while the Conservatives were much too interested in who was and who was not kosher, which caterers could be trusted, and purely local issues. I was used to exchanging ideas with men and women whose interests embraced worldwide problems.

I realized that I would have to fall back on my own resources and turned to some writing and editing. I put together a group of papers which appeared under the title *Judaism Under Freedom*, and I revised and edited a translation I had done some years earlier of Feierberg's *L'An* (*Whither?*). The latter was accepted by Abelard Shuman. I wrote a few articles, notable among them an essay which won first prize in a contest run by the London *Jewish Chronicle* on "Who Is a Jew?" I prepared a pamphlet on a *Reconstructionist Approach to Jewish Education.*

The life of the lonely student or writer was never my choice. I always enjoyed working with others. Rabbi Kaplan and my other associates were nowhere around. But my personal problem was less serious than the problem of the Reconstructionist movement. It was certainly not moving. If anything, it was gradually going to pieces. The magazine was edited for two years by David Sidorsky, a very capable intellectual (he was working on his doctorate at Columbia, where he later joined the faculty in philosophy); but David's ambition for the *Reconstructionist* was to make it into a sort of poor man's *Commentary.* He sought out distinguished contributors, which made for good reading. But the main purpose of the magazine, as I saw it, was to disseminate the basic principles of Reconstructionism.

For this reason and others, support for the Foundation declined. The Foundation Board had engaged Rabbi Herbert Parzen, who served for a time as executive director; Harry Rosen tried very hard to generate financial strength. Before then, Harold Weisberg, a brilliant rabbi and philosopher (later of Brandeis University) who died prematurely, struggled with the problem. And I, the savior from Chicago, was not doing so well myself. I had managed to interest about a dozen people from the congregation in contributing to the Foundation, but the total sum they gave was insignificant. Rabbi Eugene Kohn was getting older and thinking of retiring, and when David Sidorsky announced early in 1959 that he was withdrawing as editor so that he could devote himself entirely to teaching at Columbia, a crisis situation arose.

Rumors began to circulate that the Board of the Foundation was getting very discouraged. It seemed to be going down nowhere, and they were getting weary of holding up a sagging structure. While I was making some progress with the Anshe Emet project and was about to launch a campaign for the adoption of the High Holiday prayerbook, I was assailed by the dreadful prospect that I might be fighting for a cause the headquarters of which were about to disintegrate. If my home base disappeared, I would be left isolated. It became clear to me that the Foundation had to be saved.

I confided my fears to my brother-in-law, Sidney Musher. He agreed with me wholeheartedly, but he added that there was only one person who could save the Foundation, and that was I. Was I prepared to leave Chicago, return to New York, and take over the magazine? This meant that my five years at Anshe Emet might have to be sacrificed. It also meant that I had to be ready for a personal sacrifice in income. Judith had never been happy as a *rebbetzin*, but she had adjusted to living in Chicago. However, when the question arose: shall we move back? her response was immediate: Yes. I called Sidney to tell him that if the leaders would guarantee my salary (a much lower one) for a period of five years, I would accept the invitation.

Thus, in May 1959, I called my congregation's president and broke the news to him. I explained why I simply had to go back to save the home base. He was gracious enough to reply that he was sorry to see me go, but I am not so sure he meant it with his whole heart. I offered to return for the High Holidays, for I knew they could not replace me on such short notice.

My leaving provoked a full page editorial in the *Sentinel*; the editor said that Anshe Emet and Chicago had now gotten what they deserved. They never fully appreciated me, and I was right to walk out on them. I tried to explain to him (and it was true) that I was not leaving in pique, but what he wrote seemed to make a better story, and he never bothered to correct the impression he had made.

The congregation surprised me by presenting me with a brand new Pontiac and a check for $5000. This did not prevent some of my detractors from repeating again and again that I had been fired.

I was later informed that, shortly after my departure, the Sunday School was reinstated and the fashion show restored. But I had planted some seeds which later sprouted. One of my adult students at Anshe Emet, Leroy Shuster, organized a Reconstructionist congregation in Evanston.

14

Reconstructionism
Begins to Move

We returned to New York in July of 1959. My original plan was to take over the editorship of the magazine, which I believed would occupy only about half my time, and devote the rest to writing or perhaps to teaching, if I were invited to teach at some institution. The most exciting prospect in that respect was the Jewish Theological Seminary. While I had often fantasized about being on that distinguished faculty, I never really expected to be asked to join it, mainly because I was not what the Seminary regarded as an authentic Jewish scholar. Furthermore, Dr. Kaplan was still functioning as Professor of Philosophies of Religion, and it was unlikely that they would add another Reconstructionist to the staff.

Nevertheless, I was led to believe that the fantasy was not entirely a product of my imagination. As we were preparing to leave Chicago, indeed as the movers were taking the furniture out of the apartment, I received a call from Moshe Davis. He insisted that I come to see Dr. Finkelstein *immediately* upon my arrival in New York, saying it was with regard to my teaching at the Seminary. I replied that I would be there as soon as possible. In two days I announced my presence at Dr. Finkelstein's office, and I was ushered in with great cordiality.

It did not take long, however, before I realized that something was wrong. Dr. Finkelstein began to explain why all members of the faculty were required to observe the same ritual regimen which was expected of the students: Shabbat, *kashrut*, daily prayers with *tefillin*, and the like. Could the Seminary, he asked rhetorically, demand less of its teachers than of its pupils? I was flabbergasted. I had said nothing about the reason for my visit; he had said nothing about having invited me in. I was not applying for a position. I had come at the urgent summons of Moshe Davis, and he wanted without delay to disabuse me concerning my chances of an appointment.

Dr. Finkelstein rose to conclude the interview. He threw his arm around my shoulder and said, "I hope you don't mind my being frank with you. Anyhow, it will be a pleasure to have you back in New York. We missed you." I thanked him and went home. There I wrote a letter to Dr. Kaplan, who was vacationing, in which I poured out my heart. In effect, I said that the whole thing reminded me of a line from Groucho Marx. He had been suggested for membership in a golf club. When notified of this, he remarked that he would never join a club which would have him for a member. I wrote Dr. Kaplan that I would never accept an appointment to teach at JTS on the terms which I would apparently have to accept in order to gain the appointment. If the Seminary could be satisfied with me in the knowledge that I was observing the rules not out of conviction but in order to get a job, I could not respect the Seminary.

I wrote the letter in white heat. Fortunately I did not send it. I knew it would hurt Dr. Kaplan. But getting it out of my system made me feel better. It also confirmed, if further confirmation were necessary, that I could not have any further dealings with that institution. I turned my full attention to the Jewish Reconstructionist Foundation, hoping to make something of it other than what I found. The Board had asked me to assume the presidency—whatever that meant—and now I faced the challenge of saving the Foundation.

My first task was to diagnose the problem. What was wrong? Why had a series of executives given up, feeling frustrated? Harold Weisberg, Hannah Goldberg, Mordecai Kessler, Jacob Katzman, and others had, at one time or another, tried their hand at building up the Foundation; each had to admit defeat. Some, I fear, blamed themselves. Upon reflection, I came back to my old thesis; we did not know what we were asking them to do. The Jewish Reconstructionist Foundation offered members subscriptions to a magazine, access to the books published by the JRF at a discount, and the satisfaction of knowing that they were helping to spread the word. What activities should they engage in?

Get together and study, we told them. But while studying is a noble activity, it is generally not enough to keep the students constant. Study groups at best involve a small number of people. Membership in such groups does not afford people the sense of belonging to a large body; they have little experience of Jewish peoplehood, especially when they do not conduct services or observe Shabbat and holidays together. The congregation is the natural instrument for these experiences—and as yet Reconstructionism had not done anything to establish such institutions. A school of thought cannot survive so long as it lacks the cement of organization and institutionalization to hold it together. Reconstructionism would have to build institutions. I knew that Rabbi Kaplan opposed this philosophy, but I was determined to demonstrate to him and to the Board that there was no alternative. I had not returned to New York merely to carry on as before.

Before anything, I had to try to get the Foundation out of the red. The office was inefficient. Unnecessary expenses had to be pared down. This was a boring but important step to reduce the worrisome deficit. My next task was to acquaint myself thoroughly with the state of the magazine. David Sidorsky was kind enough to sit down with me and review the articles which had already come in and those which had been commissioned.

I hoped to change the character of the journal, to make it a more self-conscious voice of the Reconstructionist point of view without at the same time turning it into a house organ. Despite the lack of systematic promotion, the *Reconstructionist* had maintained its circulation of about 5000. This indicated that we had friends "out there" who were unusually loyal. The question was whether we could translate that loyalty into active support. Obviously, the readers were interested in what the magazine stood for. Surely they would want, sooner or later, to move from passive approval to some kind of organized effort. Hence I felt that what was needed at that point was to stimulate a greater awareness of the unique character of the journal and of the ideology which it articulated.

What seemed at first to be a wistful wish turned out to be a reality: the years of publishing, preaching, lecturing, and pamphleteering had indeed produced a small but earnest constituency which was not waiting for New York to make up its mind about the next steps.

Congregations were being started, without direct guidance by the Foundation, but clearly inspired by its published writings. Rabbi Sidney Jacobs, for example, persuaded a group in the new suburb of Skokie, Illinois, to form a Reconstructionist congregation. Rabbi Abraham Winokur did the same in Pacific Palisades, California. Louis Bunis, a respected businessman in Buffalo, N.Y., had asked me (before Chicago) to help him set up a congregation similar to the SAJ, which he had observed in New York. There was one difference, with respect to Buffalo, however; the Foundation did help, providing the services of Rabbi Harold Weisberg (who was serving as Executive Director of the Foundation), Rabbi Jack J. Cohen, and me. We spent many weekends assisting the group in getting started.

In the meantime, Rabbi William Greenfield, in consultation with one of his leading laypeople, decided to affiliate his congregation in Indianapolis with the Jewish Reconstructionist Foundation, to the extent of pledging a fixed amount each year to its support. Rabbi Milton Steinberg had been the rabbi there from 1928 to 1933, and in his memory they established a Steinberg Memorial Lecture, the fee going to the Foundation.

By 1955 the four congregations—the SAJ, Skokie, Indianapolis, and Buffalo—agreed to meet in Buffalo to establish a Reconstructionist Fellowship of Congregations. My only regret was that I could not participate, since my own congregation, Anshe Emet in Chicago, was still new to the whole idea of Reconstructionism. I had been there only one year, and while I was working diligently to move the congregation toward our philosophy, they were by no means ready for affiliation. Indeed, as I described above, they were still recovering from the misinformation that I had agreed to abandon my ties with Reconstructionism.

Obviously, no matter what Rabbi Kaplan believed about

the proper character of Reconstructionism, that it was and should remain a school of thought, events developed a logic of their own. People who had been convinced that the Reconstructionist approach was the correct one were not content for long to remain lone voices in Jewish institutions which were either indifferent or hostile to that approach. A few courageous souls were prepared to withdraw from the established organizations and strike out for themselves.

I was delighted to see this happen because I had always believed that the way to change the habits of thought and action of others was by example, not by writing books alone. The written word is read and variously interpreted by its readers. Soon the vocabulary is appropriated, often without the substance of its message. This had already happened to Reconstructionism. Even the Orthodox had come to use words like "civilization" and "dynamic"; the Conservatives had begun to refer to "evolving civilization." Reform had virtually monopolized the process of adapting to the forces of contemporary society.

To such a degree had this development occurred that frequently our friends were puzzled. They asked why there was any further need for Reconstructionism when the basic ideas had already been adopted by the three major groups. Some went so far as to contend that what was valid in Reconstructionism had been accepted, and what was false had been rejected.

Observers had already noted this phenomenon operating in other fields. Freud's writings, for example, had provided many with a vocabulary which they had denuded of its substance, and thus casual conversation is peppered with phrases like "defense mechanism" and "Oedipal complex." Adler had supplied "inferiority complex." Einstein gave them "all things are relative." And Darwin is the source of the glib remark, "survival of the fittest." Kaplan gave Jews convenient phrases too, but these phrases were lifted out of the context of his philosophy, distorting them and at the same time blocking the progress of Reconstructionism.

The creation of a Fellowship of Congregations was therefore something I warmly welcomed. For the first time, people would have an opportunity to see what happened when Dr. Kaplan's teachings were put into practice, illustrating what Reconstructionism was and not merely supplying other movements with legitimizing slogans.

By the fall of 1959, after I had taken over the presidency of the Foundation, a new mood had been introduced; the sentiment was now in favor of organizing new congregations and consolidating the union of those already in existence. A meeting was arranged, to be held in a newly established congregation in White Plains, N.Y., of which Rabbi Ludwig Nadelmann was the spiritual leader. He had been associate to Rabbi Jack Cohen at the SAJ, and his ties to Reconstructionism were strong. The 1959 meeting was the first bringing Reconstructionist congregations together after the initial one in 1955.

The White Plains meeting was a major turning point because Rabbi Kaplan himself was present there. He recognized what was happening. Still unreconciled to this development, he insisted that the Fellowship require of each of its constituents that it belong to one or another of the three major congregational organizations. In this way, he believed, the Reconstructionists (and he himself) could not be accused of introducing a divisive factor into Jewish life. The laypeople were as eager as the rabbis not to undertake any program which was contrary to Dr. Kaplan's wishes, so that provision was added. But it soon proved unrealistic. Some congregations could not afford dual affiliation. More important, they felt that the new Fellowship's legitimacy was weakened by the tacit admission that genuine affiliation was defined only by belonging to one or another of the three major movements.

At the heart of the issue lay Dr. Kaplan's continued association with the Seminary. As long as he remained a member of the faculty, he would never consent to launching a fourth movement. To him this spelled disloyalty. We tried to understand his position, though we insisted that he would have been entirely within his rights to start an independent association. As long as the Conservative movement refused to accept his plan, whereby Reconstructionists would comprise the third or "left" wing of a coalition, he had the right to strike out on his own.

At this point a new type of Jewish association began to appear on the American scene. It has since come to be known as the *havurah*, or "fellowship." The impulse to create small "fellowship" groups was stimulated in part by a series of articles which I published in the *Reconstructionist*. The first, by Prof. Jacob J. Petuchowski of Hebrew Union College, was entitled "Toward a Modern Brotherhood." In it Petuchowski proposed a revival of the old Pharasaic *ḥavurah* (Vol. 26, no. 16, Dec. 16, 1960). This was followed by an article by Professor Jacob Neusner entitled, "Five Principles of Fellowship." In this essay, Dr. Neusner advanced the idea of the *ḥavurah* in more specific terms (Vol. 27, no. 11, October 6, 1961).

Inspired by these two essays, I then wrote a series of three pieces in the magazine ("In Passing," Nov. 3, Dec. 1, and Dec. 29, 1961, Vol. 27, nos. 13, 15 and 17) in which I urged our readers to take action. I described the possibilities which the *ḥavurah* idea offered, explaining the reasons why large congregations are often unable to meet the needs for fellowship and intellectual stimulation. Shortly thereafter I brought these articles together, and the Reconstructionist Foundation published them as a pamphlet entitled "The Havurah Idea."

From that point on *ḥavurot* began to appear in ever larger numbers. Some of them blossomed out into full-fledged congregations; others, like the Whittier, Calif. *ḥavurah*, have maintained their character for many years.

Thus it came about that the group which met in 1959 as The Reconstructionist Fellowship of Congregations (modified the following year to read, "The Fellowship of Reconstructionist Congregations") changed its name in 1960 to "The Federation of Reconstructionist Congregations and Fellowships." For by then nine *ḥavurot* had joined the group, while the number of congregations grew to ten. Since the word "fellowship" had been used to describe both the organization and individual *ḥavurot*, it was decided to name the organization, "The Federation of Reconstructionist Congregations and Havurot." And the name has remained until the time of this writing. [For short, the acronym FRCH (pronounced *firch*) has been used.]

Thereafter conferences were held yearly. The Federation produced a *Guide to Jewish Ritual* in 1962, and the following year, meeting in Buffalo, the delegates voted upon a first draft of a *Guide to Education* which I had been asked to prepare. It was similar to the first draft of the ritual guide which had been adopted the previous year. Rabbi Emanuel Goldsmith, serving then as leader of a congregation in Halifax, presented the outline of a plan for the "Ben Torah," an innovation in adult education leading to an adult version of the bar/bat mitzvah ceremony for those who had never become bar or bat mitzvah when they were young. Enthusiasm ran high, for a genuine breakthrough had occurred at the Saturday evening session, one which set Reconstructionism definitely on a new path.

It was reported in the May 17, 1963 issue of the magazine (Vol. 29, no. 7):

> The Saturday evening session did not confine itself to the Ben Torah, however; the delegates devoted the occasion to a long heart-to-heart talk about the movement and its future. Dr. Kaplan, the rabbis and the laity participated wholeheartedly, and the decisions which grew out of that session will, it is hoped, do much to put the movement on the road to a greater impact and influence on Jewry in the United States and Canada.
>
> At this point it may be said that the group achieved a consensus with regard to the functioning of Reconstructionism as a "movement." As is well known, for many years Reconstructionism was regarded by its leaders, its followers, and its critics as a "school of thought." The activities were confined to the publication of the magazine and books. Since 1959, however, when Dr. Eisenstein took over the leadership of the Foundation, he has been pressing for the adoption of a more active type of program, including the establishment of agencies and institutions which would embody the ideas and concepts of the movement.
>
> As a result of the discussions held in Buffalo, it seems assured that those identified with Reconstructionism are now convinced that if the philosophy and program of Reconstructionism is to have a fair hearing by American Jewry, they will have to be translated into the kind of terms which will render them part of an actual *movement*.

This subtle double-talk was the best I could manage in order to convey to the public the implications of what happened without actually reporting what happened. Those of us who were present will long remember that Saturday evening. The delegates had been invited to a local congregational dance, but a dozen of us remained behind for a special, unscheduled meeting with Dr. Kaplan.

The meeting lasted until 11 o'clock. At the end we had extracted from him a promise that he would write to the Seminary requesting retirement.

He gave as his reason for remaining so long on the faculty (51 years at that point) despite their active efforts to neutralize his teachings, the fact that he needed to teach in order to remain productive. The stimulation of students was indispensable to his thinking. We replied by promising him students from among the rabbis in metropolitan New York, who, we were certain, would be delighted to sit at his feet. Some of the laypeople went so far as to offer to contribute to the Foundation the same funds which they were then donating to the Seminary. While he was reluctant to do anything which might divert funds away from the institution to which he owed so much, he was nevertheless impressed with the seriousness of the offer.

We sensed that we had turned a corner. If Dr. Kaplan really intended to terminate his official relationship with the Seminary, we could turn our attention to making Reconstructionism into a movement. But we had not anticipated some of the pitfalls. Prof. Finkelstein went to visit Dr. Kaplan and urged him to change his mind. The Seminary needed him. The fact is that Dr. Kaplan was really, by this time, strongly attracted to the idea of retiring, but he found it very difficult to admit to Finkelstein that this step was intended to enable the Reconstructionists to move forward. Instead he proposed in his letter of resignation that he wished to create a Research Institute for the purpose of "doing research in Reconstructionism." Just which he had in mind I did not know, and to this day I am not sure I understand what he planned for such an Institute. But it gave him what sounded like a credible reason for stepping down without causing a rift between himself and the institution.

217

At a meeting of the SAJ membership called especially for this purpose, he announced that he was prepared to retire from the Seminary if he were given assurances by the membership that they would help him to establish a Research Institute on Reconstructionism. The members were probably as puzzled as I was, but they voted for his retirement, and the letter to the Seminary was duly posted.

How did Dr. Kaplan intend to go about establishing the institute? One Shabbat morning after services, he asked several leading laypeople to meet with him briefly in the library of the SAJ. He said he wished to talk to them about something important. They always responded to any request of his. Once in the room, he explained to them that he wanted to create an institute for research, and if each one present would contribute one thousand dollars, it could be started. The men were taken by surprise; they asked questions, which were answered in a vague but reassuring way. I got the impression that, despite their promise to think it over, they would not provide the funds. The whole idea was too amorphous.

Indeed, the idea never materialized. But we who had promised to provide Dr. Kaplan with students went ahead with a plan to invite local rabbis to a series of sessions at which Dr. Kaplan would lecture on some of his new ideas. The response was fairly good; an average of about 15–18 rabbis came more or less regularly. But Dr. Kaplan was not sure just what he intended to do with these students, and from time to time he asked me to take over the group.

The Seminary announced that Dr. Kaplan, having reached the age of 83, had been retired and would now be Emeritus. This sounded sensible enough. After all, who goes on teaching at that age? His reason for retiring was, of course, never mentioned. Virtually no one outside the family circle of Reconstructionists knew that he had yielded to pressures from us, pressures which we had applied for the precise reason that we wanted his sanction to go ahead and make something institutionally out of Reconstructionism.

Once the umbilical cord had been broken, there was no longer any need for Dr. Kaplan to resist the idea of a new rabbinical school. The leadership of Reconstructionism, until that time, had come from Conservative and Reform rabbis who had openly declared themselves to be Reconstructionists. But if a movement was to be launched in earnest, provision would have to be made to develop leaders who were not defectors from other groups. The growth of the Fellowship (which was now renamed Federation of Reconstructionist Congregations and Fellowships *[Havurot]*, almost a spontaneous growth, created the need for leadership. Groups were naturally reluctant to form as Reconstructionist groups—either *havurot* or congregations—if their members could not be assured that rabbis would be available. Hence the idea of a training school began to take shape.

For a while I became active in a rabbinical school organized by Rabbi Louis I. Newman and a small group of his colleagues. It was called the *Academy for Higher Jewish Learning*, and had been organized by alumni of the Jewish Institute of Religion after the JIR had been absorbed by Hebrew Union College. They felt that the purpose for which Rabbi Stephen S. Wise had established the JIR had been subverted. It had become an integral part of the Reform movement, while Wise had wanted to make of it a nondenominational institution.

When Rabbi Felix Levy of Chicago retired and came to New York to live, he was persuaded to assume the presidency of the Academy. Although himself a leading Reform rabbi and former president of the Central Conference of American Rabbis, he sympathized with the aims of the Academy and accepted the post. But he would not make his final decision until he had persuaded Rabbi Newman and me to teach at the school. Since I always enjoyed teaching, and had had little opportunity (except for one semester at JTS) to teach rabbinical students, I agreed.

The more I learned about the Academy, however, the less enthusiastic I became about it. There was a small and ineffectual board of trustees; the students were a mixed group of varying talents and backgrounds; there was no library, and (a minor point?) the school had nowhere to meet. In a moment of impulsive generosity, I offered the one spare room available in the SAJ building. When we discovered that the fire laws were being violated, the classes were moved to the building of Temple Rodeph Sholom (Rabbi Newman's congregation).

One graduation exercise was held at the SAJ; thereafter I

begged off, claiming that I could no longer afford the time which the Academy was costing me. Soon thereafter, Dr. Levy's health worsened, and he had to step down. It seemed that the Academy would soon have to close down. At that point I was asked whether the Reconstructionist Foundation might be interested in taking it over. Much as I wanted Reconstructionism to conduct a rabbinical school, I could not bring the offer to the attention of my board. We certainly did not need the burden of revitalizing a school whose assets were virtually nonexistent. If we were to begin a rabbinical training program, we would want to start from scratch.

Dr. Kaplan, having been convinced that a new school was needed, decided to take the bull by the horns and raise one million dollars for that purpose. Without giving the matter too much thought, he seized on the sum of one million and proceeded to call upon an individual to ask him for the money. At his request I went with him to the home of a wealthy man who was deeply involved with the Jewish Theological Seminary. This should not have been an obstacle, thought Dr. Kaplan; a man of such wealth could easily afford to support two institutions.

The evening was a disaster. When we arrived we found the gentleman entertaining an old schoolmate, a vulgar and ignorant man of even greater wealth. Dr. Kaplan, after a few innocuous comments about the weather, said he would like to discuss a very important matter with the host. He implied that he would prefer a private conversation. But the host insisted that his guest remain. After all, they were old friends, and they had no secrets from one another. Dr. Kaplan had no alternative but to plunge directly into his prepared remarks. He came out boldly with his proposal for the establishment of a new rabbinical school, one which would put less emphasis on the glories of the past and stress more the problems of the present and the future. For one million dollars such a school could be set up.

The host, loyal to the Seminary, naturally asked what was wrong with the JTS. Dr. Kaplan began somewhat gingerly, but he soon warmed to his subject, and before long he was pouring out his heart, listing his accumulated grievances. The host sprang to the defense of the institution which he was so generously supporting. The guest meantime added his uninvited remarks, expounding on the futility of organized religion. Indeed, he added at some length, he didn't see why all that money had to go to academic studies. He himself had never graduated from college, and look where he had managed to get without such an irrelevant education.

The wife of the host joined the melee. She was better acquainted with some of the ancillary activities of the Seminary, such as the Jewish Museum, and defended that institution with warmth. By this time Dr. Kaplan had cast prudence overboard. The result was anger, frustration, and a deep pessimism regarding the possibility of setting up a new school. "You see," he told me on the way back, "it is impossible to get people to understand the need for still another institution. You saw their reactions. They are certainly typical. What would be the use of approaching others?"

I had come to quite another conclusion—that this was precisely how not to generate support for a rabbinical school. One did not invade someone's home without adequate preparation and ask for a million dollars. This was the ultimate in fantasy. Only in poor fiction does this kind of strategy work. If we truly meant to go about raising funds, first we would have to work with our tried and true friends, the men and women who had stuck with us throughout the years, whose loyalty was primarily to Reconstructionism and not to other movements or institutions. Just who they were I did not know at this moment, but I was certain that the decision to go ahead would have to be made collectively, by the small but loyal forces which comprised the Federation of Congregations.

The fact that Dr. Kaplan had been turned down proved nothing about the feasibility of our dream. Why then did Dr. Kaplan immediately lose heart? Why was he so quick to come to the conclusion that no one would support the establishment of a college? Did he believe there was no interest in launching a movement (rather than a school of thought)? I believed then, and I am still inclined to believe, that Dr. Kaplan was not convinced that we were on the right track. He still had faith that in the course of time we Reconstructionists could influence the existing groups to change their ways. Moving out was a risky affair. We might fail, and that would be worse than not being altogether effective as a school of thought.

It occurred to me that in this controversy, he was taking the position classically represented by the anti-Zionists, while I was on the Zionist side. That is, he, like the Bundists and the early reformers, urged that we stay where we were and fight it out, changing the society which was causing us trouble rather than leaving and setting up house for ourselves elsewhere. The Zionists, on the other hand, had lost faith in the possibility of significantly revising the system and urged the establishment of a new home in a new place under a new program. I was therefore puzzled that Dr. Kaplan, the Zionist, was unprepared for the *halutziut* which would be required in transforming Reconstructionism into an independent movement. (On the other hand, perhaps I too would have been reluctant if I had been 83 years old, instead of 25 years younger.)

In the fall of 1964 I suffered a heart attack, and for several months thereafter I was not sure that I could go on or that I wanted to. I am told that I fell into a depression—not serious enough to disable me but enough to lead me to considering early retirement. The latter alternative was unrealistic because financially neither the Foundation nor I was able to provide adequate funds for such a program.

At this point my spirits were lifted by a visit to my office by Sam Blumenthal, a leading member of a group which had formed in the Great Neck area of Long Island. He invited me to become associated with that small *havurah*, for it had been struggling to make headway. The people who comprised the group were all convinced Reconstructionists, and they were eager to develop a vigorous institution on the North Shore, but they had no one to lead them properly. They had been depending on various rabbis who could find the time to spend Shabbat with them, but the lack of continuity had been deleterious. They were not progressing.

I did not think that I could take the offer seriously, having so many other responsibilities. But apparently they were prepared to have me come out for the Holidays and for every other Shabbat to conduct services, adult classes, and maybe lead a teenage group. This program struck me as moderate; in addition, I wanted to develop a burgeoning congregation which would add to the strength of the movement, and (not to be ignored entirely) the additional income would be welcome.

Judith and I went out to meet the group. From the beginning we were strongly attracted to them. They were bright, interested, some of them fairly well educated in Judaism, and imbued with a missionary spirit. They sincerely wanted to share their pleasure in being Reconstructionist-minded Jews with others who, they believed, were in similar circumstances. Many of them had belonged to other congregations and had been disappointed or disillusioned; they were certain that many families found themselves in the same stage of spiritual growth.

The *shiddukh* (match) was made; and for the following ten years we served as their bi-weekly rabbinical leaders. Judith took over the congregational singing, and even gave a series of lectures on Jewish music over a period of Friday nights. They provided the chorus for the first performance of her *The Binding of Isaac*, a liturgical drama. I experimented with Friday evening discussions, which were both stimulating and fun. The group grew from some 25 to 125 in the years that followed our first season. All in all, the congregation became one of the pillars of the movement—when it became a genuine movement. Its members contributed generously, and several of the people took on positions of leadership in the college which emerged, finally, in 1968.

Only my second heart attack in 1977 ended my active relationship with the Reconstructionist Synagogue of the North Shore.

15

The Reconstructionist
Rabbinical College

The convention of the Federation in 1967 took place in Montreal. The choice of that city was a happy one: first, Expo '67 was scheduled to open, and that would bring many people. Second, our friend and colleague, Lavy Becker, and his congregation were about to celebrate the bar mitzvah of the synagogue and the dedication of their new building. If the reader can still remember the early pages of this chronicle, you will recall that Lavy had become my friend as I was about to enter the Seminary. He had been a loyal and loving companion throughout the years, and he had organized a Reconstructionist congregation in Montreal by the simple device of advertising in the local paper that such a congregation was about to be created and asking all interested parties to appear at a certain hotel one evening.

The response was immediate and very encouraging, for Lavy had by this time become a distinguished member of the Montreal Jewish community, and any project which he led was bound to evoke enthusiasm. By 1967 the synagogue was well established. The convention was not only successful. It was actually memorable, because it was then and there that the delegates voted their support for the establishment of a rabbinical school under the auspices of the Reconstructionist Foundation.

I record the bottom line first, but no one should infer that the sessions were smooth, calm, or without the raising of voices.

The Six Day War was about to break out, but we strove mightily to keep our attention fixed on our immediate business, the future of the movement. Several delegates spoke vehemently about the need for a school for the training of our own leaders. At one point Dr. Kaplan rose and delivered an impassioned speech, saying, in effect, that enough time had passed and that action was called for. He urged the delegates to pass a resolution calling for the immediate establishment of a rabbinical school. All that was needed was one million dollars. Everything else was already in hand.

I was guilty, at that moment, of doing something I had vowed I would always avoid. I rose publicly to disagree with my teacher and to ridicule his simplistic proposal. Once again he had plunged into a fundraising effort without the slightest preparation and with no knowledge of how these things are done, inevitably inviting a slap for his naive strategy or, as in this case, producing an irresponsible motion. It was moved, seconded, and passed, that the Federation go on record in favor of raising one million dollars for the purpose of setting up a rabbinical school!

The net effect was to put me in the position of appearing dilatory about implementing the idea of a college and reluctant to push the movement forward in that direction. And of all things, it made Dr. Kaplan seem the proponent of action, as though I had not for years been vainly striving to make of Reconstructionism a fourth movement. I nearly had another heart attack. I spoke with too much anger, to my own hurt. I challenged Dr. Kaplan to read again the minutes of the meetings which recorded my many efforts to get the school going in his absence (he had been away to Israel). Dr. Kaplan shouted back that he did not see the minutes because they had not been sent to him. Why did we keep him in the dark? I shouted back, repeating that the minutes were scrupulously forwarded to him, but he never took the trouble to read them . . . and so on.

When we returned to New York, and the delegates had returned to their respective cities, I was left with the burden of doing something about that resolution. I began to search for an associate to replace Emanuel Goldsmith, who left the Reconstructionist Foundation to teach at Brandeis. Rabbi Arthur Gilbert, a member of our Editorial Board and a long-time avowed Reconstructionist, had just been dropped from the Anti-Defamation League and was looking for a position. He asked me whether I knew of an opening. I immediately suggested he come to see me. I could not offer him his accustomed salary, but he was willing to come aboard with the understanding that he be free to teach at Marymount College to supplement his income.

He came to my summer house in Hunter that summer to discuss with me his duties at the Foundation. I was happy to be able to tell him about our plans for a rabbinical school. This made the job much more palatable, for the rest was not as interesting as the work he had been doing with the ADL and the National Conference of Christians and Jews.

That fall we laid plans for launching the school. By January 1968, we had persuaded one of our Board members, Abraham Goodman, to hold a meeting in his home, to which we would invite as many as we could muster of old and new friends of the *Reconstructionist.* Among our new friends were members of the North Shore Reconstructionist congregation.

On a very snowy Sunday afternoon, the group came together. We had asked Rabbi Judah Cahn to supplement Dr. Kaplan and me as speakers. The idea of the college was dramatically presented. We made it clear that we were at a crossroads. If we did not move ahead with vigor, Reconstructionism would remain a set of fine ideas, written about in many books which would eventually gather dust on shelves. With the college, we would be a full-fledged factor in American-Jewish life.

Apparently, the laypeople were more eager to act than we had hoped. From that group of about thirty men and women we received pledges amounting to $140,000. By the time the afternoon was over, we were more elated about the prospects for the future than at any previous time. We thought that with approximately fifty thousand dollars a year for three years, we could venture forth. As it transpired, that amount of money would by no means be adequate, but fortunately we did not know that at the time. Otherwise we might not have started.

The Reconstructionist Rabbinical College

I had been working for some time on the basic concept of a curriculum for a Reconstructionist college. If Judaism was to be understood as an evolving religious civilization, it would be necessary for the curriculum to reflect that idea. In other words, in each of five years, the students would recapitulate, as it were, the total experience of the Jewish people during one epoch in Jewish history, devoting one year each to the biblical period, to the rabbinic, medieval, modern, and contemporary periods. Arthur and I spent several exciting evenings working out some of the implications of this approach.

The more immediate problem was where this new school would be located. The determining factor would be the presence of a university with a strong department of religion. I was intent upon requiring that our students be as sophisticated about religions in general as about Judaism in particular. With congregations now frequented by well educated men and women, rabbis would have to know the secular world as well as they knew the Jewish world. Where could one find such a university?

My first choice was Brandeis. Already in the spring of 1967, I had attended the annual meeting of what had originally been called the Jewish Philosophical Society; it grew into the Association for Jewish Studies. While at Brandeis, where the sessions were held, I asked my friend Dr. Harold Weisberg whether he would arrange an appointment for me with Dr. Sachar. I wanted to present to him the basic idea of a school for the training of rabbis which would be adjacent to a university with a department of religion. I was curious to learn whether he approved of the idea, and whether he could accommodate such a school near the campus of Brandeis.

My appointment in Dr. Sachar's office, scheduled for ten minutes, developed into a visit of an hour. He seemed fascinated by the project. But as he pointed out, Brandeis had no department of religion. I told him I was shocked to find that religion was overlooked at a university which purported to be a center of liberal arts education. Our conversation happened to coincide with the observance by Harvard of the 150th anniversary of its Divinity School. Sachar often jokingly (but quite seriously) compared Brandeis to Harvard; in religion, I said, Brandeis should not be outdone. Religion is a serious discipline.

He agreed, and he promised to look into the entire plan. He would consult with his faculty and board and be in touch with me. I do not know at this writing—nor am I likely to learn hereafter—whether Dr. Sachar was serious about adding a department of religion, but he did get in touch with Abraham Goodman, inviting him to have breakfast in New York to discuss my visit. Abe Goodman quite properly urged that I be included in the invitation, and the three of us met at the Waldorf in New York one morning.

Dr. Sachar praised my idea. He thought that the combination of a Reconstructionist school for rabbis and a department of religion at Brandeis would be original and constructive. He then proposed to Goodman that he—Goodman—donate five million dollars to Brandeis for such a project. He—Sachar—promised to raise another ten million. With fifteen million dollars the project could be started. It would require a building, a library, faculty, scholarships, and the like. Mr. Goodman said he was glad to know that the idea was a good one, but he did not have that kind of money, and he would not give that much to Brandeis.

In a word, Dr. Sachar priced the project out of possible attainment. We were accustomed to his grandiose vision, and without it Brandeis could never have become what it is. But was he serious? Or did he deliberately make such a school impossible of achievement in order to avoid being charged with getting into the "religion business"? After all, most of his supporters were associated either with HUC or JTS. Was he simply staying out of trouble?

By the summer, when Rabbi Gilbert had joined our staff and I had recounted to him my experiences with Dr. Sachar, he put his mind to the problem of locating the college (when and if it really came into being) in the proper city. He came up with the suggestion that Temple University might be the best place. The university had just become a state-supported institution, and to compensate it for the removal of the theological seminary which had played a prominent role, a substantial budget had been set aside for a department of religion under the leadership of Professor Bernard Phillips. Arthur proposed that we meet with Phillips.

The three of us had lunch together at Steinberg's, the once

famous dairy restaurant on Broadway. Phillips told us he had brought together a distinguished faculty, consisting of scholars in the major religions of the world. He had insisted that a Moslem should teach Islam, a Jew teach Judaism, a Chinese teach Chinese philosophy. This, he felt, was the only authentic way to convey the true spirit and meaning of any religion. Four people were already teaching Judaism: Robert Gordis, Jacob Agus, Gerald Glitstein, and Maurice Friedman.

Phillips was enthusiastic about the idea. While Temple could not enter into official relations with us, the authorities would encourage the project in a variety of ways. For instance, students would not be required to take a full course load. They could spread their masters or doctoral program over a longer period, inasmuch as they would be engaged in their rabbinical studies at the same time. He suggested that Hebrew might be accepted as one of the required languages, provided it was an integral part of a dissertation. He went so far as to propose that we come to Philadelphia and meet with Dr. Anderson, president of the university. The visit was arranged. Dr. Anderson was most cordial and promised to help in any way that he could. He subsequently wrote a letter to that effect.

If indeed Temple was our choice, we would have to find a building nearby to house the school. Students should not have to spend too much time going from one program to another. Rabbi Gilbert, himself a former Philadelphian, was very helpful in this matter too. He found an agent who offered us a building on Broad and Dauphin, once a luxurious private home, then a funeral parlor which, in 1968, was defunct. It was a depressing looking structure, but solidly built.

Events moved quickly. A committee of our supporters visited Philadelphia, examined the building, accepted the price of $25,000, and engaged the services of Beryl Price, a popular architect in Philadelphia who had worked with many other Jewish organizations. Just at that time Charles Tishman, a member of the SAJ, died and left to the Foundation the sum of $25,000. It came precisely when we needed it, for with less than fifty thousand dollars to work with the first year, we would have been in financial straits immediately if we had had to draw on that fund for the purchase and renovation of a building.

How to furnish the school? A dear friend and generous supporter, Reuben Isaacson, came forward with a pledge of $1500 to be used to provide the basic tables, chairs, files, and shelves so that we could begin to operate.

Did we not need to obtain official recognition from the government of Pennsylvania? If we hoped to achieve status in the eyes of the world, we would require at least a temporary charter. Isaacson and I traveled to Harrisburg, consulted with the education department, and came away with the necessary information. We could indeed proceed on a temporary charter, but for final approval we would need an endowment of $500,000, an adequate library, a building, a board, a full faculty, an acceptable curriculum—all that went into the making of a full-fledged institution. A letter from Dr. John Pettinger confirmed our understanding. He even praised the basic concept on which the school was to be established, stressing the originality of the notion of combining secular and rabbinic curricula.

Would we attract students? We had no way of knowing, but we printed a large poster, and it went to all the Hillel Foundations, announcing the formation of a new school for the training of rabbis to be opened in the fall of 1968. It is important to recall that this was the season of discontent for virtually all students. The Vietnam War was raging, and the protests against it were raging as well. The Woodstock generation was operating in full force. We were not surprised, therefore, to find that those who inquired about the school were typical of their time. Some of them were brilliant; some even possessed rich Jewish backgrounds. But they were radical: they questioned all inherited values and concepts.

While that first entering class knew little about Reconstructionism, they presumed that we were unconventional, innovative, and therefore about to establish an institution unlike any that had ever existed. To be more precise, they felt that it should function like a commune—no structured curriculum, no requirements, no examinations. All would be students, but all would also be instructors. Just how they visualized the program was not quite clear, certainly not to me. Thirteen students entered in the fall of 1968; most of them eventually dropped out. Only two graduated, one after five years, the other after six. But the members of that first class were not just irresponsible people. They were confused. They cherished lofty if unrealistic visions of what society should be like and how Judaism should function. Rabbi Gilbert was more understanding of them than I, possibly because he was nearer to their age.

But I am grateful that I did not yield altogether to the spirit of the 60's. I insisted that while we represented a new approach to rabbinical education, we were not about to become a "hippie" institution. Faculty was faculty; students were students. A curriculum would be followed. If examinations were abolished, written evaluations would take their place. I was not opposed to having students participate in discussions which led to decisions, but the final decisions had to be made by the administration. I tried to make clear to the students that they might enter, study, and leave, but that responsibility for the institution remained in the hands of its permanent staff.

The term "staff" seems to connote a large body of people. Actually, only a very few were involved. Rabbi Kaplan came once a week to lecture, and I offered an introduction to Reconstructionism. Rabbi Gilbert presided over a seminar in the contemporary Jewish community, and the core program for the first year, which centered on the biblical period of Jewish civilization, was in the hands of Rabbi Ivan Caine, a rabbi and scholar recommended to us by Professor Moshe Greenberg, at that time of the University of Pennsylvania.

I was pleased and somewhat surprised to find that Rabbi Caine was willing to identify himself with our school. Considering the precarious nature of our finances and the tentative character of the institution as a whole, considering the risk which any scholar took in associating himself with a new and untried institution, Rabbi Caine displayed a faith in us which we deeply appreciated. As of this writing, he remains the oldest member of the faculty, from the point of view of service.

The name of this school was a matter of some discussion. While I sought to get Rabbi Kaplan to agree that we should name it for him, he vigorously refused and made me promise that neither during nor after his lifetime would we call the instituion by his name. He did, however, permit us to name the library the Mordecai M. Kaplan Library. This was entirely appropriate, since he donated his large personal library to the school, and it formed the nucleus of the collection, which has since grown. The late Rabbi Max Schenk also turned over his entire personal library to us.

The name finally chosen was the Reconstructionist Rabbinical College, and so it is called. I was asked by the Board of the Foundation to serve as president. Rabbi Gilbert was chosen to be dean, a post he held until his untimely death a few years later.

A dedication of the College took place on the campus of Temple University during Sukkot of 1968 (5728). Representatives of Temple University and the Board of Rabbis of Greater Philadelphia brought greetings, and a major address was given by Rabbi Kaplan. A procession with lulav and etrog marched up Broad Street later to the building still in the process of being renovated, and the *mezuzah* was affixed on the door by Rabbi Kaplan.

This was, for me, a moment of fulfillment and of challenge. I had hoped since 1940 that some day we might emerge as a movement on the American Jewish scene. This hope was now realized, but in the years that would follow, we would be tested. We would have to establish that this historic step was indeed a step forward, and that it would be followed by other steps indicating that we had set out on a path which the Jewish community would consider a blessing.

Some old-time devotees of Rabbi Kaplan saw in the opening of the College a betrayal of all he had stood for and much that he had written about. They had loved and admired their former teacher even though they had not been able to accept all his views, but their reverence for him was strengthened by his frequent declarations that he did not come to add a fourth denomination to those already on the scene. They saw in his reluctance to encourage Reconstructionists to form a movement a dedication to Jewish unity. They could not get themselves to believe that he had willingly given his consent to this turn of events. He was obviously unduly influenced by Ira Eisenstein.

Perhaps they were right. Perhaps Rabbi Kaplan simply could not any longer resist the pressures of his disciples and the demands of the laypeople who were looking for a new and different option. Perhaps he would have preferred to let Reconstructionism continue as before. If so, he must be praised for the strong words he used thereafter in public addresses and in print, urging his followers to support the new college and the movement which it helped to rejuvenate.

For rejuvenation was the immediate consequence of the establishment of the College. More progress was made in the first few years after its creation than in decades prior to it. New congregations and *havurot* were organized. New support was forthcoming. And whereas in the discouraging days of the 40's and 50's, Reconstructionism was synonymous with Mordecai Kaplan, Ira Eisenstein, Eugene Kohn, and Milton Steinberg, in the 70's it denoted a College, a Federation of Congregations and Havurot, a Reconstructionist Rabbinical Association, a Women's Organization, and a Foundation which functioned as their parent body and sponsor. After 1968, the literature on contemporary Jewry frequently mentioned *four* major groups in the religious community.

I do not know what the next generation of Reconstructionists will do to reconstruct Reconstructionism. There are already some indications that changes are in the offing: liturgy needs to be thought through carefully with a view toward re-editing the major prayerbooks; attitudes toward ritual are being revised; a new consensus regarding *halakhah* will be on the agenda; a rethinking of theology and the God-idea is being suggested.

But whatever new directions the new generation will take, I hope that we shall remain faithful to the basic principles which form the basis of the Reconstructionist conception of Judaism as an evolving religious civilization.

16

Valedictory

I have been very fortunate that my life since my adolescent years has moved in a single direction. I have been spared the false starts and frequent changes of direction which have been the lot of others. Early on I chose to be a Jew, a committed Jew, dedicated to making Judaism a source of moral and spiritual strength. Having met Mordecai Kaplan at a time when I was seeking precisely the guidance and inspiration which he provided, I was fortunate enough to seize the opportunity to link my life with his and with his daughter's.

Our life together has been a rare collaboration. Her interest in music and musicology has meshed with my own love of music. We play duets at the piano, and while this sometimes (as expected) leads to disagreements about whose fault it is that Mozart or Shubert is not coming out the way it should, on the whole our playing has been a source of wholesome recreation and an escape from the petty, or not so petty, worries of the day.

Our common involvement in Judaism has been the major force molding our lives. The fact that Mordecai Kaplan was her father and my superior and then colleague has provided a focus for our activities which has yielded many creative experiences. Judith did not have to be the conventional rabbi's wife while I served the SAJ; her mother Lena was an ideal *rebbetzin*. But this did not mean that Judith was detached from the Society. For some years when money was tight, she taught at the school. Together we produced five cantatas, which have had phenomenal success. Judith provided the music for the *New Haggadah*; she sang in the synagogue choir. In many other ways she was a willing and active partner in all our Jewish undertakings.

This was a blessing but sometimes a problem because she was her father's daughter, and when I was irritated by him or annoyed by his attitude toward the Seminary, she was caught between her husband and her father. One of the reasons she welcomed the invitation to move out to Chicago despite her dislike for living in a "second city" was that we could both get out from under Mordecai Kaplan's dominating presence. Yet, like me, she was proud, and she considered herself privileged to be his daughter. Such ambivalence, I am sure, is not uncommon.

As a preacher's kid, a p.k., she recognized the difficulties of her position as she was growing up, and she was determined to spare our daughters some of the ordeal which she experienced. This meant that we tried very hard to arrange for them to be like other children their age, not necessarily conforming completely, certainly not to the undesirable habits and values of their peers; but surely we did not impose standards upon our girls just because they were appropriate for a rabbi's children. We have known rabbis who believed that their little sons and daughters must be models for other children. This could only lead to hostility to Judaism in general and religion in particular, not to speak of the misery which is the lot of children who bear the burden of being paradigms.

The ones who most enjoyed my being a rabbi were my parents. Fortunately for them, they lived to see me selected for the post at the SAJ, which by their standards included "the best people," and they were greatly excited by the invitation to go to Chicago. For my mother, who, I am sure, was appalled at the prospect that her boy (!) would be almost one thousand miles away, the thought that I was to be the rabbi of a very large, prestigious congregation was enough to compensate for the imminent separation.

She had reacted very differently when our engagement was announced. It catapulted her into one of her worst migraines. The separation then was, of course, not geographical. She had wanted me to get married, she said, but (like Saint Augustine) not yet. She dreaded the change in me that marriage would effect. And indeed I changed. The liberation which my impending marriage represented to me produced a revolution, first and most important, in my relation to my mother. Her migraine was prophetic; I became a quite different human being, one which she did not recognize. I no longer acted like her loving son; I became cold, perhaps colder than I should have been. But the radical change was necessary if I was to make a clean break.

By the time we were preparing to move to Chicago twenty years later, a *modus vivendi* had been worked out, an *entente cordiale*—or whatever the English equivalent is. While in Chicago, we gave them both all the *nachas* (pleasure) they could have wished for. They were welcomed at the Covenant Club, the next-to-the-most-fancy Jewish club in town, of which we were honorary members, and of course everywhere they went, they were introduced as the "proud parents" of our rabbi.

We thought, when we returned to New York, that they would be overjoyed, but we were wrong. Nothing, not even our physical presence (and our children's) could make up for the loss of this lucrative and prominent position. Being the editor of a small and virtually unknown magazine, the *Reconstructionist*, was definitely a comedown. They never did fully understand why I preferred the smaller salary, the precarious financial condition of the Reconstructionist Foundation, and the comparative financial anonymity of my official post to the glamorous pulpit of Anshe Emet in Chicago. Having almost all of my life nurtured the hope of becoming a rabbi, I should surely have reveled in the climactic achievement which this large congregation symbolized. No wonder they were puzzled by my ready acceptance of the chance to return to New York, to take over the magazine.

The fact is that I never did fully enjoy being the rabbi of a congregation. I was reconciled to the post at the SAJ because it gave me the opportunity to be close to Mordecai Kaplan. As I mentioned earlier, the Roxbury synagogue was larger and better paying, and in it I would have been the sole leader. But it did not appeal to me as much as the prospect of thinking alongside a major thinker, writing, editing, and addressing a larger audience than the one (and the same one) sitting before me week after week.

I did not relish visiting hospitals, officiating at funerals and weddings, or attending bar mitzvah parties, and the pressures of the weekly sermon were always oppressive. I would begin to worry on Monday about my talk the following Shabbat; it would hang over me all week. The shadow of the High Holidays began to shut out the sun beginning in July.

Despite the problems, I was content to be a rabbi at the SAJ. It was different, as my colleagues repeatedly told me. It was not typical, and for that I was indeed grateful. I did not realize how right they were until we moved to Chicago. *This* was the typical large congregation. Here they insisted that I wear a clerical robe, the uniform I had never worn at the SAJ, thanks to Rabbi Kaplan who eschewed the priestly garb for the civilian suit. Chicago Jews, at least those we came to know on the North Side, were unlike the community we had known in New York. They rarely went to the theater. They attended the opera, when they did, because it was fashionable. They did not read. Their major concerns were interior decoration, trips to Florida or Las Vegas, clothes, television sets (as many as possible), and the "temple." I suppose we should have been grateful for their interest in their local synagogue, but this annoyed me because it was unrelated to what the synagogue stood for.

The congregation was the focal point of their narrow lives. It provided them with their gossip. Fundraising, at which they were very competent, occupied a major part of their consciousness. Study, an intelligent grasp of Jewish religious concepts, discussion of vital issues facing the Jewish people—these were the concerns of a very small nucleus. For most, the synagogue offered a social life. This is what my colleagues meant when they said that the SAJ was not typical.

In sum, standard congregational life in the United States does not, cannot, attract the literate Jews, the academicians, or other professionals, who hunger for intellectual stimulation— except for those Orthodox synagogues which offer strict tradition for those who have embraced the new Orthodoxy. This type of highly educated, scientifically trained, deeply pious Jew did not exist in my childhood or my early adulthood. It is a new phenomenon, the product, perhaps, of the Holocaust experience and the establishment of the State of Israel. These young Orthodox Jews are proud, disciplined and enthusiastic. They take their Judaism seriously, and though one may disagree (as I do) with their theology, the rigidity of their observance, and their attitude toward those who do not share their views, one must concede that they command respect.

This does not mean that they are unaffected by the bourgeois values which I found predominant in my Chicago constituents. They like their clothes, vacations, homes, and televisions as much as anyone else. But in their scale of values, Torah and *mitzvot* (observances) rank very high, and being a rabbi in one of their congregations could conceivably be rewarding, provided, of course, that one shared their conception of Judaism.

But being a rabbi in any kind of congregation means living a life almost totally devoted to the duties of the office. For most people, synagogue activity is a leisure-time occupation; they spend their days at their chosen work. The evenings are set aside for synagogue programs. This means that rabbis are occupied virtually every evening of the week. They are rarely at home with their families. And on Shabbat and holidays they are twice as busy. The popular joke has it that rabbis preach the joys of family life but can never enjoy them because they are always busy preaching the joys of family life.

This kind of schedule leaves no room for friendships which are not by-products of synagogue life. I cannot think of a single friend I made at college with whom I am in touch. And those men and women whom we have met over the years through other associations have drifted away. Judith believes that this need not have happened, that I have little patience for those who do not share my interests. Perhaps that is so, but the broad truth remains that the rabbi's social life narrows down to those who are directly concerned with Jewish affairs.

This accounts for the character of this memoir. In the early chapters, the reader may be able to detect the person behind the events; as the book progresses, the person recedes into the background. The growth of the Reconstructionist movement is the major theme, and at times the only one. But, of course, my life went on. We spent summers at our little cottage in Hunter, N.Y.; our children grew. They went through the usual, sometimes painful, stages of growing up. They went to college. We took trips (to Israel, to England, and the continent). We worried about money. We cheered for Adlai Stevenson and grieved at his defeats.

In a word, the years were occupied with the daily routines. I cannot believe that anyone would be interested in knowing, blow by blow, just how we spent our time. The central theme of my life has been my constant search for meaning in Judaism and in life as a whole. This chronicle, therefore, eclipses almost everything else, and this fact troubles me, not because I regret for a moment my preoccupation with Judaism, but because that preoccupation and the relative uneventfulness of my life reflect a seeming callousness which I do not believe is characteristic of my nature.

I refer to the horrifying events of the late thirties and half of the forties: the extermination of one-third of the Jewish people in the greatest holocaust history has ever recorded. True, millions were being destroyed in war. That was tragic enough, but tragic as war itself is tragic. I mean that for no reason than that they were Jews, my brothers and sisters were being murdered in the most unspeakable manner, while I was leading discussions and delivering sermons and attending meetings of the Board of Trustees, deciding whether to increase the dues, to fix the roof, or to add another hour to the religious school program.

We knew, and we did not know. Reports reached us of persecution and special laws restricting the lives of Jews. But we did not know nor could we imagine the depths of depravity to which the Jews' tormentors had fallen. We fluctuated between wringing our hands at the seeming docility of the Jews, and thrilling to the news that they had revolted, as in Warsaw. We wept when we read about boats loaded with refugees sunk by the wretched passengers themselves after being turned away in this country and others. We gave money to the United Jewish Appeal. But then we went to the movies and spent July and August in the country.

Perhaps self-flagellation for sins of omission relieves the mind somewhat, but it neither accounts for nor makes up for the failure of American Jews to do more than we did. What more could we have done? I really do not know, but the nagging sense of failure persists.

I go further. I feel guilty about the fact that the sense of failure does not persist without letup; it goes away for weeks, months at a time. Elie Wiesel writes a book, and for a time we realize that we did not do enough during the Holocaust, to prevent—or at least, protest—the horror. A television program depicts the Nazi "final solution," and for an evening we are assailed by waves of guilt for having not merely survived, but for having prospered while all this was going on. Indeed, my father enjoyed one last brief period of affluence during the war. The day after our pangs of guilt, we are back at our daily routines.

We all rejoice at the establishment of the State of Israel. We visit the country and swell with pride at the extraordinary achievements of a nation of survivors who brought with them nothing but their nightmare memories and their highly developed intelligence. To be sure, many millions of dollars have been contributed by Jews in the free countries, and the American government has given or loaned billions more. But the work has been done by those who went to Israel and stayed there. We tourists return to this country and go around making speeches about how wonderful the Israelis are, how creative, how brave, how self-sacrificing! And this too is vanity.

A historic opportunity presented itself to my generation to take part in the rebuilding of a nation, to reestablish a commonwealth after twenty centuries, to end the long era of homelessness for the Jewish people, and we found a thousand reasons for not doing so, discovering comfortable ways of feeling involved in that historic process without actually planting our feet on the soil itself.

Some of my colleagues who remained behind in the Diaspora use the revival of Israel to serve their theological ends. They were deeply shaken by the Holocaust. Their faith in a providential God was challenged by God's apparent indifference to the suffering of God's chosen ones. How to save God became their major project. Tradition taught that God works in history. Could God indeed have been working through the Nazis? This was too sacrilegious a thought! They fell back, some of them, on the theological conceit of God being hidden, permitting people to work out their own salvation. After all, God had given humans moral freedom. How convincing this thesis was I do not know. I found it to be metaphysical hair-splitting. But the State of Israel came to the rescue for these theologians. Here was the answer: God works in mysterious ways the divine purpose to achieve. If not for the Holocaust, the State of Israel would never have come into being. Israel reborn is God's purpose.

I cannot accept any of this. I am not concerned about saving God's reputation for omnipotence or goodness. My theology does not call for this kind of apologetics. For me God is the name we attach to those powers in nature and in humanity (more prominent in humanity, though still largely undeveloped) which "makes for" (in Kaplan's terms) harmony and growth, for interdependence and for self-realization, for the polar values of cooperation and individualization. God is not a personal Being; and referring to "Him" is only a device for articulating thought, not a commitment to belief in the existence of a supernatural Somebody. To speak, therefore, of justifying the ways of God to humanity, or to the Jewish people, is to speak in anachronistic terms.

Theodicy has no place in my scheme. I cannot account for evil any more than I can account for good, or for existence itself. My purpose is otherwise: I want to improve the world; the question is: can it be done, and how? The first question demands faith, that is, faith in the potency of that Force or those powers to which I have referred. Is the potential powerful enough to overcome the chaos of human nature? If the answer is yes, then the next item on the agenda is: how? What are the means available, and how can those means be best utilized to achieve the desirable ends?

That is why I have little patience with theologians who claim to know more than they can possibly know. They base their knowledge on revelation, but they cannot agree on how that revelation is to be understood. Each one cherishes his own dogma.

Nor can I abide those who, also latching on to the Holocaust, come to the conclusion that it finally and incontrovertibly proves that there is no God at all. For them the Holocaust revealed the total meaninglessness of existence. I have often wondered why, if life is so meaningless, they take the trouble to write one book after another on the subject.

Without minimizing the horror of the Holocaust (who would dare do that?), one can rightly say that it differed from other, previous slaughters quantitatively but not qualitatively. With the use of technology, the Nazis could destroy as many as 20,000 souls a day. In former times, when work had to be done by hand, the total number murdered had to be smaller. But the purpose was the same, the motive no different. Somehow, pious Jews were able to explain these events. They were God's will. Religious people did not need theodicies. And theodicies did no good for those who were not religious to begin with.

While all this theological discussion was going on (and it still goes on), I wondered what good it was doing, how much suffering it was alleviating, how much rebuilding of the ruined places it was causing, how much peace among nations and people it was advancing. For one who has devoted his entire life to the Jewish religious enterprise, these are disturbing thoughts, for religion today seems to be slipping back to either simple dogmatic fundamentalism, or to escapist mysticism.

The pragmatism which informed Kaplan's thinking is in disrepute. The very word "pragmatism" has developed the connotation of cheap, short-sighted self-interest. It has lost its original thrust. Pragmatism grew out of the spirit of activism, the intuition that an idea, to be meaningful, must be translatable into action—whatever may be the nature of reality. Speculation concerning ultimate things is a pleasant occupation, but there is work to be done, and that work presupposes only one affirmation about the nature of life, namely, that the potential is there. That is the simple faith on which I have based my life. I believe it is enough to carry us through even the most difficult times.